Other, Please Specify

Other, Please Specify

QUEER METHODS IN SOCIOLOGY

Edited by

D'Lane Compton, Tey Meadow,
and Kristen Schilt

UNIVERSITY OF CALIFORNIA PRESS

University of California Press, one of the most distinguished university presses in the United States, enriches lives around the world by advancing scholarship in the humanities, social sciences, and natural sciences. Its activities are supported by the UC Press Foundation and by philanthropic contributions from individuals and institutions. For more information, visit www.ucpress.edu.

University of California Press
Oakland, California

Library of Congress Cataloging-in-Publication Data

Names: Compton, D'Lane R. (D'Lane Rebecca), editor. | Meadow, Tey, editor. | Schilt, Kristen, editor.
Title: Other, please specify : queer methods in sociology / edited by D'Lane Compton, Tey Meadow, and Kristen Schilt.
Description: Oakland, California : University of California Press, [2018] | Includes bibliographical references and index. |
Identifiers: LCCN 2018001554 (print) | LCCN 2018006215 (ebook) | ISBN 9780520963993 () | ISBN 9780520289260 (cloth : alk. paper) | ISBN 9780520289277 (pbk. : alk. paper)
Subjects: LCSH: Queer theory. | Sociology—Methodology.
Classification: LCC HQ76.25 (ebook) | LCC HQ76.25 .O84 2018 (print) | DDC 306.7601—dc23
LC record available at https://lccn.loc.gov/2018001554

Manufactured in the United States of America

25 24 23 22 21 20 19 18
10 9 8 7 6 5 4 3 2 1

Contents

Acknowledgments

This book has been an exercise in what it might look like to do queer collaboration within academia. We are deeply grateful to all of the contributors who believed in the project and worked with us over the past two years: Amanda Baumle, Cati Connell, Tina Fetner, Gary Gates, Amin Ghaziani, Melanie Heath, Jody Herman, Kimberly Hoang, Trevor Hoppe, Cayce Hughes, Angela Jones, Emilia Lombardi, Mignon Moore, CJ Pascoe, Carla Pfeffer, Evren Savci, Amy Stone, and Jane Ward. This amazing group of scholars committed not just to writing a chapter but also to participating in paper-in-progress workshops and to peer-reviewing one another's pieces. We are immensely proud of this volume and of the community that we created with one another in the process.

The "collaboration pods" were possible only through the generosity of the people and institutions that provided us with space and food for thought (and body). For the Boston pod, we thank the Department of Sociology and Women and Gender Studies at Harvard University, and most especially Deb DeLaurell. For the Los Angeles pod, we thank the Williams Institute at the University of California at Los Angeles, Jody Herman, Reilly Nelson, and Andrew Flores. For the Austin pod, we thank Christine Williams, the Department of Sociology at the University of Texas at Austin, and all of the graduate student participants—many of who are now doing queer work as assistant professors. We also thank our contributors, who were willing to self-fund their travel to these workshops.

Many people gave us critical feedback and inspiration throughout this process. Naomi Schneider at the University of California Press believed in this project from its most nascent stage and shepherded us across the finish line with her guidance and vision. We thank also the anonymous reviewers who read and evaluated the prospectus and the book manuscript. The detailed and generative comments we received helped us to hone our intervention. We thank Matt Brim and Amin Ghaziani, who generously cited our then-forthcoming volume in their 2016 *Women Studies Quarterly* special issue on queer methods. Kimberly Hoang tirelessly read versions of the introduction and several chapters and offered enthusiastic, critical comments that always pushed the project further. Paige Schilt provided us with her invaluable editorial skills. Lauren Berlant, Patrick Jagoda, Chase Joynt, Susan Mann, Dudley Poston, Gayle Salamon, and Jane Sell were our sounding boards, cheerleaders, and inspirations.

Introduction

QUEER WORK IN A STRAIGHT DISCIPLINE

Kristen Schilt, Tey Meadow, and D'Lane Compton

Evelyn Hooker was ahead of her time. Best known for her 1957 paper, "The Adjustment of the Male Homosexual," she was one of the first research psychologists to decouple homosexuality from psychopathology and to argue for a new view of sexual diversity as benign human variation. In staking that maverick claim, she had no idea how broad her impact would be on cultural conceptions of gay lives, but she already knew a great deal about the personal and professional costs it would bring.

Hooker's project was a combination of insight and serendipity. A student introduced her to the gay world of Los Angeles, which was, at the time, largely invisible to heterosexuals (White 2009). There, Hooker learned about the social function of gay bars, witnessed the LA Police Department's notorious gay-baiting vice squad in action, and observed the emergence of a nascent gay rights movement. Through her ethnographic fieldwork, she experienced a crisis of faith in the representations of homosexuality in her field of psychology. Using the psychological tests most prevalent at the time, she collected her own data on gay men's mental health and concluded that many of the problems her respondents faced came from social stigma rather than individual pathology.

Pushing against disciplinary conventions and orthodoxies, Hooker worked at the margins of her field. Her research in gay communities brought, at best, ridicule from her colleagues and, at worst, police surveillance and harassment. Mentors told her it was impossible to study "normal male homosexuals," because "no such a person" existed (Hooker 1993: 451). The McCarthy-era government agency that unexpectedly agreed to fund her research referred internally to her work as "The Fairy Project" and assigned police to tail her every move. She eventually destroyed most of her archive to protect her research subjects. Describing the emotional costs of working at such ideological odds with her home discipline and with the dominant legal and cultural conceptions of her time, she wrote in a retrospective essay near the end of her life, "Without a colleague with whom to share the sympathetic knowledge of human suffering, sometimes one's own vicarious suffering becomes unbearable" (1993: 451). She remembered vividly the relief she felt when she first encountered another researcher, Finn Carling, who shared her commitments. After comparing their research findings about gay men over tea, Hooker remembered, Carling turned to her and said hesitantly, "I want you to know that I am on their side." Hooker leaned in and conspiratorially replied, "So am I" (452).

Like the scholars we showcase in *Other, Please Specify: Queer Methods in Sociology*, Hooker believed deeply that rigorous empirical data could inform the tactics of progressive social movements and change public and scholarly opinions; and, indeed, her research set the wheels in motion for the removal of homosexuality from the *Diagnostic and Statistical Manual* of the American Psychiatric Association in 1973 (Minton 2001). Yet it was her willingness to look at how gay men made sense of their worlds, rather than to accept the taken-for-granted assumptions about gay men in psychology at the time, that allowed her to think outside the prevailing discourse in her discipline. This volume is a reflection and reference manual for scholars who, like Hooker, are seeking to harness social scientific methods for a politically informed research agenda, who are navigating the professional and emotional challenges of doing such work within a traditional discipline, and who are willing to invest time and energy into building community with others who are, so to speak, on their side.

We locate this volume within the critical conversation about what it might mean to "queer" research methods that have developed over the past decade in conference panels, workshops, edited volumes, and journal symposia. This complex question explores the possibilities and pitfalls of knitting insights from poststructuralist queer theory, a body of scholarship that renders the subject destabilized, multiple, and fluid, with social science research methods that utilize categories and explicitly bounded concepts as a starting point (Browne & Nash 2010). Such engagement between queer theory and the social sciences is an important development. More recent critical interventions into the early discourse of queer theory (see Butler 1990; Sedgwick 1990), such as queer of color critique (see Hong & Ferguson 2011; Puar 2007), black queer–diaspora studies (see Allen 2012; Johnson & Henderson 2005), and transgender studies (see Stryker & Whittle 2006; Stryker & Aizura 2013), have shaped the development of an interdisciplinary field of queer studies that "insists on a broadened consideration of the late-twentieth century global crises that have configured historical relations among political economies, the geopolitics of war and terror, and national manifestations of sexual, racial, and gendered hierarchies" (Eng, Halberstam, & Muñoz 2005: 1). Yet, in this move from queer theory to more socially oriented queer studies, little widespread cross-pollination has happened.

The dominance of the humanities in queer studies reflects, to some degree, a "queer suspicion" (Brim & Ghaziani 2016, 16) that empirical methods are reductionist. And, even among researchers invested in building bridges between queer theory and empirical research, there can be a lingering discomfort with the social sciences, disciplinary fields with a historical legacy of categorizing populations and practices as "normal" or "deviant" in ways that uphold racialized formations of hetero- and cisnormativity. The conversation around queer methods signals a willingness among some social scientists to reevaluate the axioms and knowledge claims of their disciplines, and offers a chance to take stock of how, thirty years after the emergence of queer theory, "queer conceptualizations have intersected . . . with research design" (Browne & Nash 2010: 4). As Matt Brim and Amin Ghaziani argue, turning such critical attention to queer methods creates new avenues of inquiry that move beyond the question "What is queer theory?" to ask, "How is queer theory done?" (2016: 14).

Building on these discussions, *Other, Please Specify* turns a queer lens on the production of knowledge in sociology in the United States. A disciplinary context caught in a (very long) moment of quantitative hegemony, U.S. sociology has a tendency to push to the margins any work that problematizes (or, we might say, *queers*) the field by bringing to the forefront the experiences of people and groups consider too "indecent," too "fringe," or too "micro" to warrant attention from the established sociological center. Steven Seidman's pathbreaking edited volume, *Queer Theory/Sociology* (1996a), incited this critique, focusing predominantly on the long erasure of gay and lesbian lives from mainstream sociological research. Seidman and his colleagues provided a provocative roadmap for creating a "more queer sociology." Two decades later, we see that while sociology has become more "gay-friendly"—a change we appreciate and applaud—it does not look decidedly queerer. Since the 2010s, studies about LG (but still rarely B, T, or Q) populations have found a home in survey and demographic research through the increasingly more common inclusion of "sexual orientation" as a variable (see, for example, Ueno, Roach, & Peña-Talamantes 2013; Mize 2016). Yet the investment in positivism in U.S. sociology makes the academic field less receptive to work that engages in a poststructuralist critique of scientific knowledge production or to research on identity formations and practices outside the bounds of hetero- and (more recently) homonormativity.

The barriers to a "more queer" sociology are complex. The lingering discomfort with research that takes an appreciative approach to identities and practices widely held to be nonnormative or "fringe" by the sociological center—for example, gender fluidity and sex work in this historical moment—creates professional legitimacy problems for sociologists invested in such research.[1] These are problems that colleagues working on more sociologically acceptable areas of study, such as income inequality, are less likely to face even when they draw on qualitative methods of inquiry. Queer work has made some inroads in U.S. sociology, most notably in the subfields of sexualities and gender. But the lack of disciplinary support for critical queer theory as a legitimate epistemological underpinning for sociological research, coupled with the continued stigma associated with research on identities and practices that go beyond the binary formulations of man-woman and gay-straight, can keep early-career sociologists invested in doing this work in the proverbial closet. We see this volume as an opportunity to show the value of bringing a queer critique to both our research and to the disciplinary conventions that disparage politically engaged work as too ideological to be "good" (i.e., objective) research and too nuanced to be "useful" (i.e., abstract) theory.

This critique of U.S. sociology has much to contribute to the growing conversation about queer methods. In its "ideal type," a queerer method of social science inquiry would work to dismantle essentialist disciplinary conventions and exclusionary epistemological traditions from the inside out, thereby engendering a research practice that seeks to grow, rather than codify, possibilities for how to be in the world. At the heart of this project is a desire to find ways to gather empirical data about the experiences of people who are politically and socially marginalized without reproducing such marginalization through practices of research and theorizing that conflate objectification with "good science." To date, however, most attempts at putting queer methods into practice have come from researchers working in academic fields that as a whole prioritize archival or ethnographic methods (see Brim & Ghaziani 2016 for an exception). We see much to be gained from looking closely at the experiences of researchers who do social data analysis from a queer vantage point in a disciplinary context in which ethnography, interview, and archival methods exist alongside, but are not always afforded the same gravitas and legitimacy as, survey and demographic methods. While many sociologists doing queer work do draw on qualitative methods in an effort to prioritize people's self-understandings and phenomenological worldviews, they face, unlike their colleagues in history or cultural anthropology, evaluation from a disciplinary center that privileges causal mechanisms and generalizability over locally situated knowledge and meanings.

Highlighting the dominance of quantitative methods of inquiry in U.S. sociology, most PhD programs require students to take statistics courses, while qualitative methods are almost always an elective. A quick perusal of the top three general-interest journals in the field further demonstrates that qualitative research is published much less frequently than statistical work—a pattern that holds true particularly for qualitative research on queer areas of study. Sociologists seeking to publish queer work in these journals often navigate positivist gatekeepers who evaluate the significance of research in terms of p-values, and generalists who prioritize broad "so what" claims. These demands to make qualitative research about nonheteronormative identities and practices that are often locally situated and in flux matter to sociologists invested in generalizability and "large N" metrics of evaluation creates a paradox for researchers. Abstracting from people's lived experiences can feel like turning agentic subjects into theoretical objects, drawing a line between "us," the researchers, and "them," the people we study. Yet keeping an analytic lens on the center from a vantage point of the margins can limit publishing and job opportunities, a professional barrier that can push early-career scholars away from doing queer scholarship or lead them to leave sociology altogether. As we show in this volume, the experiences of people doing queer work in a disciplinary environment in which positivist logics form the basis for evaluating "good" or "bad" work bring into high relief a range of epistemological and institutional challenges—as well as strategies for navigating these challenges—that can advance the queer methods discussion and motivate sociology to be more receptive to critical queer work and the people who do it.

In *Other, Please Specify*, the contributors present an array of experiences, insights, and approaches that show the power of queer investigations of the social world and of disciplinary conventions. All of the authors undertook their graduate training in a U.S. sociology program, though some of us have made our professional homes in other fields. Working at the intersections of LGBTQ studies, the sociology of gender and sexualities, and queer and trans studies from within many different subfields, we often felt isolated during our training, underprepared for the complex professional field we were entering, and in great need of others who were on our side. We speak from varied social locations, methodological approaches, and epistemological investments but share a common goal of making more space for queer research and researchers within sociology.

In the chapters that follow, some authors engage explicitly with methodological issues, offering discussions of how they transformed or, at times, abandoned conventional sociological research methods in their queer work. Others elucidate the challenges and pleasures of putting a critically queer research agenda into practice and offer strategies for world building in the academy. Taken together, the book's chapters provide roadmaps for getting queer research off the ground, present models for what Amy Stone in this volume calls "queer persistence" in our research and our careers, and highlight strategies for continuing to push back on the disciplinary conventions that can keep queerly disruptive research on the margins. We use the term *strategy*, rather than *solution*, purposefully. As Matt Brim and Amin Ghaziani suggest, the mandate of a queer methodological approach should be to "clarify, but not overdetermine, the conditions that make life livable" (2016: 19). In this spirit, our book aims to elucidate practical strategies for livable world making, not merely for the communities we study but also for ourselves, for our colleagues who strive to expand the space for pluralistic gender and sexual discourses, and for our students and the academic world within which we want them to flourish.

FROM *QUEER THEORY/SOCIOLOGY* TO QUEER SOCIOLOGY

One of our initial goals when we conceptualized this book in the mid-2010s was to capture a snapshot of the state of the field of queer work in sociology since the publication of the edited volume *Queer Theory/ Sociology* (Seidman 1996a). This now-canonical book began as a symposium in a 1994 issue of *Sociological Theory*—to date, the only such symposium in a general-interest sociological journal—and then expanded to become the definitive text for sociologists seeking to harness critical insights from humanistic queer theory in their research (see also Gamson & Moon 2004). The volume's contributors take as a central problematic how to think about the anti-normative and deconstructionist challenge that humanistic queer theory poses to the positivist epistemology of sociology without surrendering a disciplinary investment in "fundamentally sociological questions" (Epstein 1994: 199) grounded in empirical methods, such as how political contexts and social institutions enable and constrain particular forms of gender and sexual identity formation, and how social actors come to embody, disrupt, and transform such possibilities through collective action. As Charles Lemert, the series editor for *Queer Theory/Sociology*, notes in his introduction, the slash in the book's title was "one of the rare instances where such an odd editorial mark is required—here to signify that two distinct traditions of study are being brought into a still indefinite relationship" (1996: x).

Seidman and colleagues acknowledge at the outset that while queer theory as an interdisciplinary endeavor has built bridges with some social sciences, particularly anthropology and history, theorists in the humanities showed little interest in possible queer contributions from sociology, a discipline that, with its prioritization of positivism and categorization, could seem "irrelevant, or at the very least, a bit stuffy" (Epstein 1994: 188)—a fair critique, in many ways, for a discipline that resisted the critical interventions of feminist theory (Stacey & Thorne 1985), gay and lesbian studies (Stein & Plummer 1994), critical race studies (Zuberi & Bonilla-Silva 2008), and transgender studies (Namaste 2000). Yet, the contributors posit, the seeming irrelevance of sociology to the project of queer theory resulted from contests over epistemologies and knowledge claims in the discipline rather than an inherent incompatibility. To this point, Steven Epstein argues that the social constructionist approaches to homosexuality that emerged in sociology in the 1960s pushed back against "naturalized conceptions of sexuality as a biological given, against Freudian models of the sexual drive, and against the Kinseyan obsession with the tabulation of behavior" (1994: 188) to assert that sexual categories, meanings, and identity formations were "intersubjectively negotiated social and historical products—that sexuality was, in a word, constructed" (188). This theoretical paradigm, he notes, predates the work of theorist Michel Foucault, the figure most widely held up as the progenitor of humanistic queer theory, and, thus, represents a lost queer lineage that is uniquely sociological.

Bracketing the missed potential of a queer theory rooted in sociological traditions, the authors make a case for what is uniquely exciting about poststructuralist queer theory for sociologists who wish to "rethink sexual (and gender) nonconformity in ways that do not reproduce marginality" (Stein & Plummer 1994: 178). Steven Seidman highlights the importance of queer theory's destabilization of categories and its move toward seeing identities as "multiple or at best composites with an infinite number of ways in which they can intersect or combine" (1996b: 11). This theoretical intervention disrupted the idea of a unified homosexual identity long central to the organization of Western gay rights politics and to gay and lesbian studies in the academy. Queer theorists, in other words, sought to "shak[e] the ground on which gay and lesbian politics has been built, taking apart the idea of a 'sexual minority' and a 'gay community,' indeed of 'gay' and 'lesbian' and even 'man' and 'woman'" (Gamson 1996: 395). Moving past a unified, essential identity created analytic possibilities for exploring how "identity constructions function as templates defining selves and behaviors, and therefore excluding a range of possible ways to frame the self, body, desires, actions, and social relations" (Seidman 1996b: 12). And queer theorists did not stop with the self, but also trained a critical lens on the "institutional practices and discourses producing sexual knowledge and the ways they organize social life" (Seidman 1996b: 13).

This focus on social power and the institutional and interpersonal regulation of identities and bodies allowed queer theorists to shift the direction of the analytic gaze, offering a critique of the center from the margins (Stein & Plummer 1994). In particular, the work of Judith Butler (1990) and Eve Sedgwick (1990) transformed heterosexuality from a naturalized and unmarked identity into an object of analysis—a shift later encapsulated in the concept of "heteronormativity" (Berlant & Warner 1998). Making such a queer turn in sociology was crucial for building more reflexive studies of sexuality, Viviane Namaste argued, noting that "if we focus only on the 'subculture' of homosexuality, and if we never interrogate the conditions which engender its marginalization, we shall remain trapped within a theoretical framework which refuses to acknowledge its own complicity in constructing its objects (and subjects) of study" (1994: 204). Further, this view of the center from the margins could push the study of sexual identities in sociology away from a narrow and stigmatizing focus on *sexual deviance* and into a pluralistic view of *sexual difference*.

Bringing queer theoretical insights into sociology could, many of the authors suggest, engender a "more queer sociology" (Stein & Plummer 1994: 183), one that is "critical of its categories" as it considers "the ways that knowledges [*sic*], including sociology, shape sexual and social orders" (Seidman 1996b: 17). Putting the analytic lens on the social construction of *sexualities*, rather than on homosexuality, would also enable sociology as a discipline to take seriously the queer idea that the psychic and institutional life of sexual power permeates all aspects of the social world. With greater reflexivity, sociologists could more clearly illuminate their unique disciplinary contributions to the queer theory project, particularly a commitment to understanding people's lived experiences through empirical research. Emerging from traditions of philosophy, political theory, and literary criticism, queer theory rarely moved past textual or discourse analysis. For sociologists, such a focus created a "dangerous tendency . . . to ignore 'real' queer life as it is materially experienced across the world" (Stein & Plummer 1994: 184). Viviane Namaste extends this critique, noting that while queer theorists have dedicated much analytic attention to drag and gender performativity, "these works have shown very little concern for those who identify and live as drag queens, transsexuals, and transgenders [*sic*]" (1996: 183). In contrast, a queerer sociology would "integrate the emphasis on discourse in queer studies with a sociological focus on social institutions" (1996b: 17) and strive for empirical and theoretical work that simultaneously understands identities as multiple, stable, and subject to culture while keeping close to the subjective experiences and meaning making of individuals and communities.

More than two decades after *Queer Theory/Sociology*, this vision for a "more queer" sociology has, to some degree, come to fruition, embodied in theoretical and empirical research that encompasses a range of methodological approaches and topical areas. The subfields of sexualities and gender that house most of the queer research in the discipline have grown and thrived, supported by a series of institutions, such as the Sexualities and Sex & Gender Sections of the American Sociological Association (ASA), the LGBTQ Caucus, the ASA Committee on the Status of LGBTQ People in Sociology, and, most recently, Sociologists for Transgender Justice. LGBTQ studies has held a place on the list of recurring "regular sessions" at the ASA annual meeting since the early 2000s, joined in 2018 by transgender studies. These forms of institutional support, though perhaps normative from a radically queer anti-assimilationist position, create space for queer research to flourish in sociology. Further, these institutions bring people together to form communities of support and to problematize and challenge the marginalization of LGBTQ sociologists and queer work in the broader discipline (see Irvine 2014; Taylor & Raeburn 1995).

Yet the preponderance of queer work within the niche of sexualities and gender has provided a ready excuse for sociologists in other subfields to neglect queer topics in their own research, in their conference panels, and in their teaching. Highlighting this point, queer theoretical work is rarely taught in contemporary sociological theory courses or published in sociological theory journals (for an exception, see Green 2002; 2007). While research on the workplace and health outcomes of gay and lesbian people or the dynamics of gay and lesbian social movements can now be found more readily in general sociology journals, it is still uncommon to encounter research on non-heteronormative identities and practices that draws explicitly on queer theory (for an exception, see Pfeffer 2014). The lack of legitimation of queer work in our journals and in our conference halls, coupled with the continued association of queer research with "dirty work" (Irvine 2014; see also Hoang, this volume; Jones, this volume)—work that is considered inappropriate, indecent, or immoral in the professional imaginary—creates barriers for sociologists interested in entering this field. Further, the persistent undercurrent in the discipline that queer work is "not sociology" (Schilt, this volume), can lead sociologists to migrate to interdisciplinary fields, such as area studies or gender and sexualities studies, where they can find colleagues who see the value in their work (see Ward, this volume).

While U.S. sociology has not undergone a queer paradigm shift that transforms "the orienting assumptions and conceptual frameworks which are basic to a discipline" (Stacey & Thorne 1985: 302), the developments of and in queer research since the millennium highlight exciting new terms of engagement with both interdisciplinary queer studies and sociological conventions. Sociologists doing queer work from the starting point of sociological theories of gender and sexuality have brought empirical weight to theories of performativity, notably in C. J. Pascoe's ethnographic study (2007) of how high school boys engage in "a constellation of sexualized practices, discourses, and interactions" that she terms "compulsive heterosexuality" (86). Pascoe analyzes the ways in which compulsive heterosexuality, which reproduces male supremacy over bodies coded as female or feminine, or both, is legitimated by boys' interactions with peers and teachers, as well as through institutional logics and practices. Queer sociologists also have used their empirical research with LGBTQ people to highlight the limits of a deconstructivist approach to queer lives, such as Adam Isaiah Green's slightly tongue-in-cheek critique of performativity theory in which he argues: "Even as an individual gay man will intellectually apprehend the epistemological limitations of sexological classifications and their central historical role as a disciplining apparatus, it will do him no good to cite [Judith] Butler when confronted with a pack of gay bashers (or a homophobic landlord or employer), and protest that his identity is multiple and unstable, thus exempting him from the ensuing beating (or discrimination)" (2002: 530; see also Johnson 2001). Pascoe and Green's work shows a shift that we imagine in this volume as a move away from sociological anxieties that we are "not yet queer enough" (Valocchi 2005) in the eyes of our humanistic colleagues, toward the development of a body of queer research that is informed by poststructuralist critiques of knowledge production but remains grounded in a commitment to empirical investigation—a definitively sociological endeavor that takes the insights of queer theory as a useful provocation rather than as an aspirational how-to guide for doing our queer research.

SOCIOLOGY/QUEER THEORY: REDEFINING THE RELATIONSHIP

Imagining an agenda for a "more queer" sociology in the early 1990s, the contributors to *Queer Theory/Sociology* put forth several areas of inquiry that might be fruitful: sexual meanings and categorizations, social movement dynamics, and the construction and regulation of sexual identity categories and meanings by institutions like the state, the law, and medicine. Taking stock of the current state of the field, we see that while many of these areas of study have a central place in the sociology of sexualities, the range of topics and salient questions in what we identify here as "queer sociology" have developed in ways perhaps unimaginable even a decade ago. This body of work reflects the growth of institutional space for LGBTQ studies within sociology, the greater visibility of transgender scholarship and activism, and the rapidly shifting cultural and political landscape of contemporary LGBTQ rights in the United States. Further, much of this work has been responsive to interventions from queer of color critique and transgender studies, interventions that render visible the racialized and hetero- or cisnormative domain assumptions of much social science research—including work within the sociology of sexualities and gender. Finally, conversations about the "doing" of queer sociology, particularly around questions of the relationship between anti-normative political commitments and methodological orthodoxies, have emerged and developed as quantitative researchers begin to consider the possibilities of a queer (or queerer) demography. Here, we provide an overview of these developments.

The lives of gay men, and, more specifically, white, cisgender gay men, long dominated critical sexualities research in sociology. As progressive gay studies expanded to include the experiences of lesbians and, less frequently, bisexual and transgender people, researchers started to address the lack of empirical research on LGBTQ lives with research on topics like family and kinship (see Moore & Stambolis-Ruhstorfer 2013 for an overview; see also Baumle & Compton 2015; Pfeffer 2016); workplace discrimination (Connell 2014; Schilt 2010); the racial and class politics of so-called "gayborhoods" (see Greene 2014; Ghaziani 2015); the rhetorical strategies, political shifts, and internal divisions within social movements and organizations (see Ghaziani, Taylor, & Stone 2016 for an overview), and political and religious opposition to LGBTQ rights (Fetner 2008; Stone 2012). Alongside these important developments in LGBTQ studies, researchers drawing on queer theoretical interventions have shifted the focus to sexual identity formation and practices in general, rather than on homosexuality exclusively; and from initial investigations of the alternative kinship structures that organize gay life (Weston 1997), to the very relational structures we consider familial.

One central body of queer work examines the institutional regulation and interpersonal formation of nonnormative sexual practices. In *Beyond Monogamy* (2016), for example, Mimi Schippers studies polyamorous communities to identify "how compulsory and institutionalized monogamy is constitutive of and legitimates the discursive construction and institutionalization of gender as a racialized, hierarchical binary" (2016: 5). Schippers's work is in conversation with critical heterosexuality studies that take the reproduction and maintenance of heteronormativity as a central problematic (see Dean 2014; Ingraham 2004; Ward 2015). As Jane Ward and Beth Schneider argue in their introduction to a special issue of *Gender & Society* on heteronormativity, "The attention to the social construction of heterosexuality has challenged conceptions of difference limited to the triad of 'race, class, gender' while also demonstrating that the realm of sexuality encompasses far more than marginalized, essential (gay and lesbian) identities" (2009: 434).

Building on the insights of heteronormativity, another queer area of inquiry examines the co-constitutive relationship between gender and sexuality—the concept of "gendered sexualities" (Gagné & Tewksbury 2002). The importance of understanding this relationship began to emerge in *Queer Theory/Sociology,* but often remained a parenthetical aside for most contributors who adopted the formulation of "sexual (and gender) identity" (Stein & Plummer 1994: 178). The critical investigation of gendered sexualities opened up areas of inquiry around gender performativity and identity formation in queer communities (Rupp & Taylor 2003; Shapiro 2007). Sociological research in transgender studies also offered a corrective to the long-standing positioning of transgender and gender-nonconforming people as objects, rather than subjects (see Rubin 2003; Namaste 2005; Vidal-Ortiz 2008; Lombardi, this volume) by building "a research agenda which accounts for the intersections of race, class, and gender in the context of the lived social relations of transgender people" (Namaste 1996: 195). Transgender studies in sociology examine areas of inquiry such as sexuality, family, and kinship (Dozier 2005; Meadow 2011; Pfeffer 2016); the legal and medical regulation of gender identity (Meadow 2010; shuster 2016; Windsor 2011); and experiences of violence and discrimination (Miller & Grollman 2015; Nordmarken & Kelly 2012; Schilt & Westbrook 2009). Building on critical developments in the interdisciplinary field of queer and transgender studies, more recent work has begun to examine "cisnormativity," an ideology that "assumes and expects that all people are and should be cisgender by disallowing transgender experience and enforcing cissexism in beliefs and practices" (Sumerau, Cragun, & Mathers 2016: 294; see also Mathers 2017; Westbrook & Schilt 2014).

Recent work from a queer of color or "quare studies" (Johnson 2001) perspective urges greater reflexivity concerning the unmarked racialized assumptions and historical erasures of the complex intersections between race and sexuality. Much of the "interventionist work" on racialized sexualities has come from the humanities (Johnson & Henderson 2005: 2), since sociology, for its part, has often been antagonistic to black and brown sexualities, both normative and nonnormative, "exclud[ing] and disciplin[ing] those formations that deviate from the racial ideal of heteropatriarchy" (Ferguson 2004, 18; see Johnson & Henderson 2005).

Efforts to "quare queer," or to extend its service to the interests of blackness (Johnson 2001), employ a three-pronged epistemological agenda. First, its proponents recognize that "as sexuality was rendered into a social construction, it was turned into a technology of race, imagining African American culture as the antithesis of compliance, discipline, and normativity" (Ferguson 2005: 59). Sexuality itself was conceptualized in an ethnocentric context that, rather than offering it up as an alternative formation to race, invested in its very contours an articulation of racial privilege (Johnson & Henderson 2005). In important response to that legacy, some queer sociologists center the experiences of communities of color within the field (see Battle & Barnes 2010; Moore 2011; Ocampo 2012; Vidal-Ortiz 2005), uncovering institutional practices, cultural logics, and psychic structures that reproduce the racialization of erotic desires (see Han 2015; Hoang 2015; Jones 2015). This marks a disinvestment from a politics of identity that opposes queer and heterosexual, recognizing that differing communal ties can be crucial for individual survival, and disinvestment from notions of radical politics built not on identity per se, but on the idea that different identity categories are invested with differing degrees of power (Cohen 1997).

Whether through performing insurgent readings of classical texts (Ferguson 2004), writing into the scholarly center subjects previously relegated to the margins (Allen 2012), examining the sexual politics of racialization (Hong & Ferguson 2011), or tracing the racialized histories of trans identities (Snorton 2017), scholars of color are merging social science scholarship with political pursuits in novel ways. If, as Jasbir Puar writes, "queer times require even queerer modalities of thought [and] analysis" (Puar 2005: 121), we might look for its evidence in creative empirical investigations such as those found in Cathy J. Cohen's book on the racial and sexual dimensions of HIV-AIDS (Cohen 1999) and Juan Battle's Social Justice Sexuality Project. Despite the ever-present tension between the normative pull of academia and the urgent need for cogent empirical investigations of state violence (Cohen & Jackson 2016), scholars are making headway on these issues as we write, including expanding the sociological canon to include meaningful engagement outside the English-speaking world (see Carrillo 2018; Puri 2016; Savci 2017). Finally, in conversation with a growing body of interdisciplinary rural queer studies (see Gray, Gilley, & Johnson 2016), queer sociology has started to fill the lacuna of empirical research on LGBTQ lives in rural and southern cities in the United States (see Abelson 2016; Crawley 2008; Kazyak 2012).

The development of methodological discussions in queer research is the last innovation we examine. The majority of queer research in sociology utilizes qualitative research methods, such as interviews, ethnography, and media analysis. The prevalence of qualitative studies reflects in part an epistemological commitment to methods that can more readily capture the phenomenological dimension of people's worldviews and feelings (Rubin 2003). Yet sociologists invested in making quantitative interventions into sexual and gender discrimination are exploring ways to potentially "queer" survey and demographic research. Such research includes examinations of heterosexual attitudes toward gay communities and gay-rights activism (Powell, Bolzendahl, Geist, & Steelman 2010), as well as statistical estimations of the size of the LGBTQ population in the United States (Flores, Herman, Gates, & Brown 2016; Gates & Herman, this volume). Other research, often done collaboratively with queer and transgender activists and communities, seeks to develop best practices for designing more open and inclusive gender and sexual identity categories on surveys (see GenIUSS Group 2014; Lombardi & Banik 2016; Westbrook & Saperstein 2015). A final strand of research seeks to problematize the normative and heterosexist assumptions built into much quantitative research, and to find ways to make more space for queer demographic and attitudinal research (see Grzanka 2016). This push for a "more queer" demography (see Baumle, this volume) reflects a growing demand in mainstream LGBTQ political activism to be counted in order to achieve larger-scale changes in anti-discrimination policies. Such quantitative investigations in queer sociology are far afield from the anti-categorical imperative of humanistic queer theory that takes the position that "it is illogical to 'count' subjects once one has argued that a 'countable subject' does not exist" (Browne & Nash 2010: 11). Yet we see the inclusion of these attempts as critical to the conversation about queer methods even while we acknowledge that the ability to effectively "queer" quantitative methods in a way that would disrupt normative power hierarchies is still very much up for debate.

TOWARD A QUEER AGENDA FOR SOCIOLOGY

So, what, then, is queer sociology, once we remove the idea that "queer" is just shorthand for LGBTQ studies or that it requires a shared commitment to qualitative modes of inquiry? We identify a set of tenets that connect the disparate epistemological and methodological investments, areas of inquiry, and social locations of researchers and research that we discuss under the umbrella of "queer sociology." First, these works prioritize bringing empirical data to bear on analyses of gender and sexual formations that are set apart from the normative center. Second, these works adopt a perspective from the margins to illuminate the hidden workings of power and normativity around racialized gender and sexual categories and to provide critical investigations of how investments in hetero-, homo-, and cisnormativities are deeply embedded in much sociology theory and practice. Third, queer sociology remains sensitive to the ways in which people draw on identity categories to make sense of their lives and desires while accounting for how these regulatory socially constructed identities emerge and shift across historical, political, and national landscapes. Fourth, queer sociology employs intimacies, erotics, reflexivities, intersectionalities, and hybridities that from a positivist position may seem to weaken a method but that are, we argue, crucial for understanding social and sexual life. And finally, building on important interventions from queer, feminist, and critical race theory, queer sociology examines how institutions, communities and social networks, and social locations, such as race, class, and nationality, shape people's lived experiences with sexuality and gender in ways that both enable and constrain the possibilities of achieving a livable life.

In *Other, Please Specify,* we bring together sociologists working at the queer intersections of gender and sexualities who embody these tenets in complex and sometimes contradictory ways. We sought contributions from early-career scholars who had discussed in the appendices of their often field-defining first books, on conference panels, or over late-night drinks at local gay bars near the annual meeting hotel the limits of conventional sociological methods—and the disappointment of receiving conventional responses from the sociological center—that make queer innovation and community building difficult. We asked people to write about these experiences and, if they felt able, to share personal accounts of the joys and quandaries of being queer and doing queer work in sociology. Understanding the feelings of professional and personal risk that accompany "talking out of school" about one's discipline, for the most part we approached potential contributors who were, or who hoped to be by the time of publication, on the other side of tenure—a privileged location that can afford more stability for taking career risks. But we also acknowledge that our strategy omits the voices of our graduate student, adjunct, and tenure-track colleagues. The majority of contributors also are white and cisgender—a demographic characteristic that reflects who is most likely to be tenured in sociology, as well as who often has the most institutional resources for doing queer work. We hope this volume will open up more room for a greater diversity of queer voices in sociology by making the case for the value of this area of inquiry to the broader discipline and encouraging more scholars—queer or not—to mentor the graduate students and junior colleagues who are, as we write this, developing the next critical interventions in the field. We see this book not as the definitive word on queer sociology but rather as an opportunity to take stock of how the field has developed and shifted since the first attempts to blend queer theory and sociology in the 1990s. We remain critical of the voices and topics that are still missing, and seek to help foster and make space for the next iteration of queer—or whatever comes after queer—sociology.

Drawing on their research and career experiences, our contributors engage with questions of epistemology, methodology, and political commitments across a range of topical areas that include transnational sexualities, queer communities of color, sex work, queer kinship and family formation, transgender studies, and queer demography. Connecting to the legacy of queer and feminist "tales from the field" (see Lewin & Leap 1996; Laslett & Thorne 1997), some authors share personal experiences from their research that reflect the "queer vulnerability" (Meadow, this volume) that many of us faced in the communities we studied and in our broader discipline. Other chapters address how LGBTQ communities can challenge methodological conventions, such as those defining what constitutes an ethnographic field site or an archive. Some contributors flip the gaze to show how queer work can bring into high relief the sexist, racialized, Western-centered, or positivist assumptions embedded in sociological epistemologies and methodological logics, as well as the limits of a queer theoretical approach that neglects the social. As a whole, this book provides methodological advice and practical strategies for getting queer research off the ground, and for navigating the absence of mentorship that many queer scholars face in sociology, first as graduate students and often again as faculty members. We see this volume as a way to transmit the emotional support and informal advice we give one another in conference hallways and offer our students during office hours.

While we engage with methodological challenges and quagmires, we, like other editors of collections on queer methods, resist the allure of offering a (or even multiple) solution(s) or the promise of a new queer method. Instead, taking a page from the early conversations about feminist methods in the social sciences, we make a decision not to say what a queer sociological method is but rather to "illustrate by example what it includes" (Reinharz 1992: 5). This decision allows us to embrace the "messiness of everyday life" (Browne & Nash 2010: 14) that occurs once we move away from texts and into the field (or the survey lab, as it might be). Further, in this way we can more fully capture the diversity of epistemological traditions and methodological investments and disinvestments of our contributors. What we mean when we invoke the idea of queer methods, then, has less to do with technical advice (though, we throw some of that in for good measure) than with the vein of C. Wright Mills's classic formulation of methodology as the practice of making visible "actual ways of working" (1959: 195). In the spirit of Shulamit Reinharz's (1992) engagement with feminist methods, we are not interested in telling queer sociologists what methods to use, but rather wish to document, and encourage the expansion of, the diversity of voices in queer sociology.

The vision of queer sociology we present here—critical of ossified categorical systems, reflexive about the constitutive power of knowledge on the social world, and integrative of queer studies discourse with a practical focus on institutional life—requires directing a fine lens on our daily practices. To do this, we must acknowledge the ambivalent relationship many of us have with both the level of theoretical abstraction found in much humanistic queer studies work and the positivist and normative yardstick by which our work is measured in our discipline. Most of us maintain commitments to empiricism and the processes of categorization that expand understanding and generate political and rhetorical force while taking seriously critiques of the reductionist tendency in much social science. We put this ambivalence on the table for discussion to highlight our "practical strategies" (DeVault 1999: 2) for negotiating the tension between doggedly following disciplinary conventions and utterly rejecting them—particularly for scholars early in their careers, as most of us were when we started the studies we write about here. Strategies for managing a middle ground generate the potential for opening lines of inquiry that simultaneously produce and critique knowledge. Such strategies often require, as Marjorie DeVault has argued about efforts to do feminist sociology, participating in existing institutions of knowledge production and accepting that our efforts "will always be only partially successful" (DeVault 1999: 3). We discuss strategies that have worked for us while acknowledging that these same strategies may not translate to other researchers or settings, and present methodological and theoretical ideas for pushing queer sociology forward. Above all else, we share details of strategies that have not worked for us in an effort to embrace what J. Jack Halberstam (2011) has termed "the queer art of failure."

Opening up the conversation about queer methods and strategies in sociology will, we hope, provide some collaborative, pedagogical advice for new generations of sociologists. In these pages, we acknowledge our embarrassments and missteps and, for many of our contributors, our experiences of stigma within the broader discipline. We do this not to suggest that we came of age in the "bad old days" of sociology that today's graduate students have the luxury not to face (though we wish that were true), but rather to demystify the process of career building and world making within queer sociology. Further, we want to challenge the professional delegitimation that many of us have faced—and that we still see junior colleagues face—from peers and colleagues, experiences like having our work dismissed as "me-search," "too political," or "too micro." While all of the contributors have found ways to navigate these forms of professional dismissal, we see it as critical to make visible the prevalence of these kinds of stigmatizing experiences in an effort to emphasize the difference between doing work strategically *from the vantage point of* the margins and *being* marginalized by one's colleagues and peers.

ORGANIZATION OF THE BOOK

Appreciating the irony of ending a book about queer interventions into social science methods with a series of categories, we move now to this volume's chapter organization. Finding an organizational schema that respects the different and sometimes conflicting epistemological and methodological investments of the authors, but manages to avoid leaving the reader with a sense of vertigo, is not an easy task. In an attempt to bring some order to the following pages without sweeping the messy reality of how research actually happens back into the sociological closet, we locate the chapters across four broad themes: (1) anti-orthodoxies, (2) relationships, (3) strategies, and (4) epistemologies—though, in the interest of full disclosure, these categories are neither exhaustive nor mutually exclusive (a little sociology humor for the humanists who may be reading this), nor are they intended to be stable or universal (a little queer theory humor for the sociologists who may be reading this). Within these themes you will find varied strategies and approaches for studying gender and racially diverse queer communities and nonheteronormative practices alongside the shared problematic of how to do collective world building within the field of sociology.

We open with "Anti-Orthodoxies," a section that brings together authors who identify, and offer strategies for navigating, disciplinary barriers to a more politically engaged sociological project. From a range of approaches and areas of inquiry, the authors in this section discuss the challenges of doing research that pushes back against methodological, epistemological, and moral conventions in the field. Some authors end with strategies for building a more inclusive sociological field, while others show the power and impact of working in other disciplinary fields, such as gender studies and public health, or in public policy advocacy.

In "The 'Not Sociology' Problem" (chapter 1), Kristen Schilt lays out a set of interactional practices that limit any research that seeks to disrupt the disciplinary status quo by locating it outside the realm of "real" or "good" sociology. Arguing for the importance of mentoring innovative queer work even when it may challenge our own theoretical commitments and ontological realities, she ends with a discussion of collective strategies for expanding what "counts" as sociology. We then move to Jane Ward's "The

Methods Gatekeepers and the Exiled Queers," which examines the tense relationship between sociological methods and queer modes of inquiry. Showing how queer work in sociology is often dismissed in the discipline through methodological critiques, Ward argues that such methods talk masks disciplinary anxieties about race, gender, and sexuality by operating as a seemingly neutral set of concerns by which to undermine politically invested research. In "Trans Issues in Sociology: A Trans-Centered Perspective," Emilia Lombardi continues this conversation by highlighting how years of activism and advocacy by transgender scholars has begun to reshape how data about transgender and gender-nonconforming people are collected and used in policy research in sociology and public health. Lombardi emphasizes the power of a trans-centered sociology that locates transgender people as active participants in knowledge making around their experiences and lives. Keeping the focus on quantitative research, Gary Gates and Jody Herman discuss the importance—and potential pitfalls—of doing public sociology that pushes back against controversial policy initiatives that uphold discriminatory cultural conceptions about queer and trans lives. In "Beyond Academia: Strategies for Using LGBT Research to Influence Public Policy," Gates and Herman assert that policy advocates, activists, media, courts, legislatures, and even voters, all become potential critics of scholarly work and research design, and caution that when data are relatively rare and populations are stigmatized, the importance of new research findings can be heightened and even lead to misuse. We end part 1 with Angela Jones's "Pornographics as Queer Method." Drawing on the institutional barriers she faced when she began to study sex workers, Jones elucidates how cultural conceptions of nonheteronormative practices as "dirty" and "immoral" that are deeply embedded in the discipline operate as a constraining force on sociologists who seek to study sexual behavior rather than sexual identity formation. She ends with a manifesto that calls for queer sociology to develop a "pornographic imagination" that brings the study of sex (real, actual sex) back to the study of sexualities.

The second section highlights relationships with our work and in the field. Continuing the tradition of "tales from the field," contributors discuss how issues of embodiment and social location impact possibilities for queer presence and relationality across an array of field sites. Taken together, these chapters underscore empirical research as an investment involving both intellectual and emotional risk and further illuminate the difficulties of working at or beyond the limits of traditional sociological frameworks.

In "Not Out in the Field: Studying Privacy and Disclosure as an Invisible (Trans) Man" (chapter 6), Cayce Hughes discusses his decision to come out as a transgender man in his professional life while conducting his dissertation research on motherhood and poverty. Hughes's chapter shows how, even when we do not consider our research to be queer, our queer experiences with gender and sexual identity in the field can shape our research questions and methodological commitments—though in ways that are not always visible to our respondents, our colleagues, or, at times, ourselves. Catherine Connell's chapter, "Thank You for Coming Out Today: The Queer Discomforts of In-Depth Interviewing," introduces a number of ethical and epistemological challenges for qualitative researchers who have queer commitments. Connell highlights how the dependence on coming-out narratives in queer fieldwork shapes data collection in ways that can have unexpected effects on researchers and participants. In "Studying the 'Right' Can Feel Wrong: Reflections on Researching Anti-LGBT Movements," Tina Fetner and Melanie Heath discuss the specific challenges and emotional costs that can arise for queer and queer-supportive scholars who do research with groups that embrace a politics of disgust against LGBTQ people. In the final chapter of part 2, "The Mess: Vulnerability as Ethnographic Practice," Tey Meadow describes the anxieties that can arise for researchers who seek to resist typical ethnographic orthodoxies, like the complementarity of subject-object and the predator-prey model of erotic engagement. Meadow explores moments in her fieldwork with parents of trans and gender-nonconforming children that show what happens when these well-hewn distinctions break down, when the researcher becomes a site of study, and when erotic encounters are neither benign nor exploitative.

We move then to "Strategies," whose chapters offer examples of the many ways that scholars expand and adapt traditional sociological frameworks to create work-arounds that more closely align with specificities of queer populations, topics, and epistemologies. Illuminating where we are willing to go to find and answer our questions, contributors discuss the

complexities of recruiting participants, conceptualizing and reconceptual-
izing sociological concepts and measures, creating quantitative-qualitative
synergies, and achieving rigor. They further offer insights on and strategies
for negotiating struggles with legitimacy, believability, and validity in queer
work.

In chapter 10, "Challenges, Triumphs, and Praxis: Collecting Qualitative
Data on Less Visible and Marginalized Populations," Mignon Moore
details approaches to creating spaces and community for diffuse and
hard-to-reach populations, such as queer communities of color. Detailing
what she describes as "the inverted order of the gatekeeper" technique of
locating an informant, Moore exemplifies how the researcher can be
resourceful and inventive in recruitment, rather than succumbing to the
myth of "invisible populations" that can stop queer research before it even
gets under way. Relatedly, D'Lane Compton's "How Many (Queer) Cases
Do I Need? Thinking Through Research Design" discusses the long-
standing idea in sociology that LGBTQ populations are too challenging or
too small for traditional sampling frames and research designs. Speaking
to these popular misconceptions, Compton provides a model for designing and assessing queer research. Amin Ghaziani, in "Queer Spatial
Analysis," lays out both theoretical and logistical issues in defining and
studying gay neighborhoods. Ghaziani concludes with a field-shifting
assertion that sociologists must move beyond binary conceptions to generate creative indicators of sexual geographies. From spatial analysis we
move to Amy Stone's chapter, "Queer Persistence in the Archive." Detailing
how queer archival work often requires her to go, literally, into the closet,
Stone asserts that scholars must be open to research in unexpected places
and willing to follow leads, and must realize the power of making alliances. She further elucidates how dealing with dead ends and pushing
through self-doubt is part of the process of doing queer research, in which,
more often than not, we have less to work with because of omissions and
the invisibility of queer experiences. We end part 3 with Kimberly Hoang's
"Gendering Carnal Ethnography: A Queer Reception," a chapter that
explores how informal disciplinary reactions to our work can limit our
attempts at methodological innovation. Highlighting sociological
responses to her embodied ethnographic research with sex workers in
Vietnam that were simultaneously salacious and dismissive, Hoang argues

that unpacking the gendered double standard in status that ethnographers receive from their colleagues when they literally put their bodies into their research can illustrate tensions, struggles, and trade-offs that come with bringing queerly disruptive research out of the field and into the academy.

In the final section, "Epistemologies," we present chapters that engage with some of the structural, intellectual, and emotional barriers to building more complex thought around queer work in sociology. These chapters think through the possibilities and limits of a queer theory of knowledge in the authors' specific field sites and areas of inquiry. While all of the authors maintain commitments to empiricism, they seek simultaneously to push back on processes of categorization, calcified traditions, and historical erasures in ways that expand our sociological understanding of queer lives and generate political and rhetorical force.

We start with Evren Savci, who makes a case for "translation as queer methodology" in her chapter (15) about doing transnational sexualities work on queer identities. Drawing from ethnographic research in Turkey, she argues that the framework of translation allows for the undoing of false dichotomies, particularly between discourse and practice, and can call into question the "colonized" versus "authentic" binary when talking about the non-West. In chapter 16, "Queer and Punishment: Sexual Social Control and the Legacy of 'Nuts, Sluts and Preverts,'" Trevor Hoppe considers how changes in political landscapes and social movements around seemingly non-LGBTQ issues can push sexuality scholars to explore new meanings and conceptualizations in their own work. Challenging the dismissal of "deviance studies" in the field of sexualities, Hoppe argues that studying sexuality through the lens of punishment and the state can shift the sociological gaze toward practical techniques of social control that limit the possibilities for queer lives. We then turn to another epistemological challenge to queer orthodoxies, in Amanda Baumle's "The Demography of Sexuality: Queering Demographic Methods." Challenging an easy dismissal of quantitative modes of inquiry as anti-queer, Baumle argues that the incorporation of queer theoretical perspectives and nonheterosexual experiences into population research illustrates that many "nonsexual" demographic outcomes (such as income and place of residence) are shaped by sexual identities and practices. In a related conversation about queer insights for qualitative methods, C. J. Pascoe asks in her chapter, "What to Do with Actual People? Thinking Through a Queer Social Science Method." Pascoe makes a case for adopting a queer theoretical sensibility that interrogates the basis of categories and patterns that often are taken for granted in our discipline. As Pascoe argues, such an adoption may "fail" from an established disciplinary position—but what we learn and gain from such "failures" is what makes our queer work better collectively. Finally, we end with "Queer Accounting: Methodological Investments and Disinvestments," Carla Pfeffer's challenge to the use of a positivist epistemological framework for evaluating (and often dismissing) politically engaged queer work. While scholars doing queer work are often faced with responses from journal editors, grant reviewers, and colleagues that suggest (or explicitly state) that their work is less legitimate than that in other subfields, Pfeffer makes a case for how to shift the normative center by carving out systems of support that create more spaces for queer scholarship. We end with this piece, as it serves to wrap up the conversation about queer collaboration and world building that we develop across this volume.

Coda: A final note on queer collaboration

We see this book as an experiment in collective process, as itself an instance of queer world making within a straight discipline. Many graduate programs in sociology afford few opportunities for working collectively within the subfield of queer sociology—or even the broader category of the sociology of sexualities. Most of us in this volume were mentored by the single sociologist in our department who was doing work on sexuality or gender (if we were lucky), or on related topics, such as embodiment—a situation that, while a vast improvement over previous generations, made it difficult to form scholarly community. Often, it was only as junior faculty that we began to develop such a community and were able to start more complex conversations about the craft of sociology. In casual discussions with our peers, we encountered story after story of people making initial forays into the field with an underdeveloped toolkit for deciphering queer worlds, in isolation or in direct defiance of our mentors' counsel. Taking these conversations as the starting point for this volume, we asked contributors to write up these experiences as first-person accounts.

Yet, while we were met with much excitement about this project, it was difficult at first to get the chapters off the ground. Contributors wrote to us with common questions: How personal should I get? What is everyone else writing? Is there a model for the type of chapter you are envisioning? Even as the editors, we found ourselves dragging our feet about committing our own experiences to the page. What we realized from this collective hesitation was how emotionally risky it felt to write against disciplinary convention—how "queerly vulnerable" (Meadow, this volume) we made ourselves in admitting struggle, confusion, ambivalence. Acknowledging as a group that we felt stuck in our writing, we came to realize just how difficult it is to pull back the curtain and show the messiness and anxiety that often lies behind our attempts to produce politically informed empirical work in a discipline committed to objective, depersonalized reporting of theory and data.

We chose to address what people felt to be an individual stumbling block with a collective strategy. As the chapters of this book took form, we met with the contributors in small groups in three different cities to workshop early drafts. In these sessions, we gave and received feedback and assisted one another in thinking through our ideas. Most important, we were able to try out provisional ways of presenting our experiences and linking them to broader questions and methodological considerations without the fear of being "wrong" or unable to support our ideas with "evidence." After meeting in these small groups, we edited our chapters and submitted them for a round of blind peer review from within the group. This process offered each contributor a second set of eyes on the revised work. Through this method, we worked against the isolationist model of journal review, one that expects perfection before engagement. We tried instead to cultivate an ethic of collaboration in which we helped authors execute the work in their own vision.

There are several implications of this model of collective knowledge production. It created the conditions for us to work in community, which, for most queer scholars, is rare. It offered us the unusual opportunity to glance behind the curtain at the processes that created the studies we read and used in our own work. It cut against the disciplinary convention that we are, by definition, in competition for scarce resources and thus must guard closely our intellectual product. It allowed us to see that we were encountering a similar set of practical, empirical, and emotional obstacles, even though many of us do vastly different kinds of work. Finally, it generated a pool of knowledge for future scholars doing this work to build on, critique, and extend. We offer up our model of queer collaboration to readers in an effort to encourage more dialogue around building queer community in a straight discipline.

NOTE

1. In using the term *appreciative*, we draw on the work of sociologist David Matza (1969) to distinguish between a research approach that seeks to understand a particular practice or identity from the point of view of respondents, and an approach that seeks to correct such ways of being in accordance with prevailing norms.

WORKS CITED

Abelson, Miriam. 2016. "'You aren't from around here': Race, masculinity and rural transgender men." *Gender, Place, & Culture* 23: 1535–46.

Allen, Jafari. 2012. "Black/queer/diaspora at the current conjuncture." *GLQ: A Journal of Gay and Lesbian Studies* 18 (2–3): 211–48.

Battle, Juan, and Sandra Barnes. 2010. *Black sexualities: Probing powers, passions, practices, and policies.* New Brunswick, NJ: Rutgers University Press.

Baumle, Amanda K., and D'Lane R. Compton. 2015. *Legalizing LGBT families: How the law shapes parenthood.* New York: New York University Press.

Berlant, Lauren, and Michael Warner. 1998. "Sex in public." *Critical Inquiry* 24(2): 547–66.

Brim, Matt, and Amin Ghaziani (eds.). 2016. "Introduction: Queer methods." *WSQ: Women's Studies Quarterly* 44(3–4): 14–27.

Browne, Kath, and Catherine J. Nash. 2010. *Queer methods and methodologies: Intersecting queer theories and social science research.* Burlington, VT: Ashgate.

Butler, Judith. 1990. *Gender trouble: Feminism and the subversion of identity.* New York: Routledge.

Carrillo, Hector. 2018. *Pathways of desire: The sexual migration of Mexican gay men.* Chicago: University of Chicago Press.

Cohen, Cathy J. 1997. "Punks, bulldaggers and welfare queens: The radical potential of queer politics?" *GLQ: Gay and Lesbian Quarterly* 3(4): 437–65.

———. 1999. *The boundaries of blackness: AIDS and the breakdown of black politics*. Chicago: University of Chicago Press

Cohen, Cathy J., and Sarah Jackson. 2016. "Ask a feminist: A conversation with Cathy J. Cohen on Black Lives Matter, feminism, and contemporary activism." *Signs: A Journal of Women and Culture* 41(4): 775–92.

Connell, Catherine. 2014. *School's out: Gay and lesbian teachers in the classroom*. Berkeley: University of California Press.

Crawley, Sara. 2008. "The clothes make the trans: Region and geography in experiences of the body." *Journal of Lesbian Studies* 12(4): 365–79.

Dean, James Joseph. 2014. *Straights: Heterosexuality in post-closeted culture*. New York: New York University Press.

DeVault, Marjorie L. 1999. *Liberating method: Feminist and social research*. Philadelphia: Temple University Press.

Dozier, Raine. 2005. "Beards, breasts, and bodies: Doing sex in a gendered world." *Gender & Society* 19(3): 297–316.

Eng, David L., J. Jack Halberstam, and José Esteban Muñoz. 2005. "Introduction: What's queer studies now?" *Social Text* 23(3–4): 1–17.

Epstein, Steven. 1994. "A queer encounter: Sociology and the study of sexuality." *Sociological Theory* 12(2): 188–202.

Ferguson, Roderick A. 2004. *Aberrations in black: Toward a queer of color critique*. Minneapolis: University of Minnesota Press.

———. 2005. "Race-ing homonormativity: Citizenship, sociology and gay identity." In *Black queer studies: A critical anthology*. Ed. E. Patrick Johnson and Mae Henderson. Durham: Duke University Press, 52–67.

Fetner, Tina. 2008. *How the religious right shaped lesbian and gay activism*. Minneapolis: University of Minnesota Press

Flores, Andrew, Jody Herman, Gary Gates, and Taylor N. T. Brown. 2016. *How many adults identify as transgender in the United States?* Los Angeles: Williams Institute.

Gagné, Patricia, and Richard Tewksbury (eds.). 2002. *Gendered sexualities*. Advances in Gender Research, vol. 6. New York: JAI.

Gamson, Joshua. 1996. "Must identity movements self-destruct? A queer dilemma." In *Queer theory/sociology*. Ed. Steven Seidman. New York: Blackwell, 395–420.

Gamson, Joshua, and Dawne Moon. 2004. "The sociology of sexualities: Queer and beyond." *Annual Review of Sociology* 30: 47–64.

GenIUSS Group. 2014. *Best practices to identify transgender and other gender minority respondents on population-based surveys*. Los Angeles: Williams Institute.

Ghaziani, Amin. 2015. *There goes the gayborhood?* Princeton, NJ: Princeton University Press.

Ghaziani, Amin, Verta Taylor, and Amy Stone. 2016. "Cycles of sameness and difference in LGBT social movements." *Annual Review of Sociology* 42: 165–83.

Gray, Mary L., Brian J. Gilley, and Colin R. Johnson (eds.). 2016. *Queering the countryside: New frontiers in rural queer studies.* New York, NY: New York University Press.

Green, Adam Isaiah. 2002. "Gay but not queer: Toward a post-queer study of sexuality." *Theory and Society* 31(4): 521–45.

———. 2007. "Erotic habitus: Toward a sociology of desire." *Theory and Society* 37(6): 597–626.

Greene, Theodore. 2014. "Gay neighborhoods and the rights of the vicarious citizen." *City & Community* 13(2): 99–118.

Grzanka, Patrick. 2016. "Queer survey research and the ontological dimensions of heterosexism." *WSQ: Women's Studies Quarterly* 44(3–4): 131–49.

Halberstam, J. Jack. 2011. *The queer art of failure.* Durham, NC: Duke University Press.

Han, C. Winter. 2015. *Geisha of a different kind: Race and sexuality in Gaysian America.* New York: New York University Press

Hoang, Kimberly. 2015. *Dealing in desire: Asian ascendency, Western decline, and the hidden currencies of global sex work.* Berkeley, CA: University of California Press.

Hong, Grace Kyungwon, and Roderick A. Ferguson (eds.). 2011. *Strange affinities: The gender and sexual politics of comparative racialization.* Durham, NC: Duke University Press.

Hooker, Evelyn. 1957. "The adjustment of the male overt homosexual." *Journal of Projective Techniques* 21(1): 18–31.

———. 1993. "Reflections of a 40-year exploration: A scientific view on homosexuality." *American Psychologist* 48(4): 450–53.

Ingraham, Chrys. 2004. *Thinking straight: The power, promise, and paradox of heterosexuality.* New York: Routledge.

Irvine, Janice M. 2014. "The other sex work: Stigma in sexuality research." *Social Currents* 2(2): 116–25.

Johnson, E. Patrick. 2001. "'Quare' studies, or (almost) everything I know about queer studies I learned from my grandmother." *Text and Performance Quarterly* 21(1): 1–25.

Johnson, E. Patrick, and Mae Henderson (eds.). 2005. *Black queer studies: A critical anthology.* Durham, NC: Duke University Press.

Jones, Angela. 2015. "For black models scroll down: Webcam modeling and the racialization of erotic labor." *Sexuality & Culture* 19(4): 776–99.

Kazyak, Emily. 2012. "Midwest or lesbian? Gender, rurality, and sexuality." *Gender & Society* 26(6): 825–48.

Laslett, Barbara, and Barrie Thorne. 1997. *Feminist sociology: Life histories of a movement.* New Brunswick, NJ: Rutgers University Press.

Lemert, Charles. 1996. "Series editor's preface." In *Queer theory/sociology.* Ed. Steven Seidman. New York: Blackwell, vii–xii.

Lewin, Ellen, and William L. Leap (eds.). 1996. *Out in the field: Reflections of gay and lesbian anthropologists.* Urbana: University of Illinois Press.

Lombardi, Emilia, and Swagata Banik. 2016. "The utility of the two-step gender measure within trans and cis populations." *Sexuality Research and Social Policy* 13(3): 288–96.

Mathers, Lain A. B. 2017. "Bathrooms, boundaries, and emotional burdens: Cisgendering interactions through the interpretation of transgender experience." *Symbolic Interaction* 40(3): 295–316.

Matza, David. 1969. *Becoming deviant.* Englewood Cliffs, NJ: Prentice-Hall.

Meadow, Tey. 2010. "A rose is a rose: On producing legal gender classifications." *Gender & Society* 24(6): 814–37.

———. 2011. "Deep down where the music plays: How parents account for gender variance." *Sexualities* 14(6): 725–47.

Miller, Lisa R., and Eric Anthony Grollman. 2015. "The social costs of gender nonconformity for transgender adults: Implications for discrimination and health." *Sociological Forum* 30(3): 809–31.

Mills, C. Wright. 1959. *The sociological imagination.* New York: Oxford University Press.

Minton, Henry L. 2001. *Departing from deviance: A history of homosexual rights and emancipatory science in America.* Chicago: University of Chicago Press.

Mize, Trenton D. 2016. "Sexual orientation in the labor market." *American Sociological Review* 81(6): 1132–60.

Moore, Mignon R. 2011. *Invisible families: Gay identities, relationships, and motherhood among black women.* Berkeley: University of California Press.

Moore, Mignon R., and Michael Stambolis-Ruhstorfer. 2013. "LGBT sexuality and families at the start of the twenty-first century." *Annual Review of Sociology* 39: 491–507.

Namaste, Viviane. 1994. "The politics of inside/out: Queer theory, poststructuralism, and a sociological approach to sexuality." *Sociological Theory* 12(2): 220–31.

———. 1996. "'Tragic misreadings': Queer theory's erasure of transgender subjectivity." In *Queer studies: A lesbian, gay, bisexual, and transgender anthology.* Ed. G. Beemyn and M. Eliason. New York: New York University Press, 183–203.

———. 2000. *Invisible lives: The erasure of transsexual and transgendered people.* Chicago: University of Chicago Press.

———. 2005. *Sex change, social change: Reflections on identity, institutions, and imperialism.* Toronto: Canada School Press.

Nordmarken, Sonny, and Reese Kelly. 2014. "Limiting transgender health: Administrative violence and microaggressions in health care systems." In *Health care disparities and the LGBT population.* Ed. Vickie Harvey and Teresa Heinz. New York: Lexington Books, 143–69.

Ocampo, Anthony. 2012. "Making masculinity: Negotiations of gender presentation among Latino gay men." *Latino Studies* 10(4): 448–72.

Pascoe, C.J. 2007. *Dude, you're a fag: Masculinity and sexuality in high school.* Berkeley: University of California Press.

Puar, Jasbir. 2005. "Queer times, queer assemblages." *Social Text* 23(3–4): 121–39.

———. 2007. *Terrorist assemblages: Homonationalism in queer times.* Durham, NC: Duke University Press.

Pfeffer, Carla. 2014. "'I don't like passing as a straight woman': Queer negotiations of identity and social group membership." *American Journal of Sociology* 120(1): 1–44.

———. 2016. *Queering families: The postmodern partnerships of cisgender women and transgender men.* New York: Oxford University Press.

Powell, Brian, Catherine Bolzendahl, Claudia Geist, and Lala Carr Steelman. 2010. *Counted out: Same-sex relations and American's definitions of family.* New York: Russell Sage Foundation.

Puri, Jyoti. 2016. *Sexual states: Governance and the struggle over antisodomy laws in India.* Durham, NC: Duke University Press.

Reinharz, Shulamit. 1992. *Feminist methods in social research.* New York: Oxford University Press.

Rubin, Henry. 2003. *Self-made men: Identity and embodiment among transsexual men.* Nashville: Vanderbilt University Press.

Rupp, Leila, and Verta Taylor. 2003. *Drag queens at the 801 Cabaret.* Chicago: University of Chicago Press.

Savci, Evren. 2017. "Language and social knowledge." *Ethnography* 18(1): 57–67.

Schilt, Kristen. 2010. *Just one of the guys? Transgender men and the persistence of gender inequality.* Chicago: University of Chicago Press.

Schilt, Kristen, and Laurel Westbrook. 2009. "Doing gender, doing heteronormativity: 'Gender normals,' transgender people, and the social maintenance of heterosexuality." *Gender & Society* 23(4): 440–44.

Schippers, Mimi. 2016. *Beyond monogamy: Polyamory and the future of polyqueer sexualities.* New York: New York University Press.

Sedgwick, Eve. 1990. *Epistemology of the closet.* Berkeley: University of California Press.

Seidman, Steven (ed.). 1996a. *Queer theory/sociology.* New York: Blackwell.

————. 1996b. "Introduction." In *Queer theory/sociology*. Ed. Steven Seidman. New York: Blackwell, 1–30.

Shapiro, Eve. 2007. "Drag kinging and the transformation of gender identities." *Gender & Society* 21(2): 250–71.

shuster, stef. 2016. "Uncertain expertise and the limitations of clinical guidelines in transgender healthcare." *Journal of Health and Social Behavior* 57(3): 319–32.

Snorton, C. Riley. 2017. *Black on both sides: A racial history of trans identity*. Minneapolis: University of Minnesota Press.

Stacey, Judith, and Barrie Thorne. 1985. "The missing feminist revolution in sociology." *Social Problems* 32(4): 301–16.

Stein, Arlene, and Ken Plummer. 1994. "'I can't even think straight:' 'Queer' theory and the missing sexual revolution in sociology." *Sociological Theory* 12(2): 178–817.

Stone, Amy. 2012. *Gay rights at the ballot box*. Minneapolis: University of Minnesota Press.

Stryker, Susan, and Aren Z. Aizura (eds.). 2013. *The transgender studies reader 2*. New York: Routledge.

Stryker, Susan, and Stephen Whittle (eds.). 2006. *The transgender studies reader*. New York: Routledge.

Sumerau, J. E, Ryan T. Cragun, and Lain A. B. Mathers. 2016. "Contemporary religion and the cisgendering of reality." *Sociological Currents* 3(3): 293–311.

Taylor, Verta, and Nicole Raeburn. 1995. "Career consequences for lesbian, gay, and bisexual sociologists." *Social Problems* 42(2): 701–36.

Ueno, Koji, Teresa Roach, and Abráham Peña-Talamantes. 2013. "Sexual orientation and gender typicality of the occupation in young adulthood." *Social Forces* 92(1): 81–108.

Valocchi, Stephen. 2005. "Not yet queer enough: The lessons of queer theory for the sociology of gender and sexuality." *Gender & Society* 19(6): 750–70.

Vidal-Ortiz, Salvador. 2005. "'Sexuality' and 'gender' in Santeria: Towards a queer of color critique in the study of religion." Unpublished PhD dissertation, City University of New York.

————. 2008. "Transgender and transsexual studies: Sociology's influence and future steps." *Sociological Compass* 2: 433–50.

Ward, Jane. 2015. *Not gay: Sex between straight white men*. New York: New York University Press.

Ward, Jane, and Beth Schneider. 2009. "The reaches of heteronormativity: An introduction." *Gender & Society* 23(4): 433–39.

Westbrook, Laurel, and Aliya Saperstein. 2015. "New categories are not enough: Rethinking the measurement of sex and gender in social surveys." *Gender & Society* 29(4): 534–60.

Westbrook, Laurel, and Kristen Schilt. 2014. "Doing gender, determining gender: Transgender people, gender panics, and the maintenance of the sex/gender/sexuality system." *Gender & Society* 28(1): 32–57.

Weston, Kath. 1997. *Families we choose: Lesbians, gays, kinship.* New York: Columbia University Press.

White, Todd C. 2009. *Pre-gay LA: A social history of the movement for homosexual rights.* Urbana: University of Illinois Press.

Windsor, Elroi. 2011. "Regulating healthy gender: Surgical body modification among transgender and cisgender consumers." Unpublished PhD dissertation, Georgia State University.

Zuberi, Tukufu, and Eduardo Bonilla-Silva (eds.). 2008. *White logic, white methods: Racism and methodology.* New York: Rowman and Littlefield.

PART I　Anti-orthodoxies

1 The "Not Sociology" Problem

Kristen Schilt

In the 1973 supplemental issue of the *American Journal of Sociology* (*AJS*) titled "Changing Women in a Changing Society," an intergenerational assembly of scholars weighed in on the problems facing women in the United States and on the place the study of gender held within the broader discipline. Publication of an issue edited and authored almost exclusively by women in the longest running and most historically significant sociology journal—and the fact that this issue was then printed separately as a book that sold over 25,000 copies[1]—suggested a turning point in which feminist inquiry was becoming a central area of sociology. Almost fifty years later, *Gender & Society*, the feminist sociology journal started in 1987 by Sociologists for Women in Society, has nearly tied with *AJS* in terms of impact.[2] The Sex & Gender Section of the American Sociological Association also has emerged as the organization's largest member subgroup. At the same time, a quick perusal of JSTOR shows that feminist scholarship—and even research on any gender topic—continues to be underrepresented in most high-impact sociology journals that advertise their mandate as publishing research of "general interest" to the discipline. Taken together, these trends suggest that while feminist theories

37

and research might not yet be at the center of sociology, feminist scholars have staked out an influential claim in the discipline.

The evolution of a feminist community within the broader discipline of sociology exemplifies a dynamic that I wish to explore about "queer work"—and here, drawing on Amy L. Stone and Jaime Cantrell's writing about queer archives, I invoke the older meaning of *queer* as something "odd and perplexing" that can disrupt the status quo of a social milieu, such as an academic discipline (2015: 3). In the 1970s and 1980s, feminists presented such a queer challenge to sociology with their investigation into how normative gender ideologies infused traditional research methods and theories in ways that perpetuated institutional and interpersonal gender inequality (see Smith 1989; Stacey & Thorne 1985). When faced with opposition from disciplinary gatekeepers, they developed a community of scholars who served, first, as emotional support and interlocutors and, later, as feminist institutions gained ground, as editors, reviewers, and tenure-letter writers (see Laslett & Thorne 1997). A similar process of community and institution building in response to disciplinary marginalization is evident in the experiences of scholars of color working in critical race studies who have to navigate what Tukufu Zuberi and Eduardo Bonilla-Silva term "white logic, white methods" (2008), and exemplified as well by queer scholars pushing back against long-standing sociological associations between nonheterosexual identities and practices and social deviance (see Seidman 1996). The growing body of writing about the importance of community building from scholars working in areas of sociological inquiry that have been relegated to the margins of the discipline gives valuable insight into the varied strategies for resisting such marginalization, and presents a historical record from which future generations can evaluate disciplinary change.

In this chapter, I shift the focus from a discussion of how we navigate academic marginalization to an examination of the strategies used by disciplinary gatekeepers to keep us marginal. In thinking through how to conceptualize these strategies of resistance to queer work, I have come to think of them as bolstering what we might call the "not sociology" problem. I borrow this concept from Marjorie DeVault's writing about how, early in her career, sociological gatekeepers often dismissed her feminist research with the statement "But that is not sociology" (1999: 15). This sentence struck a chord with me because it is a pithy synthesis of academic resistance that I have faced—and that I have seen many others face—while doing research in the area of transgender studies. And it captures the resistance my colleagues and students have encountered when doing social justice–oriented work on a number of other "queer" areas of inquiry, such as sex work (see Hoang, this volume). While we may discuss these marginalizing experiences in small groups in dark bars at conferences, we often keep silent about them in public talks or in print because the cost of calling out the ideological character of these responses to our work can be so high. Yet there is something to be gained from transforming these reactions from embarrassing personal incidents into a politically situated analysis about how sociological gatekeeping works—and how we might disrupt it.

THE THREE R'S: RESISTANCE, REDUCTION, AND RIDICULE

In mapping out the interactional and institutional strategies that push queer work to the sociological margins, I identified the Three R's: *resistance*, the attempt to erect boundaries against an emerging area of inquiry (e.g., transgender studies, fat studies, critical heterosexualities) that pushes up against an established canon or theoretical frame; *reduction*, the attempt to dismiss scholarship on group X as too "fringe" to sociologically matter; and *ridicule*, the attempt to devalue scholarship on group X by positioning it as absurd. These strategies are not mutually exclusive—a scholar might face all three in the course of one talk—nor is my list by any means exhaustive. I see this trio simply as a starting point for a discussion about making disciplinary change and mitigating the emotional labor spent on navigating these reactions. People doing work at the margins of sociology often meet with ideological critiques disguised as objective criticism from colleagues, institutional gatekeepers, and peers. If we desire sociological careers in the academy, we can feel pressure to sit quietly while our work is dismissed with labels that fit under the "not sociology" umbrella: "too micro," "descriptive," "me-search." If we offer a challenge, we risk being positioned as "not collegial," "too ideological," or "aggressive."

Yet keeping these experiences to ourselves can make us doubt our work, can lead us to switch to new research topics that we are not invested in but that seem "safe," can encourage us to leave sociology for other fields, or can drive us out of the academy altogether.

As a tenured professor, I recognize that the costs for me in writing publicly about these strategies are less severe than the potential costs to graduate students, untenured faculty, and adjunct faculty. I also recognize that in talking about such reactions to our work, we must look at how they manifest differently depending on who is presenting the research. I received much more overt resistance to my work as a graduate student, for instance, than I do now as a tenured professor. Further, as a white, queer cisgender woman, the forms of resistance I have faced when presenting research on transgender topics have sometimes overlapped and sometimes differed from the experiences of transgender and nonbinary colleagues with whom I have collaborated. Many of us have encountered the advice that transgender research is a bad idea—it's just a fad, it's too micro, we won't get jobs (see Lombardi this volume for a larger discussion). Yet I rarely face questions about whether I am doing "me-search." I am more likely to be positioned on a continuum from someone who does intentionally "provocative" work to someone who received poor guidance as a graduate student—and who could be saved if I just moved to a new area of study. To cite a case highlighting this last point: when I was on the job market, two senior scholars at different universities asked me in what I interpreted as hopeful voices, "Do you have any other interests besides transsexuals?"

As someone who identifies in my published work as cisgender, I also have been privy to unwanted commentary from cisgender sociologists whom I often barely know about their experiences with and feelings about transgender people[3]—much in the same way that white people may assume that other people whom they perceive as white are a safe audience for racist commentary (Picca & Feagin 2007). While telling people I was politically committed to transgender social justice did little to stop such comments, letting them know that I had been partnered with a transgender man for many years usually did—though I was then often asked for details about my sexual history. I mention these experiences as a way to make my positionality visible and to demonstrate how our social locations in the status hierarchy of the discipline and our identities—and how our colleagues perceive these identities (whether correctly or incorrectly)—shape the ways in which our research is taken up and what gatekeeping strategies, if any, we may face when doing queer work. I turn now to examples of how I have experienced the Three R's while presenting to sociological audiences research about the lived experiences of transgender people.

Resistance

My early interest in sociology came from its ability to provide what I saw as an empirically grounded and theoretically rich language with which to investigate my long-standing preoccupation: how to make effective challenges to social inequality. While the Sociology Department at the University of Texas at Austin, my undergraduate institution, emphasized a particularly traditional form of sociology, I was able to take courses with feminist professors and graduate students that shaped the trajectory of my adult life. It was transformative to discover the theory of social constructionism—to take hold of the idea that unequal social relations could change, no matter how hard that change might be to accomplish, because they were not static, ahistorical, or innate. For my MA work, I built on my undergraduate thesis about Riot Grrrl, a 1990s punk rock feminist subculture that presented challenges to second-wave (1960s–1970s) feminist theory and the male-dominated realm of subcultural studies. I found generous support for this work from feminist mentors. Senior feminist scholars invited me to present at conferences as an early-stage graduate student, where I built crucial mentoring networks, and encouraged me to send my work out for review to journals. With a vibrant community of mentors who reflected to me the value of studying areas of social life that are dismissed or devalued by those in positions of social power, I grew a thick skin for situations in which nonfeminist professors and peers told me that gender scholarship was not interesting or important—in other words, was "not sociology." And, most important, I learned how to distinguish a constructive critique of my research design or theoretical argument from an ideological opinion (often stated as a fact) about what was worthy of study.

I did not realize how important this ability to distinguish between critique and opinion would be until I began presenting my dissertation research about the workplace experiences of transgender men to feminist audiences in the mid-2000s. I saw this shift in my research as a response to the body of crucial and innovative theoretical and empirical scholarship about the lives of transgender people that began to emerge in sociology in the 1990s and early 2000s (see Namaste 2000; Rubin 2003). Having the opportunity to take classes in LGBTQ studies, queer theory, and transgender studies as a graduate student at UCLA, I viewed sociological methods as well suited to bring rigorous empirical data on transgender people's experiences to bear on policy and activism around transgender rights—much in the way that feminist sociologists had done for cisgender women in arenas such as sexual harassment and workplace inequality. I saw the emerging subfield of transgender studies in sociology as poised to challenge the long-standing positioning of trans people as deviant within the sociological literature and to radically transform how sociologists conceptualized gender. As a person with political commitments to feminist and LGBTQ activism, I wanted to be a part of this work.

I had the luck to be in a department with a core group of feminist scholars who strongly supported my research even though it was outside their topical areas of expertise. Yet, in my first attempts to present my research to a broader feminist audience, I was often met with seemingly purposeful resistance from the people who held positions of authority in the subfield, such as conference panel organizers and journal editors. When I sent in papers about transgender workplace discrimination to "Gender and Workplace" sessions at the annual sociology conference, I was told that my work would find a better home in the Sexualities Section or on LGBTQ-focused panels (of which there were very few at the time)—advice that signaled to me that transgender people's experiences at work were not of interest to gender-and-work scholars. In presentations, I had feminist audiences dismiss accounts of trans men's experiences of workplace discrimination and ask if I could provide examples of how trans men might help cisgender women at work—a question that signified to me an understanding that cisgender women should always be at the center of sociological research on gender inequality. And I met with a pervasive assumption among older feminist scholars that transgender men initiated gender transitions because of internalized misogyny. I was asked many times by second-wave feminists in formal and informal settings why "those poor women" (i.e., trans men) felt they needed to "mutilate" their bodies with surgical interventions and hormones.

At first, it felt as though an unspoken message were being conveyed that research on transgender people was irrelevant to sociologists of gender—a "not sociology of gender" variant of mainstream dismissal. This message became overt, however, when I saw a prominent gender scholar tell a conference audience that transgender people could not be part of "the gender revolution," because they were too deeply invested in reifying a gender binary. I have since faced this response many times in relation to my research from people I associate with second-wave feminism. In these interactional moments, I always feel a sense of disorientation because it is often a well-coiffed cisgender woman with eye-catching jewelry or scarf telling *me*, a cisgender woman who has long eschewed pants for dresses, is usually in heels, and has a fondness for metallic lipsticks, that transgender people are reifying the gender binary. While I consciously perform what I envision as a queerly referential femme-ness, I recognize that outside queer spaces I can easily be read as reproducing traditional norms of femininity in my appearance. Yet I am not a problem for feminism.

Such a response to transgender people highlights a particular framing of gender transitions that has a long history in feminist scholarship (see Connell 2012; Serano 2007). In this line of thought, a feminist body project is one that encourages self-acceptance (e.g., love your body) while simultaneously seeking to trouble normative expectations for gender in theory, if not in embodied practice. Following this logic, transgender people who physically modify their bodies become self-hating cultural dupes of gender binarism, while cisgender women who feel they were "born in the right body" are allowed remarkable leeway for gender expression and attitudes toward feminism and gender equality. Using cisgenderism as the yardstick by which to measure the progressiveness or conservatism of a person's gender performance creates a situation in which Katy Perry on the cover of *Cosmo* may incite sighs from feminists who wish she was a better role model for young women, but does not invite the wave of condemnation and judgment that Caitlyn Jenner's *Vanity Fair* cover unleashed (see, for example, Garelick 2015).[4] And it allows feminist gatekeepers to resist and exclude an entire group of people from an imagined shared feminist project of making a "gender revolution" without questioning what assumptions about authenticity or exclusionary notions of progress are wrapped up in that particular imaginary—adopting, in other words, a similar strategy of resistance that has long been used within sociology to devalue feminist research (see DeVault 1999).

Reduction

While the "bad for feminism" response implies that transgender people have an inordinate amount of power to uphold the gender binary, a second set of responses I have received, from nonfeminist sociologists, suggests that transgender people are too "fringe" to warrant sociological study. This characterization maps on to what I term a strategy of reduction. In presentations to a general sociology audience, I have usually encountered this strategy through the question, "How many transgender people are there?" If I am interpreting this question in a generous way, I can see it as an earnest attempt to locate my interview sample size within a larger population frame. If there are, say, three hundred transgender people in the country and I conducted one hundred interviews, I would have a fairly strong basis from which to generalize. But, after getting this question many times, I now interpret it as drawing or guarding a disciplinary boundary separating a marginalized minority group that warrants sociological study from a "fringe" group that is too small or too "weird" to matter to a general sociology audience. Within this minority-versus-fringe framework, getting counted on a government document, such as the US decennial census or a large, nationally representative federal survey, often appears to be the dividing line. If transgender identification is not included in large-scale surveys that sociologists typically analyze, in other words, transgender people do not have to be taken seriously by quantitative sociology regardless of how much discrimination they may face. They are, in effect, too marginal to matter.

It is now possible to answer this "how many" question for the United States, with an estimation from the Williams Institute, an LGBTQ think tank at the University of California, Los Angeles, drawn from an analysis of national and state-level population surveys that collect data on transgender identity: 1.4 million adults, or 0.6 percent of the US population, identified as transgender in 2016 (Flores, Herman, Gates, & Brown 2016; see also Herman & Gates, this volume). As there are many potential barriers to identifying as transgender on a state-sponsored survey (see Currah & Stryker 2015), it is likely that this estimate is low. However, in my experience, the 0.6 percent figure generates just as much dismissal from quantitatively oriented sociologists as does the answer "We don't know." I have had sociologists casually tell me that I have dedicated my research career to an insignificant part of the US population, suggesting, again, that the numerical threshold for sociological significance should determine when we begin to take seriously experiences with discrimination and inequality. The dismissal of the transgender population as too small is problematic when considered alongside groups that are more readily incorporated as part of a legitimate sociological endeavor, such as Jewish Americans (estimated as 2% of the population in 2013), and, increasingly, LGB Americans (estimated as 3.5% of the population in 2011). Sociological gatekeepers' insistence on relegating transgender research to the category of "not sociology" suggests there is something underlying this "how many" question that goes beyond issues of population size and generalizability. I take up what this might be in the next section.

Ridicule

Queer work disrupts the status quo when it upsets taken-for-granted assumptions and beliefs within the established discipline—the sociological certainties upon which our academic training was based. Faced with a challenge to their worldview, gatekeepers can seek to discredit this work using the strategy of ridicule. In my experience, this tactic usually begins with an attack on the idea that transgender identities are a real social phenomenon. Such a response typically is leveled at me as a cisgender researcher, who, in the eyes of such critics, has crossed a line into absurdity by taking seriously identities and experiences that the asker positions as cultural delusions. To convey how ridiculous they find the idea of taking a transgender person seriously, audience members have asked me in talks such questions as (if the asker is white), "Well, what if I say I am black? Can I have any racial identity I want?" or (if the asker is human), "What if

I say I am an animal? Can we now just be anything we choose?" A human may claim to be an animal, askers imply, and may be able to find a small community to support that claim. Such people can alter their appearances to appear more animal-like, but, in this understanding, "we know" that they are really still genetically human. If humans cannot become cats, this logic implies, then transgender people cannot "really" exist. At the level of rhetoric, these questions are designed to be so outrageous that I will be forced by the power of analogy to admit that transgender identities are a politically correct fiction that I am propagating for ideological reasons.

What is most notable about the strategy of ridicule is its overt hostility, which was most evident to me in an anonymous review I received of one of the first articles I submitted for publication. In 2005, while a graduate student, I coauthored an article with Elroi Windsor, who, at the time, was one of the few US-based sociologists working in transgender studies. We had identified some overlap in our interview studies around trans men's experiences with the hormonal and surgical possibilities of gender transitions. Combining our data, we were able to draw on the experiences of seventy trans men from four geographic regions in the United States—a relatively large N for qualitative work in transgender studies at the time— and craft an article about the diverse ways in which the men we interviewed transformed their bodies to make their unique gender identities visible. In this article, we noted that some men sought genital surgery while others felt that it was less important to their self-making. Our point was not to support one perspective or the other, but rather to demonstrate the different ways in which transgender men embody their gender identities. We concluded with some thoughts about how considering trans men's perspectives might open up new possibilities for theorizing masculinity within sociology.

As with most articles, there was room for improvement in our organization of the data and in our argumentation. Even with that realization, however, I was unprepared for the lone review the paper received from an established social science journal. The review's author—who identified himself as a cisgender man—responded to our article with what can only be called vitriol. He repeatedly referred to transgender men as "biological women," and took issue with the idea that some transgender men were not interested in genital surgery. He ended his diatribe with the following:

These women—biologically women prior to their physical transformations—are so NOT men that they do not get the centrality of the penis. "Eh,
big deal, that penis thing" they might say, thus revealing as starkly if they
had been pantsed [sic], that they haven't the first idea of what masculinity
actually means. Let me put it this way: if pre-op FTMs do not experience
penis envy, they don't "get" the very sex they claim to already inhabit. Sorry
authors, but penises matter. Big (or well not so big) time.

The reviewer also clearly intended to discredit us as researchers—a point
further evidenced by the review's last line: "It makes me wonder if the
authors are also women, and therefore, they don't get it either."

I experienced many different emotions in reading this review. At first I
felt shame, as if I had made some type of rookie mistake. Repeatedly reading the review to myself and to others, I later began to see it as so ridiculous as to almost become a parody of cismasculinity in crisis. I wondered
what was going on for the writer—a person the journal editor assured me
was very senior "in the field" when I questioned the review's legitimacy—
and what ontological certainty was being unmoored for him by this
research. But, mostly, I felt angry. The lack of collegiality in this review—
which remains unprecedented in my experience with publishing—was
shocking. There was no discussion of the fit between theory and evidence,
or the structure of the article. There was simply a rant about the centrality
of the "phallus," and a claim that only people with penises who identified
as men could understand or make claims about masculinity. The anonymous and private nature of journal reviews made it impossible to respond
to what was clearly intended to feel like a personal attack. The article was
rejected from the journal on the basis of this one review. Eventually, however, we published this article in a special issue on trans sexualities in the
Journal of Homosexuality, a fact that shows the importance of emerging
community institutions for queer work.

CONCLUSION

At the heart of the "not sociology" problem is a resistance to research that
disrupts the center of the discipline or a well-established subfield. My
examples focus on reactions I have received when presenting research

about the workplace experiences of transgender men to sociologists in a particular historical moment; and I hope that for a new generation of scholars in trans studies and the sociology of gender, the stories I tell here do not continue to resonate. But the strategies I identify—the Three R's—can be deployed as an attempt to marginalize any emerging area of inquiry that is doing queerly disruptive work, such as research on nonbinary gender identities, asexuality, or fat positivity. In identifying these marginalization strategies, I realize the impossibility of providing any advice about "right" responses. My reactions to these incidents always involve a cost-benefit analysis in the particular context. Sometimes I feel that I give an answer that effectively pushes back on the question's underlying assumptions. Sometimes I spend the next few days stewing over what would have been a better answer, or what I wished I had said in the moment. Whatever the details of particular incidents, it has been invaluable to me to build a community of scholars working across all types of queer work to talk through these experiences. I have learned how to defend my work a little better, as well as how to support my colleagues and students when they face critiques. I have experienced the importance of intergenerational networks, and, when possible, I take on institutional roles through which I can help mentor and create more space for junior scholars. Finally, just as a feminist community did for me as a young scholar, my queer community in sociology has helped me to reframe these marginalizing strategies as less a personal embarrassment than a political problem to be worked on collectively.

I end with some thoughts about the institutionalization of once-marginalized subfields in sociology and what this means for the "not sociology" problem. That feminist sociologists could resist transgender scholarship in the mid-2000s—a resistance that appears (I hope) to be shifting with the increased visibility of transgender, gender-nonconforming, and nonbinary scholars and transgender studies and through ideological changes within feminist sociology—illustrates the extent to which feminists have made inroads into the sociological center. There is now an established canon of feminist sociology that is taught in courses, read for qualifying exams, and published in anthologies—though, in my experience, it is still unusual to see feminist theory in general theory courses or in sociological theory journals. For any marginalized area of inquiry, whether it be feminist sociology or critical race studies, to make even a slight move to the disciplinary center opens up new opportunities and brings more legitimacy to the work of scholars in this field. Yet with these gains comes more power to exclude new voices that may seek to build upon and challenge the axiomatic assumptions of this once-marginalized subfield. As queer work makes strides in sociology, we must think carefully about this power of exclusion. We might find ourselves, as we review journal manuscripts or select presenters for conference panels, resisting, reducing, or ridiculing emerging scholarship that challenges our own theoretical frameworks and worldviews. We should remember that theories and empirical findings always have a shelf life. In fact, if we are truly committed to effecting social change with our research, we should strive for future irrelevance! When we meet with new generations of students and find ourselves poised to tell them that an emerging area of inquiry or a body of theory with which we are unfamiliar, and perhaps even uncomfortable, is "not sociology," we should stop ourselves, and add, to quote Marjorie DeVault (1999, 15), "Well, at least not yet."

NOTES

1. I thank Susan Allan, managing editor of the *American Journal of Sociology*, for providing this sales figure.

2. Based on 2015 analyses publicized on journal websites, the *American Journal of Sociology* ranked 7th out of 142 sociology journals, while *Gender & Society* ranked 9th.

3. When I began interviewing people who had undergone gastric bypass surgery, I started to receive, as a relatively thin person, such unwanted commentary about heavy people from thin sociologists who imagined I must feel similar discomfort. I mention this experience to emphasize the point that these strategies are not unique to a particular area of inquiry, but show a broader process of marginalization.

4. I am not suggesting that Caitlyn Jenner is beyond critique. But thinking critically about her conservative politics or her race and class privilege is different from arguing that her gender identity and body project are detrimental to feminism.

WORKS CITED

Connell, Raewyn. 2012. "Transsexual women and feminist thought: Toward new understanding and new politics." *Signs* 37(4): 857–81.

Currah, Paisley, and Susan Stryker. 2015. "Introduction." *TSQ: Transgender Studies Quarterly* (Special Issue: Making Transgender Count). 2(1): 1–12.

DeVault, Marjorie. 1999. *Liberating method: Feminism and social research.* Philadelphia: Temple University Press.

Flores, Andrew R., Jody L. Herman, Gary Gates, and Taylor Brown. 2016. "How many adults identify as transgender in the United States?" Los Angeles: Williams Institute. https://williamsinstitute.law.ucla.edu/wp-content/uploads/How-Many-Adults-Identify-as-Transgender-in-the-United-States.pdf.

Garelick, Rhonda. 2015. "The price of Caitlyn Jenner's heroism." *New York Times.* June 3. https://www.nytimes.com/2015/06/03/opinion/the-price-of-jenners-heroism.html.

Laslett, Barbara, and Barrie Thorne (eds.). 1997. *Feminist sociology: Life histories of a movement.* New Brunswick, NJ: Rutgers University Press.

Namaste, Viviane. 2000. *Invisible lives: The erasure of transsexual and transgendered people.* Chicago: University of Chicago Press.

Picca, Leslie Houts, and Joe Feagin. 2007. *Two-faced racism: Whites in the front and back stage.* New York: Routledge.

Rubin, Henry. 2003. *Self-made men: Identity and embodiment among transsexual men.* Nashville: Vanderbilt University Press.

Seidman, Steven (ed.). 1996. *Queer theory/sociology.* New York: Wiley-Blackwell.

Serano, Julia. 2007. *Whipping girl: A transsexual woman on sexism and the scapegoating of femininity.* Seattle: Seal Press.

Smith, Dorothy. 1989. *The everyday world as problematic: A feminist sociology.* Boston: Northeastern University Press.

Stacey, Judith, and Barrie Thorne. 1985. "The missing feminist revolution in sociology." *Social Problems* 32(4): 301–16.

Stone, Amy L., and Jaime Cantrell (eds.). 2015. *Out of the closet, into the archives: Researching sexual histories.* Albany: State University of New York Press.

Zuberi, Tukufu, and Eduardo Bonilla-Silva (eds.). 2008. *White logic, white methods: Racism and methodology.* New York: Rowman and Littlefield.

2 The Methods Gatekeepers and
   the Exiled Queers

Jane Ward

In 2008, Rebecca Solnit's observation that men were constantly "explaining things" to her was so resonant with women that it birthed a new term—*mansplaining*—and set the feminist Internet aflame with testimony corroborating Solnit's insight (2008). The term is intended to describe the gendered experience of having someone, typically a man,[1] explain something to someone else, typically a woman, with condescending disregard for what the listener already knows about the subject at hand. Mansplaining, in other words, is an epistemic problem; it describes what critical theorists have long worked to illuminate: some knowledges are rehearsed, ritualized, and unleashed on others with the wild abandon afforded by privilege, while other knowledges struggle to get a word in edgewise. Solnit elaborated on the structural dynamic of being endlessly on the receiving end of mansplaining, which produces self-doubt for the mansplained subject; she not only learns to placate the mansplainer but also becomes fearful to speak.

I received my PhD in sociology nearly fifteen years ago, and since that time I have been told by numerous sociologists, mostly men but also women, that I am a methodological failure. For years, sociologists have explained methods to me: I have too many methods, not enough attention to method, too small a sample, too broad a sample, too much reliance on interdisciplinary frameworks, not enough interdisciplinarity, too much feminism, too much poststructuralism, and too much reflexivity or "personal anecdotes." Colleagues in the sociology department at University of California, Riverside, shared with me their assessment that my work was not recognizable as legitimate sociology; they warned I would not receive tenure. Consequently, after years of this sort of criticism, I fled from sociology to a gender and sexuality studies department where it came to my awareness that the very subject of sociological methods had become a source of anxiety and paralysis for me. *Queer methods,* by contrast, were central to my healing.

This chapter is a reflection on the tense but dynamic relationship between sociological methods and queer methods, explored through the autoethnographic lens of my own career trajectory—from my protoqueer training in feminist sociology at the University of California, Santa Barbara; to my three-year stint as an assistant professor in UC Riverside's racist, sexist, homophobic, and volatile Sociology Department, a department riddled with conflicts over positivist versus critical approaches to the discipline; to my current liminal position as a queer sociologist living happily in exile in a gender studies department and yet still not entirely detached—intellectually or professionally—from my disciplinary roots. As I argue in what follows, to take up the subject of "queer methods in sociology" is to examine a dynamic tension between disciplinary paradigms—a tension that can be mapped upon, or traced across, the careers of sociologists engaged in queer studies. As I have noted elsewhere, "to pair the terms 'queer' and 'methodology'—the former defined by its celebrated failure to adhere to stable classificatory systems or be contained by disciplinary boundaries, and the latter typically defined by orderly, discipline-specific, and easily reproducible techniques—produces something of an exciting contradiction, a productive oxymoron" (Ward 2016: 71-72). Here I use my career in sociology to examine how this tension can unfold for queer sociologists, and with what effects. I argue, too, that debates about proper methodology are never purely about the practice of research; anxieties about race, gender, and sexuality are frequently routed through methodological critiques, with "methods" offered as a politically neutral set of concerns that masks these anxieties.

PULLED IN: A QUEER INTRODUCTION TO SOCIOLOGY

I was trained in sociology at UC Santa Barbara (UCSB), which celebrated its fiftieth anniversary in 2015, during the same academic year in which *USA Today* reported that its undergraduate program was ranked number one in the country (Cahill 2014). In recent years, the Department of Sociology has climbed steadily in the rankings and has climbed to the number-one position for graduate training in the areas of sex and gender (Estrada 2013). These rankings point to the department's success at professionalizing and placing graduate students, especially those working in the area of gender studies.

But I am also struck by the story that these rankings *don't* make evident about the department that trained me. First, it is a story about the radical left politics of several UCSB sociologists, many of whom reportedly inspired (incited?) students to burn down the unoccupied Bank of America building in Isla Vista in 1970 and to shut down the 101 freeway in 1972, both actions taken up in protest against local police brutality and the Vietnam War. At a conference hosted by the department in 2015 to celebrate its half-century anniversary, retired professor Richard Flacks recalled his tenure as chair and bragged, only half-joking: "When I was chair, we didn't hire faculty unless they had an FBI record and were proven members of SDS" (Flacks himself was a founder of Students for a Democratic Society during his time at Berkeley). I was twenty-one years old when I began graduate school, and I naively believed that sociology was inseparable from revolution and that its purpose was to produce knowledge that exposed injustice and imagined liberatory alternatives.

Second, the story of my training in UCSB's Sociology Department is a story about dyke sexuality and queer, feminist, and critical race interdisciplinarity. I did not burn down a bank with my advisors, but I did get drunk and flirt with them in hot tubs at department parties. I performed vulgar karaoke renditions of Madonna songs (this was the mid-1990s) at department parties hosted by queer faculty in their homes in the foothills of Santa Barbara. I was trained in a sociology program that not only required I read Marx and Durkheim, but that also provided the entire context in which queer sex, feminist solidarity, and feminist drama would take a powerfully central role in my life for a decade. The department was often helmed by feminist dykes, like Beth Schneider and Verta Taylor, who knew how to keep the male faculty in check during their reign as department chairs. Beth Schneider, in particular, was a vital feminist mentor who not only introduced me to the expansive field of feminist sociology but also took me under her wing as a young straight woman who was transforming into an AIDS activist and a femme dyke. I was also inspired by brilliant interdisciplinary theorists in the department, such as Avery Gordon and France Winddance Twine, both of whom worked at the edges and beyond the boundaries of sociology. It was in sociology seminars that faculty and graduate students called me out about the blindness that accompanied my whiteness and introduced me to interdisciplinary critical race approaches. And lastly, I took a series of methods seminars from eminent qualitative sociologists Howard Becker, Harvey Molotch, and Mitchell Duneier. Conveying their embrace of unconventional methodologies and their irreverent (and arguably privileged) disregard for the rules, one of these white men affectionately referred to the seminar as "Methods Schmethods." Another of these men was an eccentric who lived in a motel and cotaught his graduate seminar with a homeless man who had been one of his research participants. Truly substantive ethnography, he indicated, was inseparable from the kinds of intimacy often deemed inappropriate by internal review boards.

My point here is that it was as a graduate student in sociology that I was first introduced to my own queerness and to the queer methods I now employ. This training in sociology led me to believe that sociological methods were expansive, malleable, and harmonious with queer ways of doing research. But what *are* queer ways of doing research? As I have argued elsewhere, queer methodology is

1) intersectional (queer projects are designed to investigate the ways that imperialism, settler colonialism, white supremacy, poverty, misogyny, and/or cissexism give shape to queer lives and queer resistance); 2) intimate, reflexive, and/or collaborative, often anchored within the extant subcultural and political affiliations of the researcher; 3) infused with the erotic, or marked by a conscious recognition of sex practices, bodies, and desires and their place within the presumably asexual realm of research; 4) interdisciplinary, or comprised of humanistic approaches concerned with the particularities of cultural representation and discourse, social science approaches

concerned with behavioral patterns, and hybrid methodologies; and 5) focused on fluid or "messy" categories, shifting classifications, and people and practices often illegible within prevailing disciplinary schemas." (Ward 2016: 71; see also Browne & Nash 2010)

I finished my PhD in sociology in 2004, and with these interdisciplinary tools in hand, I went on the job market not yet aware that in many sociology departments in the United States, queer ways of thinking and doing are stunningly absent or subject to microaggression and *methodsplaining,* or both. The thoughtful and intentional focus of queer studies on that which is imprecise, intimate, psychic, affective, and cultural instead of, or *in addition to,* that which is generalizable, rational, and singularly structural is interpreted through the lens of mainstream sociology as lacking in rigor, undisciplined, and embarrassing to science. As I discuss in the following section, the methodological tools taken up under the rubrics of critical sociology and cultural sociology certainly do integrate and overlap with queer studies methods (see Gray & Gómez-Barris 2010). But what happens when queer sociologists are hired into departments without any colleagues who work in these areas or, perhaps worse, with colleagues who have been punished for doing so?

PUSHED OUT: MAINSTREAM SOCIOLOGY

In 2004 I was hired into the embattled Sociology Department at UC Riverside (UCR). My former advisors and I were delighted that I had received a job in the University of California system, not yet knowing that I would soon, in order to preserve my integrity and sanity, be desperate to leave. Conflicts about the value of qualitative, critical sociology versus quantitative, positivist sociology had been brewing in the department for twenty years before I arrived. Feminist and anti-racist faculty were depressed and exhausted, having battled for years with senior male demographers, criminologists, and social psychologists for recognition of the legitimacy of gender and race scholarship. For several of these senior white men, gender and race scholarship were so ancillary to the mission of sociology that they perceived even the most highly ranked and competitive journals in these areas, such as *Gender & Society*, as fringe or boutique journals (at one academic personnel meeting, a male colleague proclaimed, with apparent pride, that he had "never even heard of *Gender & Society*!"). Senior white male faculty, and two white women who joined the department through spousal hires, functioned as powerful gatekeepers in the department, making no effort to hide their worry that a new generation of feminist, anti-racist, and queer sociologists were destroying the scientific legitimacy of the discipline. When feminist scholars pushed back, antifeminist faculty resisted by co-opting the language of gender and sexuality studies. They argued that they, too, "did work on gender" and cited as evidence their inclusion of readings on "sex roles" in their syllabi or the presence of gender or sexuality as variables in their regression analyses. When faculty or students of color pushed back, white faculty called them "thugs."

During my time in the UCR Sociology Department, faculty yelled at one another during faculty meetings, exchanged personal insults, threatened legal action, actually filed lawsuits, intimidated and harassed one another in myriad ways, and were forced by university administrators to undergo department-wide mediation. Twice the department was placed in receivership by the administration and an outside department chair brought in after no sociology faculty members were deemed fit to govern the department, due either to their record of bad behavior or vulnerability. Activist scholarship was publicly vilified at personnel meetings. At one meeting, an angry senior faculty member waved in the air a copy of a colleague's journal article in which this colleague documented his experience of arrest at a political event in order to theorize social movement mobilization. The angry, article-waving professor shouted, "*This* is NOT the sociology I know! This is just political opinion! Should we all just start publishing our political opinions?!" Fed up with the degradation of sociology, seven conservative white senior faculty attempted to secede from the department and form a new department; the administration denied their request.

The fervor and sanctimony with which many sociologists, such as my UCR colleagues, have guarded the gates of the discipline and asserted the privileged position of their own epistemological and methodological preferences raises some basic questions about the political stakes at hand. What, precisely, are they guarding? Why is there so much resistance to change in a discipline built upon the study of social change? How can these scholars, who are seemingly so troubled by new theories and research methods, not see the low stakes of methodological squabbles in the grand scheme of the world's social problems? It is tempting to read these turf wars at face value and to believe they are actually about things like sample size and generalizability (the stuff about which the gatekeepers harangue their junior colleagues at personnel meetings)—and hence, to dismiss them as ridiculous. But methodological gatekeeping is never only about research methods; it is also about the people (people of color, queers, women) who have brought methodological innovation into the discipline and who are pushed out when the gatekeepers succeed—thereby keeping sociology departments largely white, straight, and male. The stakes, it seems, are the preservation of white supremacy, patriarchy, and heteronormativity in the academy. Indeed, at UCR, one by one, frightened queer and feminist faculty and faculty of color left the Sociology Department, pursuing jobs elsewhere or transferring their faculty lines, as I did, to other departments on campus.

What I witnessed as an assistant professor of sociology at UCR stood in such sharp contrast with my experience as a graduate student that, at first, I imagined I had simply been unlucky to have landed in a sociology department so hostile to critical and interdisciplinary research. But this perception was hard to sustain as I began to trace the links between the epistemological violence and dysfunction in sociology at UCR and the broader discipline's tendency to use methodology as an antifeminist, antiqueer, and racist form of gatekeeping.

The story of methodological gatekeeping in sociology at UCR shares numerous similarities with the one documented by queer feminist sociologist Jennifer Pierce about her experience as a tenure-track professor in sociology at the University of Minnesota (2007). Pierce describes the striking contrast between her formative training in critical, feminist sociology at UC Berkeley, on the one hand, and, on the other, her first job in the Sociology Department at the University of Minnesota, where she encountered "'the arrogant perception' of faculty who were unable to identify with someone different from themselves" (2007: 110). Pierce describes a sociology department in which, following a now-familiar pattern, the assessment of critical, intersectional, and queer methods as unrigorous and not sociological was intertwined with a department culture in which antifeminist, homophobic, and racist forms of harassment were part of daily life. (For a profoundly chilling account of sexual harassment, homophobic slurs, anonymous threats, denials of tenure, and a department chair who advised Pierce to demonstrate her loyalty to sociology by deciding whether she was "a feminist or a sociologist"; Pierce 2007: 118). Pierce's white male colleagues, who constituted 80 percent of the sociology faculty, as well as some of the senior white women faculty, "were at best indifferent, and at worst hostile, to feminism and to my methodological expertise in ethnography" (115). They repeatedly questioned Pierce's credibility and competence, ultimately denying her tenure by compiling a long list of petty methodological complaints about her book published by the University of California Press: "The book lacked a testable hypothesis, did not use valid and reliable measures, and constituted descriptive research that could not be replicated, . . . posed unclear questions, contained only one table, used a flawed random sampling method, and did not provide an interview guide," and the list went on (122). Ultimately, Pierce—a queer feminist initially dedicated to sociology—was pushed out, exiled from sociology; with the help of colleagues at the University of Minnesota, she transferred her faculty line to American studies. Notably, the title of Pierce's prescient article—"Traveling from Feminism to Mainstream Sociology and Back: One Woman's Tale of Tenure and the Politics of Backlash"—speaks of "one woman's tale" but is, of course, a tale shared by many, including myself.

Sociologists in exile have noted that the problem is not only one of methodological gatekeeping; there is often a problem also with sociological methods themselves, at least from a queer vantage point. As the critical sociologist Roderick Ferguson argued in his groundbreaking queer studies book *Aberrations in Black* (2004), white sociologists have a long history of purporting to describe racial and sexual categories with objectivity, while actually constructing the very categories they intend to describe. For instance, twentieth-century sociology has been central to the enterprise of producing the modern, neoliberal LGBT subject, who has typically been constructed as either an "at risk" youth or a well-adjusted, homonormative adult (Duggan 2004). Moreover, policy makers have used sociological data on normative gay and lesbian families to produce reforms that benefit the most privileged lesbian and gay populations, often excluding those most in need and exemplifying the vulnerability of social science methods and data to being co-opted by the neoliberal state (McNeil 2010). Sociology's obsession with the empirical has also reproduced race, gender, socioeconomic, and sexual hierarchies by obscuring knowledge that is "difficult to describe empirically," such as knowledge conveyed through memory, trauma, and affect (McNeil 2010: 62). Critical sociologists advocate methods that illuminate "the trace" of social phenomena, such as what Avery Gordon describes as the haunting present-absence of those who have been disappeared by state violence and forgotten (Gray & Gómez-Barris 2010; Gordon 1997).

These critiques of the normative function of sociological methods, not coincidentally articulated by queer scholars of color trained as sociologists but now anchored in interdisciplinary fields, are consistent with my experience in the discipline. It was not only UC Riverside's deeply fragmented Sociology Department that pushed me out of sociology, but also my repeated encounters with the discipline's fetish for traditional methodologies—an obsession with reifying methodological conventions in such a way that leaves little room for innovation and has kept sociology at least twenty years behind the curve in its integration of queer studies frameworks (Valocchi 2005). As an editorial board member of the journal *Gender & Society* for three years, I witnessed firsthand how cutting-edge queer and feminist scholarship was dismissed for not having a large enough sample, offering too close a reading of popular culture, or being methodologically "confusing" by drawing on too many different kinds of data sources. In my assessment, some of this rejected scholarship—conducted by young queer sociologists working in queer, trans, and sexuality studies—would have been cited for years to come, but in many cases these papers were rejected without review for failure to adhere to the journal's very narrow methodological formula.

One of my favorites among the projects I've worked on during my career was a study of the "gender labor" of femme-identified women in relationships with trans men. The project included a small set of interviews (thirteen with trans men, eight with femmes), but equally important among my data were excerpted conversations from the few extant documentary films on trans masculinity, sex advice columns in queer magazines, and content from websites by and for "transsensual femmes." I was disappointed when the paper was rejected by *Gender & Society* on the basis that it "consist[ed]" of third hand rumor and unsystematic content analysis that ma[de] the paper unpublishable in its current form" (note from editor). After receiving positive feedback on the work at an interdisciplinary queer studies conference, I reached out to queer feminist scholars for advice. Queer scholars assured me that the work was good, but sociologists were simply not my audience. A handful of transformative conversations with queer scholars outside sociology (here I extend gratitude to Roderick Ferguson, Jack Halberstam, Gayatri Gopinath, José Esteban Muñoz, Ann Pellegrini, Lisa Duggan, Macarena Gómez-Barris, Deborah Vargas, David Halperin, and Robyn Wiegman) helped me to consider that perhaps the problem with my ongoing sense of failure had less to do with my lack of intelligence or the invalidity of my work than with a lack of fit between the kinds of queer interventions I wanted to make and the disciplinary requirements to which I was being held accountable.

Not only does my research focus on the particularities of participants' own accounts—that is, the kind of data gained through interviews—but I also map the relationship between people's accounts of their lives and the cultural context in which those accounts become available as rhetorical possibilities. In my work on sexual relationships between femmes and trans men, for instance, I knew that narratives about the meaning of trans masculinity were new, rapidly evolving, and disseminated through queer subcultural materials, and that because of this, interviews alone could not capture the interpersonal, collective, and cultural "labor" being done to produce trans masculinity. For this, I turned to queer advice columns, popular documentaries, and online support groups where ideas about queer genders were being collectively contested and reinvented. Similarly, when I wrote *Not Gay: Sex between Straight White Men* (2015), my aim was not to compile straight white men's stories about sex with men, but to trace cultural narratives about straight white men's sexuality across several significant cultural events, and to use these case studies to observe the contradictions and transformations in academic, journalistic, and popular accounts of the reasons straight men have sex with men. I wanted to get the long view on the erotic culture of white heteromasculinity, a project that would not have been possible with normative sociological methods, such as interviews or surveys. In both cases—the femme–trans men project and the study of "not gay" white masculinity—mainstream sociologists have criticized my methodological choices on the grounds that they are unrigorous, unsystematic, or insufficiently empirical. These critiques strike me as ironic in that they equate methodological uniformity and simplicity (a study, say, based on fifty interviews) with rigor, while methodological diversity and complexity (a study based on twenty interviews, social history, media and textual analysis, and autobiography) is perceived as sloppy.

My exile from sociology was also propelled by my recognition of the profound manipulations and compromises that would be necessary to reframe my work so as to be legible to the agencies that provide grants for social science research—an important hurdle to overcome if I were to stay in the discipline. I have received one small external grant during the course of my career, which I secured only by speculating about the "mental health" risks and consequences of straight-identified men's sex with men (a question not actually of interest to me in my work on this subject). As the neoliberal state increases its demand for goal-based research focused on assessment, evaluation, and measurable outcomes, cultural sociology and cultural studies have become virtually unfundable. From my vantage point, this demand for predictable research design and conformity to well-worn methodological conventions has also resulted in intellectual stasis. For instance, sociology graduate students conducting qualitative work on race, gender, and sexuality are trained to (re)cite methodological buzzwords such as *grounded theory*, drawing on a fifty-year-old text written by two white men that has now been cited, according to Google Scholar, 78,475 times (Glaser & Strauss 1967). The obligatory rehearsal of "grounded theory" to describe any and all qualitative research exposes the absence of a queer methods canon—one that is, thankfully, being developed in the chapters in this book.

So predictable is the default to Glaser and Strauss's method that I was unsurprised when one of the outside reviewers of my tenure file raised the decentering of grounded theory in my writing as a concern (in the UC system, outside letters are made available to tenure candidates, in redacted form). All of the letter writers strongly recommended me for tenure, except for one outlier—a white lesbian sociologist who works in the area of social psychology. In her letter recommending against my tenure, she emphasized my troubling methodology and included a specific complaint about my decision to describe my method as queer instead of as "critical grounded theory." Referring to my first book, *Respectably Queer* (2008), based on three years of ethnographic fieldwork in LGBT organizations, she wrote: "My considered opinion is that this application for tenure, while promising, is premature. A critique that ... will continue to be raised about her work is its methodology. Each of the empirical studies is based on what might be considered 'convenience' cases. Framed correctly, which is to say within a 'critical grounded theory approach,' this needn't be a problem. . . . [But] with regard to the standards for tenure, her work does not yet demonstrate integrated engagement (i.e., literacy in complex discourses of methodology, etc.) with wider networks of scholars." My colleagues in gender and sexuality studies at UCR shared with me that they were struck by the contrast between this assessment and the praise the other letter writers had expressed for what they perceived to be a richly interdisciplinary and intersectional methodology characterizing my work. While they dismissed the letter as a "personal attack," I knew that it exemplified broader and now-very-familiar epistemological and methodological forms of gatekeeping within sociology. Like Jennifer Pierce, I had failed to situate my work within mainstream sociological conventions, and for that I was being punished.

When the editors of this volume asked me if I would like to contribute a chapter, my first response was, "*Me?* But I have methodological PTSD! Methods are my absolute least favorite things to think or write about. Plus, everyone knows I'm a sociological failure" (which I meant in the most generously queer sense of the term *failure*). As one reader of *Not Gay* commented in reviewing the book on a website:

> Ugh—Jane Ward strikes again with another volume of pop pseudoscience heavily marketed to the press with best click bait titles ever! Unfortunately, most empirical sociologists cringe because she is notorious for employing weak methodology shaped by the most extreme post-structuralist/queer theory in order to justify ridiculously counter-intuitive per-determined [*sic*] conclusions that just so happen to match her politics. Ethnography is basically a non-quantitative black box that is ripe for abuse because it basically boils down to the researcher's subjective opinion that can be distorted by the anecdotal nature of the study. Ward is a hardcore social constructionist who rejects any biological explanations for human behavior, especially when it

comes to gender and sexuality. For her, there is no reality to sexual identities outside of a very extreme anti-capitalist, anti-normative politics, which the vast majority of people, gay and straight, would reject as nonsense.

Here again, methodological critique is inseparable from a conservative political agenda, expressed in the form of performative mansplaining (Ward 2016). The challenge for people who are subjected to this kind of gatekeeping is to push beyond power's demand that one's exclusion be internalized as an individual failure and to recognize the structural context of one's exile.

QUEERING SOCIOLOGY FROM THE OUTSIDE IN

One way to develop a queer analysis of the methodological and theoretical exclusions reproduced by sociological conventions is to connect with other exiled or queer sociologists, a strategy that has been essential to my comfort with the liminality of my location within, and outside, sociology. I am no longer employed in a sociology department, but my teaching and writing are indebted to the work of critical queer sociologists. I have been sustained by queer and feminist networks composed of my original mentors and, even more important, by a younger generation of sociology of sexualities scholars who are infusing sociology with interdisciplinary ideas and methods. Change is clearly afoot within sociology, though some of the spaces intended to support and animate new approaches to feminist, queer, and trans studies continue to be marginalized or undermined by gatekeepers.

In 2015, Paula England, a sociologist of sexual behavior and the president of the American Sociological Association, made what was perceived as a radical move by many in the discipline: she named "Sexualities in the Social World" as the theme of the national sociology meeting that year. Following much excitement about a sexuality-themed annual meeting, disappointment spread quickly as the conference was organized without any consultation with the Sociology of Sexualities Section, ASA's officially recognized unit of close to five hundred scholars who study sexuality (many of whom are graduate students and younger scholars working in queer and trans studies). I was personally disappointed when the "Sexualities in the Social World" program committee rejected my proposal for a panel about the concerns I have raised in this essay. The panel description read as follows:

> What does the discipline of sociology bring to the study of sexualities, and more to the point of this panel, what does it not bring? What kinds of oversights, erasures, and occlusions result from strict adherence to sociological methods and theoretical frameworks as we study sexuality? The proposed panel will examine tensions between the sociological imagination and other ways of knowing about sexuality, and will do so through a unique lens: the lens of queer scholars who have strayed from, or have been exiled by, the discipline of sociology. Each member of the panel—Roderick Ferguson (American Studies); Evren Savci (Women's Studies); Susana Peña (Cultural Studies; Ethnic Studies); and Jane Ward (Women's Studies)—is formally trained as a sociologist, and each has found their intellectual home outside of sociology, or in a synthesis of sociology and other disciplinary frameworks. The panel consists of scholars in a now growing population of "sociologists in recovery" and "sociologists in exile"—many of whom are working at the intersections of queer, transnational, and critical race approaches. Through the lens of this experience, the panel will explore the link between these "departures" from sociology and the discipline's still limited capacity to support intersectional queer scholarship.

The proposal—for a panel that would explore sociology's long-standing rejection of interdisciplinarity—was rejected.

STORMING THE GATES

This volume bears witness to a new generation of queer sociologists forging a queer school within the discipline, one that works from within by infusing queer studies with the sociological imagination, as well as from outside sociology—from the borders, the interdisciplines, and other sites of exile where expansive theories and methodologies are brought to bear in our work. As much as my story is one of being pushed out of the discipline by old-guard sociologists, it is also a story of coming into my feminism, antiracism, and queerness through the lens of critical sociology. Both of these outcomes are true of the discipline at the same time, a fact that helps to account for the success of progressive sociology departments in placing graduate students working in queer, critical race, and feminist studies in tenure-track sociology jobs at top research institutions, even as many of these scholars ultimately feel stifled, fearful, or marginalized when they pursue their genuine interests. But this dynamic, we must hope, is rapidly shifting, as sociology departments are increasingly populated by new sociologists engaged in, or friendly to, critical and interdisciplinary approaches.

Though it is perhaps a modest comfort, upcoming generations of queer sociologists can feel confident that if they are being methodsplained, or otherwise stopped at the gates, there is a solid chance that this speaks to the complexity and innovativeness of their work. Now a full professor myself, and hence a "senior" scholar, I can only say that I am eagerly awaiting to be introduced to new methodologies by younger scholars. Bring on your interdisciplinary/promiscuous methods, multiple/polyamorous methods, ambiguous/gender-queer methods, unpredictable/moving methods, and your nonreproducible methods. The discipline needs you.

NOTE

1. The term has since been expanded to describe other forms of epistemic arrogance and microaggression, as expressed by the terms *whitesplaining, blacksplaining, cissplaining,* and so forth.

WORKS CITED

Browne, Kath, and Catherine Nash. 2010. *Queer methods and methodologies: Intersecting queer theories and social science research.* London: Routledge.
Cahill, Megan. 2014. "Top ranked colleges for a major in sociology." *USA Today College.* http://college.usatoday.com/2014/12/27/top-ranked-colleges-for-a-major-in-sociology/.
Duggan, Lisa. 2004. *The twilight of equality: Neoliberalism, cultural politics, and the attack on democracy.* New York: Beacon Press.
Estrada, Andrea. 2013. "U.S. News & World Report ranks UCSB among top national universities." *UC Santa Barbara Current.* September 10. http://www.news.ucsb.edu/2013/013619/us-news-world-report-ranks-ucsb-among-top-national-universities.

Ferguson, Roderick. 2004. *Aberrations in black: Toward a queer of color critique*. Minneapolis: University of Minnesota Press.

Glaser, Barney, and Anselm Strauss. 1967. *The discovery of grounded theory: Strategies for qualitative sociology*. Mill Valley, CA: Sociology Press.

Gordon, Avery. 1997. *Ghostly matters: Haunting and the sociological imagination*. Minneapolis: University of Minnesota Press.

Gray, Herman, and Macarena Gómez-Barris (eds.). 2010. *Toward a sociology of the trace*. Minneapolis: University of Minnesota Press.

McNeil, Tanya. 2010. "A nation of families: The codification and (be)longings of heteropatriarchy." In *Toward a sociology of the trace*. Ed. Herman Gray and Macarena Gómez-Barris. Minneapolis: University of Minnesota Press, 57–86.

Pierce, Jennifer. 2007. "Traveling from feminism to mainstream sociology and back: One woman's tale of tenure and the politics of backlash." In *Feminist waves, feminist generations: Life stories from the academy*. Ed. Hokulani K. Aiku, Karla A. Erickson, and Jennifer L. Pierce. Minneapolis: University of Minnesota Press.

Solnit, Rebecca. 2008. "Men explain things to me: Facts didn't get in their way." *Common Dreams*. April 13. http://www.commondreams.org/views/2008/04/13/men-explain-things-me-facts-didnt-get-their-way.

Valocchi, Stephen. 2005. "Not yet queer enough: The lessons of queer theory for the sociology of gender and sexuality." *Gender & Society* 19(6): 750–70.

Ward, Jane. 2008. *Respectably queer: Diversity culture in LGBT activist organizations*. Nashville: Vanderbilt University Press.

———. 2010. "Gender labor: Transmen, femmes, and the collective work of transgression." *Sexualities*. Vol 13(2): 236–254

———. 2015. *Not gay: Sex between straight white men*. New York: New York University Press.

———. 2016. "Dyke methods: A meditation on queer studies and the gay men who hate it." *Women's Studies Quarterly* 44(3–4): 68–88.

3 Trans Issues in Sociology

A TRANS-CENTERED PERSPECTIVE

Emilia Lombardi

The 2015 movie *The Danish Girl* achieved critical and commercial success for its portrayal of Danish transsexual Lili Elbe. While the film garnered multiple nominations and awards—including a Best Actor nomination for star Eddie Redmayne—it also faced criticism from trans communities for its sensational portrayal of Elbe's life and for casting Redmayne (a cis man) to play her. Trans critics were concerned that Redmayne's performance, and others like it, feed the narrative that trans women are really just men. As an ironic corollary to the casting of cis men to play trans women, trans actors who compete for trans roles often hear that they "don't look trans enough," a judgment that reifies stereotypes of trans identities (Levinson 2016). Both of these phenomena demonstrate how little voice trans people have in how trans lives are presented within popular culture. In the current pop cultural landscape, it is mostly cis people who have the power to define who trans people are and how they achieve visibility.

The same concerns exist within sociology in regard to how trans people are conceptualized, how studies are conducted, and who gets called an expert. Like popular culture, scholarly research has the potential to impact how society sees and understands trans people and their issues. However, just like the Hollywood movie industry, social research is dominated by cis narratives of trans people and trans lives.

As a trans-identified researcher, I can attest to the impact these factors have had on my career trajectory. To do the work that I believe in, I have developed strategies to navigate the biases inherent in the profession of sociology. These strategies include working across disciplines and maintaining a community focus in my research. In what follows, I briefly discuss how cis and heterosexist biases hamper research on trans populations. In addition, I elaborate on the interdisciplinary, community-focused strategies that can help forge the path to a more inclusive sociology.

LIVING IN A CIS-EYE LENS

When I was in graduate school in the 1990s, Harold Garfinkel's famous study (1967) of Agnes made a big impression on me because of certain parallels to my own situation as an aspiring sociologist. As a candidate for genital surgery at UCLA Medical Center, Agnes told Garfinkel a story of physical feminization during puberty, feminine identification, and heterosexual desire. Garfinkel's interviews and analysis describe Agnes's efforts to achieve the genital surgery that would allow her to live an authentic life congruent with her gender identity. At that time, gender clinics in the United States and Europe were working to provide a new resource for gender minority populations: medical procedures (hormones and surgeries) to enable people to better live in their identified genders. However, these procedures depended on achieving the goals set out by medical professionals who acted as gatekeepers. These criteria included heterosexuality (e.g., the sexuality of those who identify as women must be oriented toward men) and physical appearance (successful candidates must be conventionally attractive in their identified gender). This was the social context in which Agnes was embedded, and to an extent the same context I was embedded within as a trans-identified sociologist, at the mercy of "experts" in order to have my life and work validated.

My own context consisted of this and other studies that viewed trans identity and expression to be problematic. Much like other trans people, I looked for answers in what had been written before, but, unlike most others, I was also learning how to be an academic and researcher. I was frustrated and angry at academic writing and research that created a narrow definition of what it meant to be trans and at the same time created numerous structures to reinforce these definitions by rewarding those who accepted them and punishing those who did not. Our understanding of trans people and trans lives has been limited by the structures that cis scientists created to provide trans people with access to needed resources (medical technologies, legitimacy), but only if those people reinforced the scientists' understanding of what it meant to be men, women, and trans.

In the 1980s and 1990s, most research by cis people working with transsexual populations focused on two issues: how to conceptualize the population and what specific treatments (hormones, surgery) could be made available to them. The majority of these studies focused on individuals who were assigned male at birth. The researchers developed a narrative of "true" or "genuine" transsexuals characterized by persistent gender identification and in some cases an acceptance of traditional gender norms and sexuality. With the help of support groups (and later the Internet) these studies filtered into trans communities, and people began to repeat the narrative back to clinicians in order to access surgeries. Thus, the studies became a form of self-fulfilling prophecy. Only "true" transsexuals could access hormones and surgeries, so trans people learned to provide clinicians the kind of narrative that would provide them the services they needed. The result was the development of a medical model of trans identity that was embedded within heterosexist gender norms. Many trans people have criticized this process, but it was cis writers' critiques that gathered more attention.

Janice Raymond's book *The Transsexual Empire* (1979) is a critique of the medicalization of transsexualism that presents transsexual men and women in a negative light. According to Raymond, transsexual women are pawns of patriarchy and should be seen as enemies by feminists. In "The Socio-medical Construction of Transsexualism: An Interpretation and Critique," authors Billings and Urban (1982) argue that sex-change surgeries reaffirm traditional gender roles and prevent radical change in society. These works (as well as many others) present a negative narrative of the process of changing sex, and essentially erase the lives and identities of transsexual men and women. While both go to great lengths to cite clinicians and other researchers, as well as to bring feminist (Raymond) and critical (Billings & Urban) theories to bear on the issue, not once does either work present the actual voices of trans men and women. The dominance of cis voices in explaining the trans experience continues to limit what we know about trans lives. The cis-centric critique of the medical model has eclipsed the complex voices of trans people who were navigating social constraints and surviving despite those who would deny their existence.

In the mid-1990s, trans people and their allies began to collect information about the health and well-being of trans populations regionally and nationally. GenderPac was one of the first organizations that focused on trans issues and was led primarily by trans people. In 1996 GenderPac sponsored a US needs assessment modeled on the New York Anti-violence Project (NYAVP) and focused on trans people's experience with discrimination and violence. I volunteered to do data entry, conduct analysis, and write up the results of the survey. We found that many trans people reported experiencing both discrimination and violence. Furthermore, we noted a link between economic discrimination and violence (Lombardi et al. 2001). Other needs assessments conducted by community organizations with input and leadership by local trans people reported similar experiences of discrimination and violence, and many organizations also began to focus on HIV-AIDS-related risks and issues because trans women (especially trans women of color) were found to be at great risk for HIV infection (Clements-Nolle et al. 2001; Kenagy 2005; Sperber, Landers, & Lawrence 2006; Xavier 2000). At the time, most health officials tended to view transgender women as a subpopulation of men who have sex with men (MSM), which meant that transgender women faced being misgendered and having their identities disrespected if they sought HIV services. This situation likely exacerbated the high HIV rates being reported by these studies. These early studies were important because they involved close collaboration between people in local trans communities and public health officials. In many cities, they led to the creation of services and resources specific for transgender populations.

My own career, as well as others', began as a result of my involvement in a project such as this, which brought together many trans people working in various settings to provide HIV and related services to trans populations. The results from my studies were similar to those found in countless others: trans people experienced high levels of discrimination, harassment, and violence, and these issues were in turn increasing the risks for numerous health problems. However, studies involving LGBT issues still encountered serious barriers. NIH officials at the time advised researchers not to include volatile terms such as *transgender* in titles and abstracts, and the number of LGBT studies was still very small (Kempner 2008). And even as support increased, the focus of these studies remained narrow (e.g., trans women and HIV-AIDS). Meanwhile, the problems inherent in how researchers conceptualized and studied trans issues were becoming more apparent to trans researchers and activists. This heightened awareness sometimes led to open confrontation, as in the backlash over J. Michael Bailey's research (special issue, *Archives of Sexual Behavior* 37[3] 2008). In 2015, a group of trans women led by trans activist Bamby Salcedo took over one of the plenary sessions at the US Conference on AIDS hosted by the National Minority AIDS Council (Ocamb 2015). The activists demanded that more resources and attention be devoted to dealing with HIV in trans communities, and that officials stop conflating trans women with gay men by identifying them as men who have sex with men.

The lack of support for trans research extends to methods and data collection. Quantitative studies tend to run upon significant barriers to including trans people in their datasets. One barrier is the lack of measures that allow for the identification of trans people either directly or indirectly. Another is the tendency of studies not to ask respondents about their gender but to depend on interviewers or others to record what they perceive the respondent's gender to be. In the General Social Survey (GSS), for example, participants have not had the option to respond to a question concerning their own sex or gender—though this may change in 2018. In previous years, interviewers have been tasked to code whether the respondent's sex is male or female (Smith 2005). I experienced a version of this problem when I participated in a phone survey asking about my political beliefs. At the end of the survey, I asked the interviewer to tell me what gender I was listed under (as I was not asked the question). When the interviewer told me I was listed as male, I informed the interviewer that this was incorrect. The interviewer indicated that the error would be corrected, but this happened only because I was knowledgeable enough about how surveys are constructed and conducted to ask the question in the first place. This is just one example of how researchers' assumptions about sex and gender inform the ways that gender is operationalized in research studies.

The importance of having trans people as active members in research can be seen in the creation of measures that differentiate between trans and cis populations on general population surveys. This level of detail is critical to providing more reliable information and guidance in a host of issues, much like measuring race and ethnicity led to more attention and work in dealing with social and health-related disparities (Institute of Medicine [US] Board on the Health of Select Populations 2013). From 2011 to 2013 I was a member of the Gender Identity in US Surveillance (GenIUSS) Group convened by the Williams Institute at the UCLA School of Law. Consisting of trans people and cis allies who had been involved in trans research for many years, the group understood the necessity of having at least two measures—gender identity and sex assigned at birth—to best differentiate between trans and cis populations, compared to the traditional "male" and "female" check boxes. Researchers without this kind of background would likely not have such understanding of trans lives and might focus primarily on gender identity.

"THE EMPIRE STRIKES BACK" AND JOINING THE REBELLION

My career could best be described as improvisational. Once I graduated, I went from a post-doc to nonprofit work. I jumped from one research project to another, all while sending out many job applications for positions and finding no interest except from public health programs. Public health is interdisciplinary, and its focus on health made it a good fit for me, but I would not have found it if I had kept to a traditional career path. Making my work interdisciplinary and being open to new challenges helped me weather the problems inherent in being a trans academic who studies trans health issues.

Fortunately, public health was the field to be in when it came to trans health issues. Public health officials were the people concerned about the health of trans people and who were devoting time and resources toward it. Public health organizations use community-based participatory research methods, which seek to involve many stakeholders in the research process—including the communities being studied. In this way, community members have a say in how data are collected and interpreted, rather than relying solely on the perspective of "experts." This orientation allows for more diverse voices and permits researchers like myself to have a role in the research process.

Collaboration provides researchers with opportunities to do research and provides materials to communities and organizations to help with advocacy. That is an important aspect of community-based participatory research: it is not done solely for an academic purpose but also to provide community resources. Communities being studied have complained about people coming into their neighborhoods and networks and conducting activities that provide no benefit to them and in fact may further stigmatize them, while providing academics with fodder for publications and promotions. Taking the opportunity to work collaboratively with communities provides important benefits for both parties. I have found working collaboratively to be very fulfilling, and it has provided me with opportunities greater than just publishing an article. The relationships I have built have helped trans studies to expand and have also helped me to see myself as more than an isolated researcher.

I have been lucky to situate myself within a network of LGBT health researchers, which took the place of a professional network within sociology. Finding alternative professional connections was a significant development that provided me the professional community in which to communicate the findings of my work and discover new opportunities. These networks require people to create and sustain them, and there were others who stepped up to generate the resources lacking in other venues. Many trans people have written and theorized about trans issues and lives for many years, especially in reaction to the research being produced primarily by cis academics. Two works in particular had a great impact on my development as a trans woman and as an academic. Sandy Stone wrote "The Empire Strikes Back" (2006) in direct response to Janice Raymond and countered many of her conclusions. Susan Stryker's "My Words to Victor Frankenstein above the Village of Chamounix" (1994) also critiques the social meanings created by cis academics and society regarding trans people. These works and others convinced me that it is important to have a public identity as a trans person in academia and to conduct research focused on the lives of trans people. These writings also advocated allowing trans people to articulate their own lives, and began to shift the conceptualization of transgender away from a cis viewpoint and to center it on trans people's actual lives. They pointed the way to involving trans people in research as active members, not just as subjects.

The invisibility of trans academics and researchers strikes at the heart of the issue. Trans people have been active in research and scholarship for many years, but few achieve the institutional positions that can impact trans research and other academic work. Currently, two universities have transgender studies programs. The University of Arizona's program was established first and is currently led by Susan Stryker. The other program is at the University of Victoria in British Columbia and is directed by Aaron Devor. Both scholars have a long history of trans-related work, and both are devoted to promoting transgender-related scholarship. An equally positive development is the creation of new venues for publishing transgender-related scholarly papers, including *Transgender Studies Quarterly* (Duke University Press) and *Transgender Health* (Mary Ann Liebert Publishers). These join *International Journal of Transgenderism* (Taylor and Francis) and other LGBT academic journals that publish trans-related academic work and include trans academics and trans allies on their editorial boards and their lists of reviewers. As a result, there are now more opportunities for publishing academic articles relevant to the lives of trans people and more opportunities to encourage and support the professional development of trans professionals. It is still too early to assess whether these developments will lead to any benefits to trans people (within and outside academia) as a whole, but they represent a definite improvement. There are more resources now for trans academics than when I first started my career.

My own experience as a trans woman and an academic has been lonely in that I have felt I had nowhere to turn as I worked simultaneously to create a field of trans health and to establish my career. Taylor and Raeburn's paper on high-risk activism (1995) is constantly on my mind as I make decisions regarding my research agenda. While stories of discrimination in employment are common among trans people and in many research studies, applying such findings to one's own life is difficult. Conclusions are difficult to make based on a sample of one. Regardless of whether I have definite evidence of discrimination in my own life, there is evidence that trans people experience employment discrimination even within sociology itself (Grant et al. 2011; Herman 2011; Lucal & Stone 2010).

I was able to secure a career by shifting my focus toward the public health field. As mentioned earlier, the discipline of public health values perspectives and actions that fit my own interests. Its emphasis on working collaboratively with communities and seeking to provide them with benefits resulting from the research activities have created a more inclusive professional environment. Public health also emphasizes cultural humility and openness to the other. It is not alone in this orientation as other disciplines that seek to improve people's lives also use this framework (e.g., social work). Cultural humility allows researchers to see the people they are investigating as the experts concerning their lives. Ultimately, this framework leads to differences in how professions see diversity and deal with issues relating to communities.

I have seen more trans inclusivity within the health sciences than in sociology. Federal agencies such as the National Institutes of Health and Centers for Disease Control have created resources and opportunities for work in trans health issues. Although they are still enmeshed in politics, these agencies have revised health surveillance tools to include trans health measures. While there is still work to be done, the support is there and more change has occurred in public health than what I have seen happen in the profession of sociology. Sociology can become more inclusive, but doing so will require significant changes in how the profession operates.

TOWARD A MORE TRANS-INCLUSIVE DISCIPLINE

Creating a more supportive environment for trans academics within sociology has to start with the ways trans issues are presented within the curriculum. Courses in sociology provide the first introduction many students have to how the discipline views trans issues and people. In my experience trans issues tended to be discussed under the topics of deviance, sexuality, or the social construction of gender. Compartmentalizing trans issues in this way tends to present trans people as the other, even when instructors have the best intentions. Trans issues encompass more than gender and sexualities studies, and an important goal is to provide these discussions more widely through the curriculum. Trans issues can provide unique perspectives on social life, and it is also important not to present trans people and issues as monolithic, as they can vary greatly by race, class, age, and many other social characteristics.

The experiences and knowledge of trans academics and a trans academic perspective need to be fostered and incorporated in order to create a more inclusive understanding of the biological and psychosocial aspects of sex and gender. The emphasis, even by allies, on a cis perspective in examining and explaining trans lives prevents the development of trans theoretical and methodological perspectives that can expand our understanding of gendered identities and lives and how social forces and individual agencies impact them. One of the major problems with trans research is that it is dominated by a cis understanding of sex and gender. Many people conflate sex and gender, and many also rely on a simplistic, binary understanding of biological sexual differentiation. In fact, the biological differences between populations identified as men and women are quite narrow, but detailed cultural narratives are created to reinforce and exaggerate these differences within social life.

The work that has been done to decouple sex from gender is evident when people discuss trans issues, but this work has been half-hearted at best when it comes to cis populations. Even the idea of cis as a concept representing the relationship between sex and gender remains unknown, unused, or even outright rejected. Rather than continuing to define trans in opposition to "normal," we need to promote cis as a parallel to trans. The goal is to problematize the construction of biological sex and which characteristics are viewed as more salient than others. For example, now that more is known about sex differentiation in the brain and other parts of the body, why are people still focused on the anatomical existence of a penis or vagina, and why are some criteria used to identify sex and not others?

To address all of these issues in trans research, we need to address the isolation and stigma experienced by trans people within academia. Students (undergraduate and graduate) should be supported in work that encompasses trans issues, but it is important to help those students become aware of the ethical issues surrounding how trans people and issues are presented within their projects. Trans-oriented research must include the voices of trans people in its conduct and the interpretation of its findings. To advise students away from trans topics is problematic in that it creates the idea that trans issues are not legitimate topics of discussion and research. To do so with the excuse that one's department lacks expertise is also a problem in that it perpetuates the idea that trans knowledge is not supported or valued within the profession. We need to stop the cycle of having no one knowledgeable about trans issues, not supporting trans studies, and not considering trans issues as worthy of study. In this climate, those who do trans work tend to move on to new topics or fields in order to advance their careers. Some, like me, will move on to new professions.

WORKS CITED

Billings, D. B., and T. Urban. 1982. "The socio-medical construction of trans-sexualism: An interpretation and critique." *Social Problems* 29(3): 266–82.

Clements-Nolle, K., R. Marx, R. Guzman, and M. Katz. 2001. "HIV prevalence, risk behaviors, health care use, and mental health status of transgender persons: Implications for public health intervention." *American Journal of Public Health* 91(6): 915–21.

Garfinkel, Harold. 1967. *Studies in Ethnomethodology.* Englewood Cliffs, NJ: Prentice Hall.

Gender Identity in US Surveillance (GenIUSS) Group. 2014. *Best practices for asking questions to identify transgender and other gender minority respondents on population-based surveys.* Los Angeles: Williams Institute, University of California. http://williamsinstitute.law.ucla.edu/wp-content/uploads/geniuss-report-sep-2014.pdf.

Grant, Jaime M., Lisa Mottet, and Justin Tanis. 2011. *Injustice at every turn: A report of the National Transgender Discrimination Survey.* Washington, DC: National Center for Transgender Equality and National Gay and Lesbian Task Force.

Herman, Jody L. 2011. "The cost of employment discrimination against transgender residents of Massachusetts." Williams Institute, School of Law, University of California, Los Angeles. April. https://williamsinstitute.law.ucla.edu/wp-content/uploads/Herman-NY-Cost-of-Discrimination-April-2013.pdf.

Institute of Medicine (US) Board on the Health of Select Populations. 2013. *Collecting sexual orientation and gender identity data in electronic health records: Workshop summary.* Washington, DC: National Academy of Sciences.

Kempner, Joanna. 2008. "The chilling effect: How do researchers react to controversy?" *PLoS Medicine* 5(11): e222.

Kenagy, G. P. 2005. "Transgender health: Findings from two needs assessment studies in Philadelphia." *Health and Social Work* 30(1): 19–27.

Levinson, Dana Aliya. 2016. "'You Don't Look Trans Enough': A Look at Trans Roles, Trans and Cis Actors, and How They All Shake Down in Hollywood." *Huffington Post,* September 18. http://www.huffingtonpost.com/entry/you-dont-look-trans-enough_us_57df1bfde4b0d5920b5b2f1d.

Lombardi, E. L., R. A. Wilchins, D. Priesing, and D. Malouf. 2001. "Gender violence: Transgender experiences with violence and discrimination." *Journal of Homosexuality* 42(1): 89–101.

Lucal, Betsy, and Amy L. Stone. 2010. "Report on the status of gay, lesbian, bisexual, and transgender persons in sociology." American Sociological Association. May 29. http://www.asanet.org/sites/default/files/savvy/about/Council_Statements/GLBT%20Status%20Cmte%20Rpt%20(Aug%202009).pdf.

Ocamb, Karen. 2015. "Bamby Salcedo and TransLivesMatter storm stage at AIDS conference, welcomed." *Frontiers Media,* 1. Retrieved October 3, 2015, from https://www.frontiersmedia.com/frontiers-blog/2015/09/13/bamby-salcedo-and-translivesmatter-storm-stage-at-aids-conference-welcomed/.

Raymond, J. G. 1994. *The transsexual empire.* New York: Teachers College Press.

Smith, Tom William. 2005. *Discrepancies in gender codes.* Chicago: National Opinion Research Center, University of Chicago.

Sperber, Jodi, Stewart Landers, and Susan Lawrence. 2006. "Access to health care for transgendered persons: Results of a needs assessment in Boston." In *Transgender health and HIV prevention: Needs assessment studies from transgender communities across the United States.* Ed. Walter O. Bockting and Eric Avery. New York: Haworth Medical Press.

Stone, Sandy. 2006. "The empire strikes back: A posttranssexual manifesto." In *The transgender studies reader.* Ed. S. Stryker and S. Whittle. New York: Routledge.

Stryker, Susan. 1994. "My words to Victor Frankenstein above the village of Chamounix." *GLQ: A Journal of Lesbian and Gay Studies* 1(3): 237–54.

Taylor, Verta, and Nicole C. Raeburn. 1995. "Identity politics as high-risk activism: Career consequences for lesbian, gay, and bisexual sociologists." *Social Problems* 42(2): 252–73.

Xavier, Jessica M. 2000. *The Washington, DC, Transgender Needs Assessment Survey final report for phase two: Tabulation of the survey questionnaires; presentation of findings and analysis of the survey results; and recommendations.* Washington, DC. https://www.researchgate.net/profile/Jessica_Xavier/publication/307464621_Final_Report_of_the_Washington_DC_Transgender_Needs_Assessment_Survey_WTNAS_August_24_2000/links/57c5cc2708ae7642019b1247/Final-Report-of-the-Washington-DC-Transgender-Needs-Assessment-Survey-WTNAS-August-24-2000.pdf.

4 Beyond Academia

STRATEGIES FOR USING LGBT RESEARCH
TO INFLUENCE PUBLIC POLICY

Gary J. Gates and Jody L. Herman

Scrutiny and critique are hardly unusual for scholars. But for most academics, that critique usually comes from peers via conferences and academic publications. Publishing research that informs vibrant policy debates, such as those over same-sex marriage or anti-discrimination laws for transgender people, opens scholars to scrutiny far beyond that from academic peers. Policy advocates, activists, media, courts, legislatures, and even voters, all become potential critics of scholarly work. At the same time, when data are relatively rare, such as those about LGBT populations, the importance of new research and findings can be heightened and even lead to misuse. This presents many challenges for the scholar, not the least of which is that graduate student training rarely includes advice or mentoring regarding how best to disseminate and talk about scholarship to wider and largely nonacademic outlets. Even less training considers how best to respond to critiques that can often be grounded less in empirical scholarship than in popular and widely held biases and prejudices about stigmatized groups. This chapter considers some of the authors' experiences in a way designed to highlight effective strategies to inform important and controversial policy debates while maintaining scholarly objectivity and credibility.

The paucity of LGBT data resources and the difficulties this creates for scholarship, particularly that designed to offer analyses that could be generalized to the population, often form the basis of critiques from both academic and nonacademic audiences. Arguments about the quality of data focused on sample size, generalizability, and appropriate measurement of sexual and gender minorities present a constant challenge to producing and defending quality LGBT scholarship.

One of the best examples of these data-focused critiques occurred after the release in 2011 of a research report that garnered substantial controversy. This research brief—published online by the Williams Institute, a research center at the UCLA School of Law focused on sexual orientation and gender identity law and policy—sought to answer the relatively straightforward question, "How many people are lesbian, gay, bisexual, and transgender?" (Gates 2011b). The brief reviewed eleven population-based surveys that included questions about three aspects of sexual orientation: identity, sexual behavior, and attraction. Two state-level surveys that considered gender identity were also analyzed.

Across surveys, estimates of the proportion of adults who identified as lesbian, gay, or bisexual ranged from a low of just above 1 percent to one survey that found nearly 6 percent. However, apart from those two extremes, the variance narrowed across seven surveys to a range of 2 to 4 percent. The transgender measures were relatively small at 0.1 and 0.5 percent in surveys from California and Massachusetts, respectively, which provided the basis for the estimate that 0.3 percent of adults in the United States identify as transgender.

Averaging across the surveys, the report suggested that 3.8 percent of adults self-identified as LGBT. Within the LGB portion, roughly half identified as lesbian or gay, and half as bisexual, though women were more likely to identify as bisexual, while men were more likely to identify as gay. The findings from the report implied that there were roughly 9 million LGBT-identified Americans.

The report also included estimates suggesting that 8.2 percent of Americans (19 million) reported having had some same-sex sexual behavior since age eighteen and that approximately 11 percent (nearly 26 million) reported at least some same-sex sexual attraction. The report of these findings was accompanied by a discussion about the importance of considering all three of these dimensions when assessing the size of the LGBT community.

The research brief drew substantial media attention and reactions from activists and advocates on all sides of LGBT policy debates (Gates 2012). The reactions offer important insights into how media, activists, and advocates frame their understandings of what it means to be LGBT and why research on this population can be challenging. For example, the Associated Press news report published moments after the study was released included the headline "US Has 4 Million Adults Who Identify as Gay." This statement demonstrated a media focus on lesbians and gay men that relegated findings about bisexuals and transgender adults to, at best, a secondary status. It demonstrates the pervasiveness of bisexual and transgender invisibility that can be all too common in LGBT-related policy debates. The headline also serves as a clear provocation, cherry-picking a single low prevalence estimate (among many reported in the research brief) that contrasted with the popular belief that 10 percent of the population was LGBT. The 10 percent figure, credited to noted sexologist Alfred Kinsey, was not grounded in population-based data. Rather, it was drawn from data derived from purposive samples of adults. The promulgation in the early 1970s of the idea that 10 percent of the population was gay constituted an action of political activists, not scholars. The figure provided as estimate of the population that was large enough to matter but not so large as to threaten a general population still quite wary of LGBT people (Gates 2011a).

Harsh responses from the LGBT community focused on this perceived low prevalence estimate. Brian McNaught, a prominent LGBT workplace diversity advocate said, "I think what Gates did was a bit irresponsible. Gay and lesbian people are homosexual even if they don't self identity." Alex Blaze, an editor at Bilerico, a popular LGBT blog at the time, observed: "A study that just asked people will produce numbers. The numbers will be useless but they will be numbers. . . . You just do all this measurement but there's so many problems with this that it's meaningless." Perhaps the most vitriolic response came from noted author and longtime LGBT activist Larry Kramer, who called the author a horse's ass and went on to say, "God save us from statisticians who, along with epidemiologists are the enemy" (Gates 2012: 700).

The question of how best to measure a stigmatized LGBT population that may be reluctant to identify itself in surveys marks an important theme in these critiques. Larry Kramer implies that demographic and statistical analyses that undercount or underrepresent the LGBT population can undermine important political and social aspirations of the LGBT community. Blaze argues that the complexity, associated with stigma and the closet, inherent in measurement of the LGBT community essentially delegitimizes LGBT research. McNaught's remark suggests that estimates of the size of the LGBT population essentially cannot be accurate, as they cannot account for those who may choose to hide their sexual or gender identity.

Curiously, while these LGBT activists and advocates focused on undermining the population estimates, opponents of LGBT rights cheered the results. For example, the finding that bisexuals accounted for roughly half of the LGBT population drew a noteworthy response from Peter Sprigg of the conservative Family Research Council: "I see this as somewhat of a problem for the gay political movement. It undermines the idea that being born homosexual is an immutable characteristic that can't be changed" (Gates 2012: 699). His comments suggest that bisexuals are indifferent to the gender of their partners and therefore can effectively "choose" to be gay or not gay.

Opponents of rights for transgender people have also latched on to the estimate that 0.3 percent of adults identify as transgender to argue against anti-discrimination protections for trans people. The North Carolina law known as House Bill 2 (HB2) was enacted in March 2016 in response to the City of Charlotte's adoption of an LGBT anti-discrimination ordinance. HB2 prohibited the adoption of such ordinances in North Carolina and requires transgender people to use bathrooms in public buildings according to the sex assigned them at birth. A common refrain among supporters of HB2 was that the rights of such a small group of transgender people should not override the rights of cisgender people. Presidential candidate Donald Trump weighed in on the controversy in support of HB2, stating in an interview with *Today*, "Everybody has to be protected and I feel strongly about that but you're talking about a tiny, tiny group of population" (Kim 2016). MSNBC countered Trump's argument by asserting that trans people should be protected regardless of the size of their population. Yet, in doing so, the reporter felt compelled to point out that the Williams Institute estimate is likely too low: "However, several researchers have acknowledged that that number is likely undercounted, as many transgender people are reluctant to out themselves in conversations with survey takers or on government forms" (Margolin 2016).

Responding to critiques made via media, particularly social media, can be challenging. Engaging critics in online comment sections or through Twitter exchanges can risk a personalization of arguments, and such forums can make explaining nuanced or complicated constructs difficult. Academics typically respond to critiques with more research, usually in journals. Outside scholarly circles, op-eds and blogs can provide forums for scholars to produce measured and thoughtful responses to criticism that are more likely to reach nonacademic audiences. They can also target responses to specific audiences and their particular reactions to a piece of research. For example, Gates used a popular LGBT media outlet, the *Advocate*, to respond to the LGBT population estimate critiques. In the op-ed "The Day Larry Kramer Dissed Me (and My Math)," Gates acknowledged the angst that estimates of the LGBT population can create, especially given the long history of discrimination and confinement in the closet that so many LGBT people have experienced. But he went on to argue: "Today, the evidence suggests that Americans care little about how many LGBT people there are. After all, even at 9 million, the LGBT population would be larger than the individual populations of 40 states and comparable to the combined populations of Jews and Mormons in this country. If anything, Americans substantially overestimate the size of the LGBT populace. A recent Gallup poll found that the average American thinks that 25% of the population is LGBT."

In the example of the LGBT population estimates, the most virulent critiques of the research came from within the LGBT community, while opponents of LGBT rights attempted to use the findings to their advantage. While this situation would seem problematic if, as in this case, the authors support LGBT equality, it actually can serve to strengthen the case for the objectivity of researchers producing such scholarship. This issue of research objectivity can be an asset and should be a serious consideration for scholars if, for example, they are called to testify before a legislature or a court.

The case of sociologist Mark Regnerus presents a cautionary tale about conducting LGBT-related research without thinking carefully about objectivity. Regnerus (2012) analyzed data from a sample of adults age eighteen to thirty-nine that he called the New Family Structures Study (NFSS). Data were collected using an online research panel maintained by Knowledge Networks, which provided sampling weights that it claimed produced a population-based sample. Respondents were asked detailed questions about their household structure throughout their childhood, as well as a range of questions that captured such outcomes as educational attainment, physical and mental health, substance abuse, criminal behavior, and sexual behavior.

Respondents were also asked if one of their parents had ever had a same-sex sexual relationship prior to the respondent's eighteenth birthday. Regnerus then compared outcomes of children who spent their entire childhood being raised by different-sex married couples with those of children who reported having a parent who had a same-sex sexual relationship (along with comparisons to children who were adopted, who lived in step-families, who lived with single parents, and who had experienced divorce). The data included nearly 3,000 respondents (from an initial panel of 15,000), with 248 reporting a parent who had a same-sex relationship. Regnerus used multivariate regression estimations to take into account differences in respondents' age, gender, race/ethnicity, level of mother's education, perceived family-of-origin's income, experience with having been bullied as a youth, and the "gay friendliness" of the respondent's current state of residence. His findings showed that respondents who reported a parent who had a same-sex sexual relationship, particularly those who reported a mother having had the relationship, exhibited many worse outcomes when compared to respondents raised by married different-sex parents.

The research project was funded by two politically conservative organizations, the Witherspoon Institute and the Bradley Institute. Publication in *Social Science Research* was unusually quick, and it was eventually determined that two of the three peer reviewers for the paper were paid consultants to the research project. One response to this article, a letter to the journal editor signed by more than two hundred scholars, expressed the widespread criticism of the methodology used in the analyses and included concerns about an inadequate review process (Gates et al. 2012).[1]

Coordinated by Gates, the letter represented a somewhat unorthodox response to a scholarly paper. In the process of soliciting signatories to the letter, Gates received feedback from many scholars who argued that "petitions" were not an appropriate response to bad research. Instead, the solution was simply better research. The concerns raised about the letter were sufficiently strong that the Williams Institute requested that Gates lead that research effort in his capacity as an individual scholar, rather than as a Williams Institute researcher.

Gates was sympathetic to the concerns raised about a petition-style letter, but argued that the specific circumstances of this paper required a more aggressive and immediate response than would be typical among academics. While methodological disagreements were part of the response to the Regnerus paper, a major component of the critique focused on irregularities in the review process. This issue was not something that additional scholarly research would likely ever address. Gates also believed that the publication of the paper was timed to influence pending litigation on marriage equality that would likely soon reach the US Supreme Court, a concern shared by LGBT advocacy groups.[2] A strong and rapid response from a wide range of respected academics was, in part, intended to blunt that influence.

A focus of the methodological criticism was Regnerus's decision to compare children who report a parental same-sex sexual relationship, regardless of the types of families in which they were raised, to children from other family types (e.g., married, divorced, step, single). Having a parent who had a same-sex sexual relationship is not a family structure. The analyses do not report on nor take into account the degree to which respondents who report a parental same-sex relationship may have experienced different family structures in their lives, differences that could affect lifetime experiences of family stability or transition. His data clearly include this information. He does take such differences at least partially into account in other comparisons made in the analyses, since adoption, divorce, and living with step-parents all implicitly measure lifetime experiences of family structure and associated family stability and transition. While he acknowledges that respondents who report parental same-sex sexual relationships likely fall into many of these other categories, he does not actually report the degree to which this is true.

The justification for this curious methodological decision can be linked to the author's objective to challenge what he called the "no difference" paradigm, his description of social science literature showing that children are not negatively affected by parental sexual orientation or gender identity composition. Regnerus indicated the motivation behind the decision to separate out respondents with parental same-sex sexual relationships, when he explained that "my analytical interest is in maximizing the sample size of Groups 2 and 3." Groups 2 and 3 are the sample of those with a mother or father who reported a same-sex sexual relationship. An inherent motivation for increasing sample size is the desire to improve the probability of finding statistically significant differences across samples. Regnerus's "analytical interest" appears to be rooted in prioritizing the need to find differences over the need to offer clear explanations for those differences (explanations that are available in his data).

In discussing his findings, Regnerus implied that taking the family history of respondents who report parental same-sex relationships into account would likely reduce the probability of finding differences in his sample. A 2015 follow-up analysis of the NFSS data by sociologist Michael Rosenfeld found exactly that (Rosenfeld 2015). After taking both actual living situations of respondents (e.g., if and how long they lived with a same-sex couple) and histories of family instability and transitions, Rosenfeld showed that virtually all of the differences in child outcomes observed in the NFSS data were not statistically significant.

The controversy over the Regnerus paper and questions of his objectivity became an important factor in one of the cases that led to the US Supreme Court's decision to declare that marriage equality is a constitutional right. This case illustrated the power of scholarly objectivity in convincing the court of the merits of research findings regarding the suitability of same-sex parents. Plaintiffs April DeBoer and Jayne Rowse challenged a Michigan ban on marriage for same-sex couples in federal court, asserting that the inability to marry unconstitutionally prohibited them from jointly adopting their three children. Judge Bernard Friedman, a Reagan appointee, set the trial for early 2014. This marked the first trial in a marriage equality lawsuit since the 2010 trial in California challenging that state's marriage equality ban, known as Proposition 8. Unlike the California trial, the Michigan trial featured social scientists testifying on both sides of the marriage equality debate, with Mark Regnerus serving as perhaps the most prominent witness on the side of the state, which sought to uphold the ban.[3] Michael Rosenfeld and Gary Gates were among the witnesses for the plaintiffs, and both used their testimony to challenge the validity of Regnerus's research.

Regnerus's testimony argued that his research offered evidence that children raised by same-sex couples experienced clear disadvantages when compared to children raised by married different-sex couples. Rosenfeld testified that social science literature actually shows that, taking lifetime experiences of family stability along with socioeconomic factors into account, there are not significant differences in outcomes of children when comparing those raised by same-sex couples with those raised by different-sex married parents.

In the trial, plaintiffs' attorneys also cited concerns about the objectivity of Regnerus's research, showing evidence that it was funded by groups clearly opposed to marriage equality. These arguments clearly influenced Judge Friedman's assessment of the research. In his opinion affirming a constitutional right for same-sex couples to marry, he wrote:

> The Court finds Regnerus's testimony entirely unbelievable and not worthy of serious consideration. The evidence adduced at trial demonstrated that his 2012 "study" was hastily concocted at the behest of a third-party funder, which found it "essential that the necessary data be gathered to settle the question in the forum of public debate about what kinds of family arrangement are best for society" and which "was confident that the traditional understanding of marriage will be vindicated by this study."

Judge Friedman's assessment of Regnerus's research differs markedly from his reaction to the testimony of both Rosenfeld and Gates. He declared both Rosenfeld and Gates to be "highly credible" witnesses:

> Although Regnerus touted the NFSS as one of the few studies to use a large representative pool of participants drawn from a random population-based sample, other sociological and demographic experts, including Rosenfeld and Gates, heavily criticized the study on several grounds. First, it failed to measure the adult outcomes of children who were actually raised in same-sex households. This is because the participants' household histories revealed that many parental same-sex romantic relationships lasted for only brief periods of time. And many of the participants never lived in a same-sex household at all. Regnerus reported that "just over half (90) of the 175

respondents whose mother had a lesbian relationship reported that they did not live with both their mother and her same-sex partner at the same time." Second, many critics voiced their concern that the NFSS made an unfair comparison between children raised by parents who happened to engage in some form of same-sex relationship and those raised by intact biological families. This is because almost all of the children in the former group were the offspring of a failed prior heterosexual union, which produced a signifi- cant measure of household instability and parental relationship fluctuation.

Academics routinely consider the credibility of scholars as objective and even-handed when they evaluate and critique their research. But the issue of objectivity for courts is of particular importance. Judges and law- yers are rarely trained social scientists, so they rely heavily on expert assessments of scholarly objectivity to help them assess the validity of research, especially when researchers disagree on findings. Scholars hop- ing to influence policy through court and legislative testimony should carefully consider decisions about funding sources and how they present research findings through the lens of objectivity.

Producing sound, scholarly research is one of the best ways to counter faulty, agenda-driven research. But creating and deploying a network of scholars that can respond to faulty research, as was done with the Regnerus response, can help to publicly establish the consensus of a group of scholars and maintain the reputation of scholarship in a particular field. It can also help lessen the influence of faulty research on policy debates.

Since 2014, a group of scholars has felt compelled to make public state- ments regarding research on sexual orientation and gender identity, in particular causes of mental health disparities and the effectiveness of gen- der transition to alleviate gender dysphoria. In the fall 2016 issue of *The New Atlantis*, a non-peer-reviewed publication, Johns Hopkins–affiliated researchers Lawrence Mayer and Paul McHugh published a special report on gender and sexuality (Mayer & McHugh 2016). They reviewed selected existing studies to argue that there is no scientific support for a biological basis for sexual orientation or gender identity, that social stress models do not explain LGBT mental health disparities, and that gender transition harms transgender children and adults. Both Herman and Gates, and other Williams Institute colleagues, were cited in this report. Mayer and

McHugh's report was released in conjunction with a filing in federal court by the state of North Carolina in response to the US Department of Justice's request for a preliminary injunction against HB2. Lawrence Mayer provided an expert statement in support of the state, reciting the arguments made in *The New Atlantis* report.

One argument made in Mayer and McHugh's report involved research about transgender people and suicide. A report that Jody Herman coauthored with Ann Haas and Philip Rodgers of the American Foundation for Suicide Prevention was cited, among other studies, to advance Mayer and McHugh's argument that surgery for transition was not an effective treatment for gender dysphoria and may be harmful (Haas, Rodgers, & Herman 2014). Haas, Rodgers, and Herman analyzed data from the National Transgender Discrimination Survey, which found that 41 percent of NTDS respondents had ever attempted suicide. They found that those who had disclosed to others that they are transgender and those who had surgical care for transition had higher prevalence of lifetime suicide attempts, noting that timing of suicide attempts was unknown. While these findings are consistent with the social stress theory of mental health, Mayer and McHugh argued that an elevated prevalence of suicide attempts among those who have had surgical care for transition calls into question the efficacy of sex reassignment surgery altogether. They conclude, "The scientific evidence summarized suggests we take a skeptical view toward the claim that sex-reassignment procedures provide the hoped-for benefits or resolve the underlying issues that contribute to elevated mental health risks among the transgender population" (Mayer & McHugh 2016: 113).

Conservative lawmakers and media quickly deployed Mayer and McHugh's arguments regarding suicide to argue against civil rights for transgender people in a variety of areas. For instance, in regard to open service for transgender people in the US military, Anne Hendershott of the Veritas Center for Ethics in Public Life cited the Haas, Rodgers, and Herman report to argue in the *Washington Times*:

> While some have suggested that the reason for the high suicide rates for the LGBT and transgender communities is due to the stigma and discrimination they have faced, the reality is far more complex. In fact, the prevalence of suicide attempts is elevated among those transgendered individuals who

are open about their transgender identity. Those who disclose to others that they are transgender have the highest rates of suicide (50 percent). The research suggests that the military's new policy of encouraging transgender individuals to "openly" serve puts these transgender soldiers at greater risk for suicide than those who continued the "don't ask, don't tell" policy. (Hendershott 2016)

Echoing this argument, US representative Louie Gohmert (R-Texas) argued that if the Veterans Administration begins providing surgical care for transition, suicide deaths among veterans will increase. "And now this administration says we're going to have the VA do sex-change operations," he lamented. "Really? Do we not have enough vets committing suicide without you increasing that 20 times?" (Hellman 2016). *The Hill* reported that Gohmert cited Paul McHugh's opinion piece in the *Wall Street Journal* titled "Transgender Surgery Isn't the Solution" to argue, "It's a generalized sense of dissatisfaction, and for that you want to cut off organs and destroy people's lives?" (McHugh 2016).

The Mayer and McHugh report did not go unnoticed by colleagues at Johns Hopkins. In a 2016 op-ed in the *Baltimore Sun*, titled "Hopkins Faculty Disavow 'Troubling' Report on Gender and Sexuality," Chris Beyrer, Robert Blum, and Tonia Poteat argued that the Mayer and McHugh report "mischaracterizes the current state of the science on sexuality and gender" (Beyrer, Blum, & Poteat 2016). They distanced themselves and Johns Hopkins from the report:

> We wish to make clear that there are many people at Hopkins who hold a profound and long-standing commitment to the health, wellness, well-being, and fair and non-stigmatizing treatment of LGBTQ people and communities. We do not believe that the "Sexuality and Gender" report cited above is a comprehensive portrayal of the current science, and we respectfully disassociate ourselves from its findings. We also vigorously support the right to academic freedom and scientific disagreement and debate. Indeed, debates are the very basis of the scientific method. That same commitment to scientific debate means we must engage the dialogue in a circumstance such as this, and not stand silently by.

The American Psychological Association's Division 44's listserv, which focuses on the study of LGBT issues, was utilized to disseminate among members Beyrer, Blum, and Poteat's responses to the Mayer and McHugh report. Whether a larger, coordinated response will be published publicly has yet to be determined at this writing.

Responses such as these to questionable research, or questionable conclusions based on others, research, are part of the tools available to researchers to maintain credibility, both as individual researchers and collectively as researchers within a field. There are other ways, as well, to help mitigate criticism that has no scientific basis and the misuse of research in media and in policy debates. As discussed earlier in this chapter, just as the media can be used to unfairly criticize or misuse research, scholars can use the media to respond directly to critics. While not without risk, this can be an effective way to use evidence-based findings to counter baseless, potentially dangerous arguments. Researchers can also use webinars and conference calls to describe and explain the research and findings for interested academic colleagues, advocacy organizations, government officials, and the public to make sure they are understood and reported accurately. These communications can also be used to describe potential critical arguments and provide a response in advance. In the end, conducting rigorous, sound scientific research is the best defense against any criticism, but that process can sometimes move more slowly than litigation, legislation, or policy changes affecting the LGBT population. Scholars who hope to inform important policy debates can and should use a variety of methods beyond scholarly publication that can influence policy and enhance (or at least not undermine) their objectivity and credibility.

NOTES

1. For the list of signatories, see "Letter to the editors and advisory editors of Social Science Research," *Family Inequality*, https://familyinequality.files.wordpress.com/2012/08/ssr-gates-letter.pdf.

2. For additional details about the responses to the Regnerus paper, see Cohen 2012.

3. The trial conducted in California's Prop 8 lawsuit (*Hollingsworth v. Perry*) included extensive social scientist expert testimony only on the side of the plaintiffs, which supported marriage equality.

WORKS CITED

Beyrer, Chris, Robert W. Blum, and Tonia C. Poteat. 2016. "Hopkins faculty disavow 'troubling' report on gender and sexuality." *Baltimore Sun,* September 28. http://www.baltimoresun.com/news/opinion/oped/bs-ed-lgbtq-hopkins-20160928-story.html.

Cohen, Philip N. 2012. "Regnerus study controversy guide." *Family Inequality* (blog), August 15, 2012 (9:46 A.M.). https://familyinequality.wordpress.com/2012/08/15/regnerus-study-controversy-guide/.

Gates, Gary J. 2011a. "Gay people count, so why not count them correctly?" *Washington Post.* April 8. https://www.washingtonpost.com/opinions/gay-people-count-so-why-not-count-them-correctly/2011/04/07/AFDg9K4C_story.html?utm_term=.3a422669218a.

———. 2011b. *How many people are lesbian, gay, bisexual, and transgender?* Los Angeles: Williams Institute, UCLA School of Law. April. http://williamsinstitute.law.ucla.edu/wp-content/uploads/Gates-How-Many-People-LGBT-Apr-2011.pdf.

———. 2012. "LGBT identity: A demographer's perspective." *Loyola of Los Angeles Law Review* 45: 693–714.

Gates, Gary J., et al. 2012. "Letter to the editors and advisory editors of *Social Science Research." Social Science Research* 41(6): 1350–51.

Haas, Ann P., Philip L. Rodgers, and Jody L. Herman. 2014. *Suicide attempts among transgender and gender non-conforming adults: Findings of the National Transgender Discrimination Survey.* Los Angeles: Williams Institute, UCLA School of Law. http://williamsinstitute.law.ucla.edu/wp-content/uploads/AFSP-Williams-Suicide-Report-Final.pdf.

Hellmann, Jessie. 2016. "GOP rep says sexual reassignments would increase veteran suicides." *The Hill,* June 10. http://thehill.com/blogs/blog-briefing-room/news/283035-gop-rep-says-sex-change-operations-would-increase-veteran

Hendershott, Anne. 2016. "Chelsea Manning and transgender suicide rates." *Washington Times,* July 12. http://www.washingtontimes.com/news/2016/jul/12/chelsea-manning-and-transgender-suicide-rates/.

Kim, Eun K. 2016. "Donald Trump denies posing as spokesman in recordings Washington Post uncovered." *Today,* May 13. http://www.today.com/news/donald-trump-denies-posing-spokesman-recordings-washington-post-uncovered-t92421.

Margolin, Emma. 2016. "Why the 'tiny, tiny' transgender population should matter to Donald Trump." *MSNBC,* May 13. http://www.msnbc.com/msnbc/why-the-tiny-tiny-transgender-population-should-matter-donald-trump.

Mayer, Lawrence S., and Paul R. McHugh. 2016. "Sexuality and gender: Findings from the biological, psychological, and social sciences." *New Atlantis* 50: 1–116.

McHugh, Paul R. 2016. "Transgender surgery isn't the solution." *Wall Street Journal*, May 13 (originally published June 12, 2014). http://www.wsj.com /articles/paul-mchugh-transgender-surgery-isnt-the-solution-1402615120.

Regnerus, Mark. 2012. "How different are the adult children of parents who have same-sex relationships? Findings from the New Family Structures Study." *Social Science Research* 41(4): 752–70.

Rosenfeld, Michael J. 2015. "Revisiting the data from the new family structure study: Taking family instability into account." *Sociological Science* 2: 478–501.

5 Pornographics as Queer Method

Angela Jones

Let's begin with a joke: what does research about a lesbian bathhouse called the Pussy Palace, a pro-sex sex toy company, BDSM dungeons, and a Nevada brothel all have in common? You'd think the answer was sex, right? Well, nope, it is not sex—and that's the joke.

Leave it to academics to ruin sex! Too often, sociologists either ignore actual sex or, when sex is actually present, they discuss it in a clinical way that equates it with disease, erases pleasure, and is boring. As a sexualities scholar and teacher, I have become increasingly frustrated with the absence of actual sex in sexualities research. Even in places where we would legitimately expect to see some discussion of actual sex, it is absent. This paradox seems interesting. As part of my current research agenda, for example, I have read much of the sex work literature, and while much of it is filled with astute analyses of labor, capitalism, and patriarchy, sociological research on sex work often excludes actual sex. In my gender courses, we read many pieces on the family and gender socialization. Here, too, even in the best sociological texts on family lives, sex is curiously absent.

As another example, the American Sociological Association's annual meeting in 2015 was themed "Sexualities in the Social World." Although I was elated, I was again disappointed that an entire conference ostensibly about sexuality was void of any major discussion of actual sex. While I certainly did not attend every panel, what I did notice in attending sessions and reading the program was a trend also detectable in multiple

intersecting literatures: sexualities research is now largely just about identity and its relationship with inequality.

In our effort to expose and examine overlapping systems of inequality,
we often dismiss actual sex, which for many people is not only the basis of
their sexual identities but also an act that brings them joy and pleasure. So
it is not just actual sex that is omitted; sexual pleasure is also neglected in
the sociology of sexualities. Recently, I have been left feeling that something is missing from our sociological imagination. Now, after analyzing
the sociology of sexualities literature, I know just what it is. Our sociological imagination has almost no pornographic imagination. In fact, the only
type of porn that seems to turn most sociologists on is trauma porn.

So, in this chapter, I am appealing to sexualities researchers to push
back against the epistemologically and methodologically conservative discipline of sociology. Specifically, we must find queer ways to penetrate the
sociological imagination with a pornographic imagination. To accomplish
this task, scholars can use a pornographic method in various phases of the
research process. Pornographics can shape how we select research topics,
design research questions, create surveys, and develop interview sched-
ules. However, as long as we refuse to ask pornographic questions, we will
continue to erase actual sexual practice and miss the richness and fullness
of people's lives and the institutions they inhabit.

A PORNOGRAPHIC IMAGINATION

Sociology lacks a pornographic imagination. In *The Pornographic
Imagination* (1967), Susan Sontag famously argued that pornography is
generally denounced as lowbrow trash. Sontag convincingly made the
case that literary texts that foray into the pornographic are, in fact, literature. She examined French works such as *Trois filles de leur mère* (1926),
Histoire de l'oeil (1928), *Madame Edwarda* (1937), *L'Histoire d'O* (1954),
and *L'image* (1956) to show the value of the pornographic imagination
to the literary canon. Sontag argued that as long as scholars in the
humanities refuse to divorce their own moral sensibilities from their evaluation of literature, they will never see pornography as interesting or valuable art.

Here, in exploring the lack of pornographic imagination in sociology and the absence of discussion of actual sex as evidence of this lack, I would like to raise a line of inquiry similar to Sontag's. What explains the lack of pornographic imagination in sociology? What explains the absence of sex in the sociology of sexualities? If sociologists construct questions that are pornographic—that is, if they ask explicit questions about sex, or if they include explicit narratives from respondents about sex acts, or if they dare to include pornographic imagery to accompany text—would these queer choices call into question the scientific legitimacy of their work?

What makes sociologists believe that a sociological imagination is antithetical to a pornographic imagination? If a sociological text reads pornographically, does it cease to be sociology? Of course not. As Sontag noted in her discussion of Bataille:

> His [works] . . . qualify as pornographic texts insofar as their theme is an all-engrossing sexual quest that annihilates every consideration of persons extraneous to their roles in the sexual dramaturgy, and the fulfillment of this quest is depicted graphically. But this description conveys nothing of the extraordinary quality of these books. For sheer explicitness about sex organs and acts is not necessarily obscene; it only becomes so when delivered in a particular tone, when it has acquired a certain moral resonance. (Sontag 1967: 223)

Sontag's words are instructive; sociologists can write explicitly about sex without compromising the quality and value of their empirical and theoretical contributions. Such explicitness does not devalue the work. In fact, it is quite the opposite—the use of pornographic questions, the inclusion of pornographic data, the use of pornographic language, and pornographic imagery give us a deeper insight into humanity and human behavior (see Jane Ward's book *Not Gay* [2016] for excellent use of pornographic data, language, and imagery).

The problem in sociology, much as in the humanities, is that the mere sight of pornographic data, language, or imagery triggers concerns around morality, stigma, and legitimacy. Thus, the rebuking of the pornographic imagination and a pornographic method are forms of strategic stigma management—a device sociologists use to protect themselves from the costs of the pornographic imagination. Put another way, as I discuss in the following section, it is not that sociologists fail to see the value of a porno-graphic imagination; they are afraid of it.

DIRTY WORK AND THE ERASURE OF THE PORNOGRAPHIC

Trying to talk openly about sex in academic settings can be difficult. Academia is a field that operates according to a neo-Victorian ethos where speech is incessantly policed and censored—particularly when it is porno-graphic speech. To achieve conventional success in this field, scholars must play by the rules. So being a good scholar means being well disci-plined—in the Foucauldian sense. Given this conservative and panoptic environment, sociologists working in the sexualities must internalize this ethos and think (sometimes obsessively) about the professional and per-sonal risks of studying sex—because we know that failure to be well disci-plined will lead to punishment.

The neo-Victorian ethos of academia puts the sociologist studying sex in an awkward and often precarious position, and scholars who fail to play by the neo-Victorian rules of academia are often punished. The stigma around what Janice Irvine called "dirty work" requires that graduate stu-dents think long and hard about how studying sexualities will affect their careers. This stigma affects the courses faculty are able to propose and teach. It affects our ability to secure funding, to carry out research, to gain IRB (institutional review board) approval, and to publish. It is important to note that the stigma of doing scholarly dirty work often marginalizes both sexualities scholars themselves and the works they produce.

In this section, using autoethnographic accounts, I examine the impli-cations of sexualities research that is construed as dirty work. Specifically, I explore both the institutional and the personal politics of doing socio-logical dirty work. This analysis is important because our reluctance to embrace a pornographic imagination can be explained by turning to both the institutional and personal costs of performing sociological dirty work.

Bureaucratic institutional mechanisms at universities can make study-ing sexuality incredibly difficult. Working with human subjects, for exam-ple, researchers can experience challenges in acquiring IRB approval. When I sought IRB approval for my current study on contemporary online sex work, I dealt with a range of issues. First, it took almost a year to obtain my first round of IRB approval. The IRB expressed many concerns about my project, ranging from legitimate to ludicrous. While my work focused on individuals who voluntarily perform erotic labor online, the IRB members were concerned about sex trafficking and what would happen if I encountered an individual who was either coerced into camming (performing erotic shows online) or who was underage. They also expressed concern for my safety, especially should I attempt to recruit, say, a performer who was forced by the Russian mafia to work online, which then might retaliate against me for attempting to talk to the performer. I found the latter concern to be an example of the paternalism that often stifles academic freedom, especially for people studying so-called deviant populations. Moreover, I wondered if and in what ways my identity played a role in these concerns for my safety. If I were a male researcher doing this work, would the IRB have had these same concerns? Maybe. However, as a black woman, I found this concern from an almost exclusively white board especially patronizing.[1] Moreover, I tried to debunk their narrow and misguided understanding of sex work by citing research, but the board was incredibly resistant. Their understanding of sex work had clearly been shaped by the mainstream media's focus on the discourses of trafficking and probably by one too many movies about violent pimps and victimized hoes. Despite my authority in the field and my explanations, these gatekeepers were intent on seeing erotic entrepreneurs as criminals with ties to international cartels, and workers as abused, traumatized, or morally bankrupted. Thus, they ultimately chose not to listen to me, allowing their own biases and moral sensibilities to condition their evaluation of my protocol.

During full board review, a biologist questioned the value of my entire project. This member said they had reviewed my entire reference page and literature review and saw no scientific work. Meanwhile, my reference page was filled with articles from top-ranking journals such as *Gender & Society* and the *Journal of Sex Research*. It was the opinion of this IRB member that what I was doing was journalism, and not science. This attitude is typical in sexualities work—research that even flirts with the pornographic and that does not study human sexuality from a health studies paradigm (e.g., disease) is not seen as legitimate scientific work. Also during full board review, I was asked to explain what made this topic different from prostitution, and during this conversation individual members expressed concern about me studying people engaged in *immoral* behavior. Apparently, some members' concerns were so great that there was discussion with the provost outside this full board review about my work and whether the college wanted to be associated with it. The provost immediately defended my academic freedom and dismissed these concerns. Nevertheless, these issues reflect the institutional politics of doing sociological dirty work. The stigma surrounding sex work meant that individual members of the IRB were able to slow down the progress of my protocol and work with their personal problems and irrelevant moral concerns about my work.

Given members' concerns and lack of experience evaluating proposals like mine, the IRB hired a consultant to assist them with my protocol, which again further delayed my ability to conduct my research. Once the IRB consultant was finally brought on and completed their evaluation of my protocol, the board required extensive modifications. In addition to addressing the issues mentioned above, I was asked to extensively alter my interview schedule. I was told that because of the nature of my work I could not have just conversational style or even semistructured interviews—that the potential for psychological harm to respondents was too great. The board seemed highly concerned about my pornographic questions. While my protocol was eventually approved, doing this dirty work meant the approval took an incredibly long time. Furthermore, time-consuming and laborious revisions were required (e.g., having to investigate and produce information about the owner of a popular webcam site to demonstrate it was not run by criminal cartels), and these struggles with IRB members had the potential to adversely affect my career.

There are also personal consequences of doing dirty work. When you research and write about sexuality, it is not just your respondents' sexuality that ends up in the petri dish. As many scholars of sex work can likely tell you, people ask you if you have ever performed erotic labor. One afternoon, I sat at lunch with a sociologist whom I did not know very well. "I hope you don't mind if I ask," this colleague began, "and you don't have to answer, but you know, given what people say about me-search, well, have you ever done sex work?" In the moment, I was unsure how I wanted to respond. The individual had originally asked to speak with me to gauge my interest in leaving my present institution. Given that I was initially interested in employment at the institution where this sociologist worked, I hid my frustrations and answered that I had in the past. I have thought deeply about this interaction and how race, gender, age, and a host of other factors shaped this conversation. What made this person think they had the right to ask me that? Privilege.

When scholars do dirty work, they become implicated in it. People will ask inappropriate questions; they will ask you about your sexual identity, desires, and behaviors. Even if they do not ask, they may still make assumptions. Moreover, as the story about the lunch conversation is meant to suggest, for researchers whose identities are situated on various axes of oppression, it becomes even more complex as these types of questions also can be racist, sexist, ageist, and homophobic. Doing dirty work often means warding off and managing harassment and microaggressions. The resolution comes not from simply growing a thicker skin (advice I've been given many times); we also have to consider how the assumptions people make about sexualities scholars will affect their ability to command respect from their peers, students, colleagues, administrators, and others. A member of the IRB asked me (not during our full board review) if I cammed, and I said no. I wondered, if they had the audacity to ask me if I was camming alongside my research participants, were they also imagining me doing so? Was my research inviting people to think of me pornographically? In considering the personal consequences of this work, it is important to take seriously that when doing dirty work, the researchers—their bodies and their careers—become entangled with the stigma surrounding their research.

The politics of dirty work outlined above helps explain the absence of actual sex in sexualities research and the general lack of a pornographic imagination in sociology. To manage the stigma of dirty work, scholars end up succumbing to what I call *heteronormative respectability politics*. In an effort to minimize the tolls of dirty work, sociologists often sanitize their work because of our fear of the consequences of having a pornographic imagination in a neo-Victorian academic field. However, we should ask ourselves what the costs are of placating respectability politics. Often, this sanitizing in the sexualities means conducting research that is heteronormative, because studying topics outside of what Gayle Rubin (1984) called "the Charmed Circle" bears stigma and studying actual sex is seen as neither respectable nor legitimate science. As scholars elect not to use queer methods, and instead conform to sociological epistemological and methodological conventions, they miss important data and, as a result, do not accurately capture the entirety of the people's lives that they are studying.

PORNOGRAPHICS AS QUEER METHOD

In this chapter, I am calling on sociologists to harness a pornographic imagination or, as Mimi Schippers so aptly put it, to strap on a pornographic imagination (2016: 30). However, to think pornographically is just a starting point. What we also need is a pornographic method. Here, I am using pornographics to refer broadly to queer ways of investigating sexual behavior and explicitly conveying sexual content. How can sociologists employ a method of pornographics that will allow them to uncover new knowledge and develop new theoretical insights? In what follows, I draw on my current research to explore the use of pornographics as queer method.

In my current research and forthcoming book with New York University Press on erotic online webcamming, I use pornographics alongside other queer methods such as autoethnography. I do this to more fully understand the multifaceted and complex motivations for entrance into the sexual economy and the workplace experiences of these workers, thereby uncovering themes such as pleasure that are frequently neglected in the sex work literature. The study of sex work is interdisciplinary, and scholars have used a range of methods, quantitative and qualitative, to study sex work. Sociologists have primarily framed their work using economically determinist theories and have been invested in demonstrating that erotic labor is legitimate work. However, most sociological studies of sex work are dismissive of the actual labor performed. In their efforts to combat the stigma around sex work, sociologists, too often invested in respectability politics and in warding off the institutional and personal stigma of dirty work, purge the sex from sex work. Moreover, not only does the sociological literature on sex work rarely talk about actual sex, but sociologists also rarely discuss the enjoyment workers often experience as a result of engaging in sex acts with customers (for notable exceptions, see Bernstein 2007;

Walby 2012; Jones 2016). Therefore, my research has been guided by a pornographic imagination—that is, by an explicit interest in investigating and writing about actual sex and pleasure.

To uncover data about the actual sexual experiences of cam performers, I had to develop a pornographic method—I had to filter all my data collection strategies through a pornographic lens. For example, I gathered data from webforums created and curated by performers. I generated a list of pornographic codes that I then used to both search through the threads on the webforums and later also used in coding and analyzing the data. These codes included terms such as *orgasm, pleasure, sex toys, enjoyment, masturbation, penetration,* and *stimulation.* I did use codes that related to labor and work; however, by also generating deductive pornographic codes and centering my analysis on pornographic themes, I was able to uncover data that would normally be lost in most sex work research, which tends to focus exclusively on clients' sexual desires and treats workers solely as rational economic actors looking to make a quick buck. Moreover, much of the sex work literature has also focused on the "myth of mutuality," which suggests that sex workers must convince their clients that they are sexually satisfying the sex workers. The underlying assumption has been that sex workers are performing emotional labor, thereby *faking it* with a motivation for money only. However, what a pornographically guided investigation uncovers is that what decades of sociological research on sex work has been missing is the sexual pleasure that many sex workers experience in their work, which is also an important contribution to sociological theories of motivation for work in erotic labor. As I discuss in a recent article (Jones 2006), many performers report that they will not fake orgasms. Part of what makes webcamming so appealing to customers is that, unlike traditional pornography, webcam performances are authentic and interactional. Furthermore, the absence online of physical contact creates an environment where many performers now feel more comfortable and safe; these conditions allow workers to more freely explore their own sexual desires with clients. Again, however, the point is that had I not intentionally turned my eye to the pornographic, and had I focused only on themes related to wages and the conditions of labor, I might have missed important data that have helped me better understand the world of erotic webcamming and that contribute to theories of sexual commerce.

During recruitment for both my survey and interviews I used pornographics and made queer methodological choices. For example, I had a
standard email that I used to recruit performers that my IRB was happy
with, but that was dry and cold. After receiving very low response rates, I
made the choice to open my invitations by telling performers something
true about me, that I was a retired sex worker now working as a professor-
researcher. This revelation helped increase response rates. Also, I am writing about sex work and, as a retired sex worker, have decided to include
autoethnographic vignettes in the book, which help to introduce important
theoretical issues and, I believe, help make the prose engaging for readers.

Thus, another valuable queer move in my current work has been to
couple a pornographic method with autoethnography. Instead of running
from my own past in sex work, I thought about how I could use my own
experiences to inform the work I am doing now. In her book on polyamory,
Mimi Schippers (2016) included both autoethnographic and fictional
vignettes. This queer methodological choice lends itself to candid and
fruitful discussions of actual sex. Schippers was not the first qualitative
sociologist to make the queer choice to use autoethnography. The most
effective use of autoethnography, however, has been in the sociology of
race (for excellent examples, see Vidal-Ortiz 2004; Buggs 2016). It may be
easier for sociologists studying race to talk about their experiences with
racism than it is for sociologists studying sexuality to talk about their sexual experiences. While the former is often seen as constructive, the latter
is seen as a self-indulgent pornographic distraction. Moreover, using
autoethnography in the sexualities can magnify the politics of dirty work
and, again, could have an adverse effect on the researcher. The fear of
exposing oneself sexually may be a deterrent for many researchers to using
queer methods such as autoethnography in sexualities research.

Using autoethnography can be challenging for sociologists studying
sex, because this method requires not only deep reflexivity but also a candid writing style. While many qualitative sociologists do reflexivity well,
writing pornographically is difficult when you have been disciplined and
trained to write and speak only in a rigid and dry tone. As Carla Pfeffer
(2017) noted, "One of the challenges of approaching sex and sexuality
from an academic perspective is that academics have a tendency to shy
away from topics and language considered 'crass.' In many instances, the

very materiality and corporeality of sex and sexuality are extracted and transformed into dry academic prose" (100). The refusal to write pornographically has consequences. First, simply put, what academic writing there is about sex is usually dull and boring. Second, there are important ethical implications here. One ethical issue arises when we extract crass talk from our texts and translate our respondents' words into an ostensibly acceptable and respectable academic vernacular. Such academic colonialism is not justified and is unethical. If our respondents speak in the language of cocks and pussies, then that is the language we should honor in our texts. We silence our respondents' pornographic voice by either not asking them about sex altogether or choosing not to include such data when presented to us, or by editing their voices to conform to the scientific community's neo-Victorian expectations.

Instead of censoring pornographic language, we must embrace it. It is not just that we miss important data when we censor the pornographic from our work; this purging of the pornographic is unethical when done out of academic self-preservation rather than to protect our research participants. I fully recognize that there are sociologists who are genuinely concerned about the politics and potential effects of presenting already-marginalized people, especially queer people and people of color, as hypersexual. However, presenting people as having sex lives does not necessarily reinforce stereotypes of hypersexuality. In addition, intentionally desexualizing respondents is an example of heteronormative respectability politics and does not necessarily help respondents, nor does it honor their wishes. If a research participant shares a sexually explicit story with a researcher, they are telling the researcher this is an important part of their life. If the researcher chooses to omit that story because they are concerned that it might, for example, reify racist stereotypes, this choice exemplifies a degree of paternalism that I find troubling—this is academic colonialism. If the researcher is concerned about the pathological way in which such data could be read and the deleterious effects it could have, the researcher can write those concerns into the analysis. But, please, let us not fool ourselves about the unequal power dynamics already present in our relationships with our research respondents. Equalizing the power relationship between researcher and participants means listening to them and letting their voices lead the direction of the pen. It is important that we document holistically all aspects of people's lives—for better or worse. Finally, for academics, writing pornographically is an exercise in power in that it allows us to push back on the boundaries of acceptable writing, all while honoring the lives of our respondents.

Intentionally writing pornographically—that is, strategically using pornographics to construct text—can have many benefits. This writing forces us to put actual sex back into work, makes our writing more engaging and readable, and often reveals important theoretical implications. For example, at the beginning of every chapter in my book (Jones, forthcoming), I weave together pornographic autoethnographic vignettes and narratives from performers as springboards for discussions about complex issues such as race, sex, and pleasure. Here, for example, is a vignette that appears in the chapter devoted to pleasure in online sex work:

> One of my regulars was an accountant, and so it went that during tax season, we both did well. For example, he'd generally pay me between $800 and $1,200 a night (not including the money showers I'd demand on stage) just to sit with him and drink and talk. We developed a friendship as a result. One night, I was sitting with the accountant, and Bianca called me into the back. She was an incredibly gorgeous caramel-skinned Puerto Rican dancer with long, thick, curly dark hair that always tickled her nipples when she danced; I knew what she wanted. Bianca and I fucked in the bathroom while the accountant waited. I spent the remainder of the evening chatting with the accountant, and having tipped the DJ well, I'd only occasionally dance on stage and always to my favorite songs. So, is being a professor so much better than being a stripper? It may jive well with the politics of respectability; I'm sure my family is pleased, but I can say that the corporeal pleasures I experienced as a sex worker will likely forever be unmatched. (Jones, forthcoming)

In this chapter in my book, I combine these autoethnographic data with qualitative data gathered from webcam performers in order to build a larger theory of pleasure as a driving force or motivation for seeking out employment across a broad range of sexual commerce industries. It is important to note that I am writing this book and these vignettes having just received tenure, which affords me a level of protection that graduate students, adjuncts, and other junior faculty do not have. It is has not been my intention to minimize the tolls of dirty work or the consequences that researching and writing pornographically can have on researchers. However, it is for precisely these reasons that pornographics and the queer methods outlined throughout this volume are so important. If new generations of scholars can continue to show the value of queer methods, we will be able to change the sociological landscape for the better. We need new generations of scholars who unapologetically ask pornographic questions and share their raunchiest field notes, who honor the language of cocks and pussies, who share with others how they grapple with their own sexual desires in the field, and who are not afraid to strap on a pornographic imagination.

NOTE

1. At this time there were three women of color on the IRB, two of whom are black. The rest of the board was white.

WORKS CITED

Bernstein, Elizabeth. 2007. *Temporarily yours: Intimacy, authenticity, and the commerce of sex.* Chicago: University of Chicago Press.

Buggs, Shantel G. 2016. "'Your momma is day-glow white': Questioning the politics of racial identity, loyalty and obligation." *Identities: Global Studies in Culture and Power* 24(4): 379–97.

Jones, Angela. 2016. "'I get paid to have orgasms': Adult webcam models' negotiation of pleasure and danger." *Signs: Journal of Women in Culture and Society* 42(1): 227–56.

Jones, Angela. Forthcoming. *Selling sex online: Work, community, and pleasure in the adult webcamming industry.* New York: New York University Press.

Pfeffer, Carla. 2017. *Queering families: The postmodern partnerships of cisgender women and transgender men.* Oxford: Oxford University Press.

Rubin, Gayle. 1984. "Thinking sex: Notes for a radical theory of the politics of sexuality." *Pleasure and danger.* Ed. Carole Vance. London: Routledge and Kegan Paul.

Schippers, Mimi. 2016. *Beyond monogamy: Polyamory and the future of polyqueer sexualities.* New York: New York University Press.

Sontag, Susan. 1967. "The pornographic imagination." *Partisan Review* 34(2): 181–212.

Vidal-Ortiz, Salvador. 2004. "On being a white person of color: Using autoeth-
	nography to understand Puerto Ricans' racialization." *Qualitative Sociology*
	27(2): 179–203.
Walby, Kevin. 2012. *Touching encounters: Sex, work, and male-for-male
	Internet escorting*. Chicago: University of Chicago Press.
Ward, Jane. 2015. *Not gay: Sex between straight white men*. New York: New
	York University Press.

PART II Relationships

6 Not Out in the Field

STUDYING PRIVACY AND DISCLOSURE
AS AN INVISIBLE (TRANS) MAN

Cayce C. Hughes

One hot Houston afternoon, I sat in the break room of a Head Start center interviewing Janice,[1] an African American mother of two young children, about her experience seeking public assistance. She sighed, looking resigned, as she described the battery of personal questions she was required to answer each time she recertified for welfare benefits. When I asked Janice how she felt about the questions she was asked, she said simply: "It's like they turn you inside out." For days after our interview, Janice's words continued to ring in my head. I remembered having a very similar feeling when I was required to disclose a great deal of personal information to medical doctors, psychologists, and state bureaucrats who held the power to determine whether or not to grant me the medical care and legal documentation I needed to transition. Like Janice, I felt as if I were "turned inside out" each time I had to recount my gender history to a new therapist or the clerk at the Department of Motor Vehicles. These experiences informed my decision many years later to pursue a dissertation on how people manage their personal privacy (and the loss of it), even though it took time for me to fully realize the extent of this professional-personal connection. Indeed, I chose to focus on an altogether different case: how poor mothers navigate the requirements to disclose extensive personal information to the state in order to receive public assistance. I made this choice in part because I did not want my personal history to be implicated in my research: I did not want to expose myself as trans, and I worried about being seen as conducting "me-search." Because of this distance I imposed between my personal history and my research, it wasn't until I was immersed in fieldwork interviewing mothers about their experiences that I began to fully recognize these parallels—and to acknowledge that the social process I was studying shed light on my own life.

For a long time, I kept these insights to myself. I did not disclose my transgender identity to my respondents or share my perceptions about our unexpected commonalities. One reason for this decision was that my dissertation was not about trans people's experiences; it was about poor mothers and welfare.[2] Also, the interviews were about them, not me. Still, I often felt uncomfortable asking my respondents to reveal a great deal about themselves while I was actively concealing a great deal about myself from them. To further complicate matters, my fieldwork in Houston happened to coincide with a fierce public debate over the passage (and later repeal) of a city ordinance that banned discrimination against LGBT people (Driesson 2014). Opponents of the ordinance dubbed it a "bathroom bill," emphasizing the purported threats to women and children that would result from transgender people using the bathroom of their choice. During this time, some of my respondents and other community members I encountered in my work who opposed the bill often made comments to me that I perceived as trans- and homophobic. I recognized that they made these comments to someone they read as a white, straight man, not someone whose civil rights would be protected by the very ordinance they decried. But when I contemplated coming out in the field, such comments reinforced my decision to be silent, as they underscored the potentially negative response I worried I would receive if I chose to disclose my identity (or was involuntarily "outed"). Yet the fact that this decision was mine to make in the first place underscores my position of privilege, as many trans people are identified as trans by others whether or not they disclose. For trans women of color in particular, the potential dangers of being involuntarily outed as trans, including facing harassment, violence, and worse, are well documented.

Throughout my time in the field, I also did not share these personal reflections and internal struggles with colleagues or my dissertation committee members, because I was not out as trans in my graduate department. While this was my personal choice at the time, it meant that I did not have an outlet to reflexively process my experience with other researchers, because doing so would have required disclosing my trans status, which I was not willing to do. As a result, I often felt overwhelmed and alienated in the field. I found that the privacy I had worked hard to achieve by *not* being out left me isolated from the support I needed to work through these thorny issues both personally and intellectually. Ultimately, my experiences in the field led me to make a major change in my own life, and I have now begun to disclose my trans status with professional colleagues—a process that continues to unfold as I write these words.

In this chapter, I discuss some of the challenges and opportunities I encountered studying privacy and disclosure as an invisible trans man. Although the anecdotes and reflections I share stem from my particular experience as a white, queer, trans man conducting interviews with African American mothers living in a high-poverty neighborhood in Houston, Texas, I emphasize common issues and questions that other researchers in various fieldwork contexts (and with different constellations of identities) may confront in the field.

BECOMING STEALTH

I did not set out to become "stealth" when I transitioned ten years ago. Rather, this process began without a concerted effort. The combination of quickly gaining social recognition as a man and moving to a new city to begin my doctoral program created the possibility for me to keep my transgender status private. Largely for professional reasons, I chose not to tell anyone. When I entered graduate school in 2010, the wave of increased trans visibility that has resulted in people such as Laverne Cox and Janet Mock becoming household names was nascent. Gender dysphoria was still a legitimized "disorder" in the DSM-IV, and there were no federal civil rights protections for trans people in the workplace. The competitive academic job market was stressful enough for graduate students without adding another layer of anxiety over whether my trans identity would hurt my chances at landing a job or whether I would have to expend energy managing others' discomfort with my identity rather than focusing on my work—a burden that people of color and other members of marginalized groups routinely face. The professional risks for trans people in the workplace in general are well documented (Schilt & Wiswall 2008; Schilt 2010), as are the barriers faced by gay and lesbian sociologists in particular (Taylor & Raeburn 1995). But there were—and still are—scant data on the professional outcomes and experiences of out trans sociologists, and few models to follow. Beyond fears about the job market, though, I also wanted to be seen by others as an academic first—to be recognized primarily for my work not for my gender history. As a sociologist, I was cognizant of how easily a "marked" aspect of my identity (e.g., being trans) could become a master status, obscuring other important parts of myself. At the same time, the fact that I had a choice here at all reflects the level of privilege accessible to me as a trans man who can pass as a member of the unmarked category: heterosexual, white, cisgender male.

As I developed my dissertation study, I knew that privacy, inequality, and institutional disclosure requirements would be at the heart of the work, but I did not trace these interests back to my transition experiences. Instead, I articulated the justification for the research on strictly intellectual grounds. When people asked me, "Why privacy?" I had a ready response about gaps in the literature, the dearth of empirical data, and theoretical holes that needed to be filled—all legitimate reasons for undertaking the work. But I never touched on what motivated me on a personal level. It was almost as if submerging my trans identity in everyday life meant that I also repressed the ways in which my research on privacy and disclosure connects to my experience as a trans man. It was only when I arrived in Houston and began hearing stories like Janice's that I began to find these parallels impossible to ignore.

PARALLEL PROCESSES OF COERCIVE INSTITUTIONAL DISCLOSURE

The parallels between my experience as a trans person and those of my research participants are not straightforward. On the surface and in demographic terms, we look quite different. The women I work with are poor, mostly African American mothers with relatively low education living in a high-poverty, high-crime neighborhood. I am a white, childless man with advanced degrees and a career path that puts me on a solidly middle- to upper-class track. I feel safe in my mixed-income neighborhood, which is an LGBTQ enclave in a major city with several such communities. And yet, countless times during my interviews, I listened to stories that resonated with my own history. As welfare recipients, my interviewees routinely endure intense questioning by bureaucrats whose job it is to determine whether clients are eligible for benefits and whether they have met the myriad behavioral conditions that participation requires. Welfare clients must disclose information ranging from documentation of income to paternity to sexual histories. In effect, poor mothers are scrutinized and monitored to ensure they comply with conditions that, if unmet, can result in sanctions and the reduction of benefits.

When I began medical and legal transition a decade ago, I underwent a similar gatekeeping process. Before being allowed access to hormone therapy or surgery (both of which were explicitly excluded from my insurance coverage at that time because they were not deemed "medically necessary"), I was required to procure a letter from a certified psychotherapist indicating that I was diagnosed with gender identity disorder. When I applied for a legal name change, I had to provide documentation of my medical procedures as proof that I had completed what the state considered to be a valid gender reassignment. I also stood in front of a judge to make the case for not publishing my name change in a local newspaper, as required by state law. In each bureaucratic encounter, I realized that transitioning was a tenuous prospect that I had little control over, as state and medical establishments held the power to deny my requests if I did not meet their stipulations (Spade 2006). I "proved" that I was a deserving candidate largely through answering deeply personal questions, telling strangers details about my life history that I would never otherwise disclose—just as my respondents do in the welfare office in order to qualify for state benefits, and indeed just as they did in interviews with me.

The content of what my research participants and I have had to prove to our respective gatekeepers is not the same, nor are the stakes. When I transitioned, I was working, I was seeking a master's degree, and I was not struggling to put food on the table. As a white person, I have never faced the racialized surveillance that follows my respondents from the welfare office into their communities, homes, and families. And when I began living as a white man, I gained additional privileges that elude many white trans women, poor trans people, and trans people of color. For these reasons, I use the term *parallel* very carefully. However, I do think both my respondents and I have occupied a structural position of vulnerability that comes with having to disclose extensive personal information in order to be granted needed services. Central to this experience is the sense that your future depends on the answers you provide and the discretion of whichever bureaucrat you might speak to that day (see Watkins-Hayes 2009). I could empathize with one of my respondents, Keisha, when she spoke of the imperative to "keep your story straight" lest a caseworker discover that she had intentionally concealed that a boyfriend was living with her or failed to disclose a gift from her child's father (both disclosures that could endanger her benefit receipt). I recalled my own dread each time I was asked to repeat my narrative of why exactly I believed I needed to change gender, and my own fears of being denied. The social and psychological costs for trans people who seek but are unable to access medical transition can be high.

The experience of being invisibly trans in the field also shaped my approach to data collection and analysis. One of the most interesting things about studying privacy is the question of how such a study is even possible. How do we study that which is intentionally kept invisible? I chose to use interviews, as my primary interest was in understanding the words poor mothers use as they think and talk about their experiences of privacy vis-à-vis the social safety net and the meanings they attach to them. But the interview format posed a curious methodological challenge. As I sat across from my interviewees, asking them to answer personal questions with the promise of a twenty-dollar Walmart gift card as a "reward," I was unwittingly re-creating precisely the dynamic of coercive information solicitation that mothers lamented in the welfare context. They wanted the twenty-dollar gift card, which for my respondents was a nontrivial amount of money, and the way to get it was to answer questions from a stranger backed by considerable institutional power.

Because of my personal history, I was acutely aware of how such questioning on the part of an "authority" can feel demeaning or disrespectful, especially when the questions are personal. Therefore, I did as much as I could to ameliorate the power differential embedded in the interview dynamic and to show my respondents respect. For example, I gave my respondents the gift card before the interview started, to signal that I meant it when I said they were free to stop the interview whenever they wished, and to assure them I was trustworthy—that I was "good for" the money I promised. It was not always easy to overcome the palpable mistrust that tended to pervade the conversation until I could make clear that I was in no way affiliated with the state, was not a social worker, and would keep everything we discussed confidential. To mitigate this mistrust, I also chose to ask a minimal amount of demographic questions and to avoid asking my respondents to provide additional contact information beyond their phone number, as I did not want them to worry about the possibility that I would share that information with someone in a position of authority (e.g., Child Protective Services). Further, when mothers indicated that they did not want to talk about a particular topic or detail—either by using a euphemism or by stating directly that they did not want to talk about it—I did not press them. I recognized their attempts to maintain privacy and purposefully let them keep these details private. For me, this was a demonstration of respect for their privacy. It was also, I hoped, a departure from the treatment they so often described undergoing at the welfare office, where a client's nonresponse is viewed with suspicion and where it is common to be asked the same questions repeatedly until an answer is given.

A researcher who does not relate in the same way I do to my respondents' experiences with the state, or for whom privacy is less personally salient, might have pressed harder and gotten more data. At the same time, it is still possible (and generative) to analyze those moments of hesitation in context to learn about when and how mothers set limits on what they were willing to disclose, and I did this work in the dissertation.

RISKY RECIPROCITY

There were times in the field when I did consider sharing some aspects of my queer personal life, in the service of reciprocity with my interviewees. Central to the contested ideals of a queer feminist approach to qualitative inquiry is that researchers can and should make efforts to "level the play-ing field" with their respondents, to share the authority for producing knowledge about respondents' experiences, and to disrupt the hierarchi-cal relationship between researcher and subject. One way to do this is through reversing the flow of power-knowledge by being open to *answer-ing* questions instead of just asking them. Such a reciprocal approach can potentially empower research subjects, enhance rapport, and also gener-ate rich data in its own right (Meadow 2013). However, as the following anecdote illustrates, the decision to be selectively open about myself in response to an interviewee's questions—in the service of reciprocity—was not without consequences.

Churches are by far the most prevalent institution in the neighborhood where I did my research, and many of the most fruitful connections I made in the early days of fieldwork came through knocking on church doors. One day I visited a local church to see if I could meet the pastor to get his perspective on the neighborhood and the church's role in providing resources for the poor. A tall, middle-aged African American man in a crisply pressed black suit, his salt-and-pepper hair closely cropped, answered the door, identified himself as Pastor Carl, and—after teasing me about my "big blue eyes"—invited me to return the next day to have a sit-down chat. When I came back the following day, we sat in his office and talked for a long time. Throughout the conversation, I was keenly aware of how intimate it felt as Pastor Carl shared stories about growing up in the area, discussed his mixed feelings about having moved to a safer and more affluent suburb, and talked about the struggles facing the more vulnerable members of his congregation. At one point, he showed me a barely legible handwritten note from a senior citizen, asking for help pay-ing for an $11.60 prescription that she needed but could not afford. Later, when the conversation turned to race relations, he told me that he saw people the way God saw people—that when he saw me walk up he saw "a human, not a Caucasian person."

At this point the conversation took a turn, and he began to ask me ques-tions about myself, referring to me in the third person: "Tell me just who is Cayce. What is Cayce about?" I immediately felt pressure to present myself in some sort of upstanding way, to give a "good" answer or at least not raise any red flags (e.g., "I'm queer and nonreligious"). At the same time, I felt pulled to be sincere and honest. This man had been warm, generous with his time, and forthcoming when I—a total stranger—had asked him about his life. I liked him and felt as if we were sharing a meaningful encounter. I started to respond with a few benign words about my career plans, but Pastor Carl interrupted to ask whether I was married. I said no, but quickly added that I'd been with my partner for seven years and that we lived together, shared a car, and were virtually married. In making that snap decision, I thought to myself that these facts could be emblematic of maturity, stability, and responsibility—all things a pastor might appreciate. Instead, he asked pointedly why we weren't married, at which point I took a deep breath and asked, "Do you *really* want to know?" He said yes, so I told him one version of the truth: that my sister is gay and my partner and I didn't feel comfortable participating in an institution like marriage until she and her partner could do the same. Earlier in our conversation, Pastor Carl had mentioned his own sister and noted how close they were, so I hoped he might have some understanding of my position.

What followed instead was first an admonition from Pastor Carl that our ideology was not a valid reason to put off marriage, since cohabitation constituted "living in sin," followed by a veritable sermon on the immorality of homosexuality. He told me in no uncertain terms that I needed to learn to love the sinner, but hate the sin—which, in this context, meant my sister and her partner's union. I shuddered to think what he might have said had I told him the version of the truth that included how my own gender and sexuality informs my approach to legal marriage. I listened patiently, nodding my head but saying little, and soon enough the encounter drew to a close. As I stood up to leave, the pastor held me in a tight embrace, a gesture that seemed to symbolize how I could in the same moment feel close to and utterly alienated from another person.

This experience was both instructive and disappointing. I left feeling foolish for letting my guard down and being so naive in that moment as to expect that even the revelation of a tangential aspect of my "real" self (via my sister's queerness) might be unproblematic. But it's also useful to consider what I hoped to gain from disclosing something potentially risky about myself. When I spoke with Pastor Carl, I was making a series of decisions on the fly about what to reveal, as was he. It is often the case that we make decisions to disclose personal information (whether consciously or not) so that we can become closer to our conversation partner. We connect through the reciprocal process of sharing pieces of ourselves, some insignificant and some meaningful. In deciding to share with Pastor Carl, I hoped to become close to him, and also to minimize the inevitable distance between the researcher and the researched. But for queer people, and others with nonnormative life experiences and invisible stigmas, disclosure can result in judgment, censure, or ridicule. The ever-present potential for a negative reaction (and the persistent hope for a positive one) shapes routine encounters and informs the ways people "do privacy" (Nippert-Eng 2010). But in this context it also raises questions about what reciprocity means in the field, especially for researchers whose identities are marginalized. Whereas Pastor Carl felt free to air his opinions about me, in my role as researcher I felt compelled to remain silent about my own views in the service of the relationship—resulting in a decidedly nonreciprocal dynamic.

In this encounter, and others, my gender presentation, whiteness, and embodiment—the fact that I pass as male—granted me the *option* to choose what to disclose about my gender. And because I am in a relationship with a woman, I am able to drop her typically female name into casual conversation to ward off any suspicion that I might be gay. Unlike people in same-sex relationships, I did not have to conjure a fake partner to shore up my performance of heterosexuality in the field. Yet the truth of our [queer] relationship—and my identity—remained obscured. While this invisibility affords me a measure of physical safety and social ease unavailable to many trans and gender-nonconforming people, it can also make it harder to do the sort of intersubjective, power-sharing work to which queer and feminist ethnographers aspire. For example, in Tey Meadow's research (2013) on transgender and gender-nonconforming youth, her gender—and genderqueerness—"became a topic of frequent commentary and speculation" with her research subjects (474). By acknowledging the symbolic investment her subjects had in her gender and allowing them to talk openly with her about it, Meadow created a relationship in which her subjects "returned [her] gaze," allowing them to negotiate categories of gender together. Not only was this empowering for her subjects, but it was also analytically fruitful, if at times uncomfortable for Meadow. This example differs from my situation in that the construct of gender itself is central to Meadow's work, but our different experiences with disclosure raise questions about how visible and invisible queerness can both open and foreclose opportunities to "do reciprocity" in qualitative research.

BUILDING TRUST

In contrast to my experience with Pastor Carl, in which it was my voluntary disclosure that prompted his expression of anti-gay sentiment, there were times when I felt unsafe as a queer trans man simply because I was present in the community at a time when LGBT rights were being openly debated. I arrived in Houston shortly before the city council passed the Houston Equal Rights Ordinance (HERO), a civil rights measure designed to provide basic protections against gender identity and sexuality-based discrimination. After a protracted public debate, the ordinance was overturned eleven months later by referendum vote. Because I was volunteering and observing at faith-based social service outreach events, and because some parts of the faith community were organizing in opposition to the bill (Swartz 2015), I often found myself included in conversations about the ordinance and about the (im)morality of LGBT people in general, despite the fact that I did not intend for sexuality to be central to my research project.

Not long after I first began spending time in Houston, I met Gerrie, an African American civil rights activist and community organizer in her sixties who worked tirelessly to bring resources and attention to the needs of the most vulnerable people in her neighborhood. We met at an outreach program she had organized, and, moments after we were introduced, she put me to work unloading bulk food from a truck and helping senior citizens carry their food boxes. I appeared to be the only white person among both the volunteers and the nearly two hundred patrons who came for the donated food. Being the only white person was typical for me in my field site, as the neighborhood was roughly 90 percent African American and less than 2 percent white. After our first meeting, Gerrie became an invaluable informant, introducing me to community leaders and prospective interviewees, including me in neighborhood and church events, and generously welcoming me into her home. I often gave her rides because her car was perennially in need of repairs, and she took every opportunity to tease me about my navigational deficits.

I was grateful for the access Gerrie gave me in the field and I truly enjoyed her company, but it came at a cost. Gerrie often shared with me her negative views about LGBT people, and helped organized a handful of pastors from the neighborhood who were vocally opposed to the HERO legislation. She referred to the ordinance in a text message to me as "madness," and spoke out on local radio against the bill. Like many other opponents to the bill, she argued that it would allow "sexual predators" disguised as women to legally enter women's restrooms. When she referred to transgender people, she put the phrase in quotation marks to indicate that such people were not, in her view, legitimate. I heard the same sentiment from other interviewees, who, like Gerrie, presumably had no idea that they were talking to one of the very people they condemned. At one outreach event, Gerrie encouraged me to pass out flyers decrying the ordinance, a request I managed to avoid by simply leaving a stack of flyers on the table without actively soliciting patrons to take them. But I grew accustomed to being included in conversations in which it was taken for granted that being gay is a sin or that transgender people pose a grave risk to orderly society if allowed to use the bathroom of their choice. Hearing these sentiments from people with whom I was developing rapport and relationships reinforced the idea that my identity and embodiment as a queer trans man would be a liability if made visible.

Researchers often encounter people in the field whose political or religious ideas are antithetical to their own (see Fetner & Heath, this volume). And it is a common strategy to keep silent about these differences—to act normatively and not speak up when doing so would alienate informants or threaten the research project itself (cf. Goodman 1996). Inserting too much of oneself in the research setting can inadvertently drown out the very people one is trying to hear, as well as cloud one's interpretation of their words. However, I found keeping silent to be doubly challenging because the object of my respondents' derision was *me*—it was my body and identity they told me should not exist. What are the consequences of being in this position? Pragmatically, I do not believe I could have done this study if I had been out as trans. The counterfactual is of course unknowable, but I think that if I were positioned as the "sinner" to be loved, I wouldn't have been able to build the relationships central to my work. The rapport I developed with those in the field felt predicated on my concealment of a central part of who I am. But beyond the practical implications of being out as trans or not for gaining entrée into this particular community, there are emotional consequences associated with the stark bifurcation of self that this kind of fieldwork requires. I found that as a researcher, these consequences affected not only me personally but also the quality of the analytic work I did. I found it difficult to hold both the empathy and respect I had for my respondents—feelings I could outwardly express—and the hurt, disappointment, and anger I felt at some of their views toward me and the people I call family—sentiments that had to remain submerged. It was only when I decided to come out as trans to my dissertation committee and professional colleagues, and to write about and talk through these experiences, that I was able to incorporate them reflexively in my analysis. Fortunately, my committee and colleagues responded thoughtfully and with encouragement, which may not be the case for others. But for me, this support was critical.

CONCLUSION

When I embarked on my fieldwork, I did not anticipate how much of my self and my history I would draw on in thinking through the privacy experiences of my research participants—in part because I was so accustomed to filtering my gender history out of my everyday work life. Even for graduate students who are not in my particular position, there is a great deal of pressure to separate oneself from one's work—to maintain a distance that purportedly allows for dispassionate analysis and also provides an emotional buffer that protects one against sustained and sometimes harsh critique of one's work. This distance can also be productive to the extent that being too embedded or personally invested can obscure one's view of the scientific object or dull one's analytic insight. Yet these can easily become false distinctions, echoes of a masculinist orientation to research that subordinates emotion, intersubjectivity, and empathy in favor of a more "scientific" objectivity. Black feminist thinkers have long argued that there can be a real danger in leaving the self out—both for the researcher and for the richness of the work itself—which can be true for queer people and other people who are marginalized, and especially for those with compound and intersecting marginalized identities (Collins 1990).

I don't know how I will manage my trans identity in future fieldwork, and I can't yet know what the professional consequences will be of my coming out as trans. Writing this chapter reflects my choice to take my chances. I do know that forging a degree of integration between my personal and professional lives has meant that I have less privacy than I would prefer. But the prospect of being able to talk openly with other scholars about these issues—and to be part of a queer community—gives me hope that the benefits are worth the risk.

NOTES

1. I use pseudonyms to protect my respondents' identities.
2. These are not mutually exclusive categories. Indeed, I may have interviewed mothers who are also trans women and did not disclose their trans status to me.

WORKS CITED

Collins, Patricia Hill. 1990. *Black feminist thought: Knowledge, consciousness, and the politics of empowerment.* New York: Hyman.

Driesson, Katherine. 2014. "Houston equality measure fails by wide margin." *Houston Chronicle.* Updated November 4, 2015. http://www.chron.com /politics/election/local/article/HERO-results-6608562.php.

Goodman, Liz. 1996. "Rites of passing." In *Out in the field: Reflections of lesbian and gay anthropologists.* Ed. Ellen Lewin and William Leap. Champaign: University of Illinois Press.

Levine, Judith. 2013. *Ain't no trust: How bosses, boyfriends, and bureaucrats fail low-income mothers and why it matters.* Berkeley: University of California Press.

Meadow, Tey. 2013. "Studying each other: On agency, constraint, and positionality in the field." *Journal of Contemporary Ethnography* 42(4): 466–81.

Nippert-Eng, Christena. 2010. *Islands of privacy.* Chicago: University of Chicago Press.

Roberts, Dorothy. 1991. *Killing the black body: Race, reproduction, and the meaning of liberty.* New York: Vintage.

Schilt, Kristen. 2010. *Just one of the guys: Transgender men and the persistence of gender inequality.* Chicago: University of Chicago Press.

Schilt, Kristen, and Matthew Wiswall. 2008. "Before and after: Gender transitions, human capital, and workplace experiences." *The B.E. Journal of Economic Analysis and Policy* 8(1): 1–28.

Spade, Dean. 2006. "Mutilating gender." In *The Transgender Studies Reader.* Ed. Susan Stryker and Stephen Whittle. New York: Routledge.

———. 2013. "Resisting medicine, re/modeling gender." *Berkeley Journal of Gender, Law, & Justice* 18(1): 15–37.

Swartz, Mimi. 2015. "The equal rights fight over Houston's bathrooms." *New York Times,* October 27. http://www.nytimes.com/2015/10/28/opinion/the-equal-rights-fight-over-houstons-bathrooms.html?_r=0.

Taylor, Verta, and Nicole Raeburn. 1995. "Identity politics as high-risk activism: Career consequences for lesbian, gay and bisexual sociologists." *Social Problems* 42(2): 252–73.

Watkins-Hayes, Celeste. 2009. *The new welfare bureaucrats: Entanglements of race, class, and policy reform.* Chicago: University of Chicago Press.

7 Thank You for Coming Out Today

THE QUEER DISCOMFORTS OF IN-DEPTH INTERVIEWING

Catherine Connell

The metaphor of the closet and the attendant language of "coming out" has come under fire from sexuality scholars for being inadequately precise, insufficiently intersectional, and increasingly anachronistic for the contemporary moment (e.g., Seidman 2002). In my own work, I have been critical of the coming-out imperative endemic to modern LGBTQ politics because of the ways it reinforces static and inflexible notions of sexuality, privileges sexuality over other intersecting identities, and puts undue pressure on those who can't afford the risks of sexuality disclosure (Connell 2015). Imagine my dismay, then, when I realized not long ago that I was inadvertently reproducing this imperative in my own research, particularly through the use of in-depth interviewing. I discovered that coming out is so thoroughly embedded in the narration of LGBTQ experience that it's virtually impossible to ask about that experience without relying on it as a framing device. Worse still, I found that using the shorthand *coming out* can have a disciplining effect on research participants that can be harmful, both to the research and to the participants themselves. The experience made me wonder, Can in-depth interviewing ever be a queer method? What kinds of queer discomforts does the method engender, and what can we learn from them? Ultimately, I argue that reflecting on these discomforts is a necessary part of engaging in queer methodological practice, regardless of the specific method chosen. In this chapter I offer an example of one such moment of turning a queer lens on a research method as a way of illustrating the productive tensions that may emerge.

In the summer of 2008, I traveled to California to conduct interviews with gay and lesbian public school teachers for my dissertation research. Short on both networks and time, I recruited participants via snowball sampling, asking the few teachers I did know in the state to refer me to others and expanding from there. This was working well until I emailed a gay teacher named Peter to ask if he was interested in participating.[1] Peter wrote back, angered and offended that someone had outed him by recommending him for the study. I was mortified at this unintentional gaffe and wrote back immediately to apologize.

After that, I didn't expect to hear from him again. To my surprise, though, he followed up, this time with a set of rather pointed questions about my research. Why was I studying this, and what did I plan to do with the information? What was my agenda? I wrote back and answered his questions, still certain he would not participate, but unexpectedly, his next email said he was willing to be interviewed after all. After several more emails about confidentiality, Peter and I agreed to meet for an interview.

Given his initial irritation, I was nervous about the interview and became even more so when his in-person affect came off as prickly and almost antagonistic toward the project. At the time, I couldn't make sense of this seeming hostility. When I asked him what bearing being gay had on his classroom experience, his reply was clipped and defensive: "I guess, for me, that's not a cross I choose to bear. I mean, most heterosexuals, they don't bring that out, they don't self-identify to their students. So I mean, I don't see why [gay and lesbian teachers] would [identify themselves]." He didn't seem to want to discuss sexuality at all and instead moved the focus to the significance of race and ethnicity for himself and his students.

Peter, who identified as Japanese, moved from Hawaii to the mainland United States for college. "Coming here," he said, "I think I kind of lost sense of who I was, because more of the people I ran around with were white." This experience sensitized him to the importance of thinking about race and racial privilege in the teaching context. He explained, "If you're going to work in areas where the people don't resemble you at all—

culturally, ethnically, even socioeconomically . . . and if your experiences don't mirror [your students'], then you need to be cognizant of that." I tried to tie the conversation back to sexuality, asking him about how teaching might also involve examining sexuality and privilege, but he demurred, repeating his early assertion that sexuality wasn't relevant for him at work.

As time went on, though, Peter's adamant stance on separating sexual and professional identities and his annoyance at questions that suggested other possible approaches faded. Toward the end of our conversation, he even evinced a certain melancholy about his decision to keep the two identities so far apart:

> I don't know if [this is] a sad testimony on my part, but I feel like there are other parts of me that I would like to explore, that I have not made time for or I have chosen not to explore. I don't know. . . . I think in the era I grew up in, [coming out] was very difficult for people to do, so I don't know. . . . So maybe in answer to your [earlier] question, it would have [helped to have role models]! It would have, you know? If there were people that you could identify with and saw that, oh yeah, they're just like me! You know? . . . You wouldn't feel so badly growing up [with] a range of ways you could see and you could identify with. I think it would be much easier to cope.

When we finished, Peter clasped my hand with both of his, looked into my eyes, and told me how happy he was to have had the chance to think about these issues, despite his initial reluctance. We both teared up a bit in parting, overcome by the intensity of the emotions unearthed in the interview process. I was relieved, exhausted, confused, and exhilarated all at once, and he seemed to feel similarly. Why had things been so antagonistic at the beginning? And how, after an hour of what felt more like pulling teeth than interviewing, did we end up here, crying and holding hands? It was one of the most surprising interview experiences I've had, to go from such guardedness to vulnerability in one encounter. In the moment, it felt electrifying, but the more I thought about it afterward, the more uncomfortable I became. I couldn't quiet this nagging sense that something was unresolved about this exchange, something of both ethical and analytical importance.

Untangling the thicket of methodological and epistemological issues implicated in this experience was tricky. First, it introduced an ethical question regarding my sampling strategy. While I had given a lot of thought to how to protect the confidentiality of my respondents in terms of de-identifying data, I hadn't fully considered how contacting potential respondents directly could itself constitute a threat to their privacy. Peter's reaction to my initial inquiry sensitized me to that possibility and made me reconsider how to sample going forward. Since that interview, I've shifted to asking participants to contact potential interviewees on my behalf; this strategy, while less effective generally, adds an extra layer of protection for potential interviewees.

What was thornier, though, was unpacking what this encounter meant about some of the project's epistemological assumptions that were invisible to me until this moment and dismaying when they made themselves known. Upon further reflection, I realized that my almost single-minded focus on sexual visibility was both crowding out other important dimensions of teachers' experiences and leading me to conceptualize sexuality in a narrow and normative way that reflected neither my political nor my personal understanding of sexual identity.

PRESENTATION IN THE FIELD

Part of what I think Peter was bristling against was the implicit privileging of sexual identity over all others that was threaded through my project, from the way I framed the project in my email, to the questions I asked in my interview. For Peter, being a teacher and a person of color were more salient identities than being gay, at least while on the job. Yet my project's framing left little room for that prioritization to be validated. I found myself a little confused by his anger in our encounter, which in retrospect feels embarrassingly naïve. If you'd asked me at the time about the discourse of coming out, I would have railed against its lack of intersectional understanding as well as the essentialized notions of sexual identity that predominate it. Yet, somehow in my own research, I was falling into all the same traps without even realizing it. What's more, this version of sexual identity I was inadvertently privileging didn't even make sense to my own experience.

In a chapter in *Queer Methods and Methodologies*, Alison Rooke (2012) discusses the dilemmas of being "queer in the field." Rooke problematizes the "assumed stability and coherence of the ethnographic self" inherent in traditional ethnographic practice—in this case, the way that a researcher's sexual identity is articulated in the field while conducting LGBTQ research (25). In the course of her research, Rooke experienced a shift in her own sense of her sexual self—from that of a lesbian identity rooted in a particular geographic and political history to something more fluid as she began a relationship with a transgender man. This shift created a number of methodological dilemmas for Rooke—was she still doing "insider research" within the lesbian support group she was studying? Was she misrepresenting herself as a "confident, secure lesbian role model" (38) to the participants? Should she be writing these dilemmas into her work? Ultimately, Rooke understands these struggles as an integral part of queer methodology—a way of understanding one's research positionality as less stable and coherent than we typically assume and therefore a crucial site of queer knowledge production.

In my eagerness to develop and maintain rapport with my participants, I realize now, I too was projecting a version of my own sexuality and sexual politics that, while not disingenuous, did not reflect the full range of my experience and that possibly unduly influenced my interviews. As a stranger, a relative outsider in both fields I studied (public schools in California and Texas) with few insider allies to vouch for me, I was quick to assure potential participants that I was, in fact, not just well intentioned but one of them. While I did not, as a matter of course, announce my sexual identity in the process of recruitment, I readily identified myself as a fellow "gay teacher" to those who asked, and often explained that my motivation for the study was making schools safer and more just for teachers like "us."

I emphasized my belonging, as both gay/lesbian and as a teacher, as a way of signaling my kinship, my acceptance, and perhaps more dangerously, my *understanding* of their experiences. While this no doubt did promote rapport and perhaps a sense of intimacy for some of my participants, it also had the unintended consequence of limiting what they were willing to say and shaped how they said it. In my effort to gain their trust in the project and myself, I rushed to assure them that I already *did* understand, which limited my ability to have them explain themselves to me. For example, when teachers used common in-group concepts like "cruising," "reading," or "flaming out," I didn't ask them what they meant in this particular context—I rushed in with a knowing smile or nod, hoping to reassure them I was, of course, in the know about such terms. Some of this behavior can be chalked up to the inevitable growing pains of becoming a skilled interviewer, but I also think it reflects a flaw endemic to "insider research" that must be contended with.

What is perhaps murkier is that my positionality within the field could not truly, accurately be summed up as a "gay teacher," and that there were repercussions to this inaccuracy. First, I was not truly a teacher in the same structural sense as my research participants. Everyone in my sample taught (or had taught) in public primary and secondary schools, and all were therefore especially vulnerable to the discrimination, harassment, and violence associated with being nonheterosexual in close proximity with children (for more on this vulnerability, see Connell 2015). While I *was* a teacher in the sense that I was a graduate teaching assistant at the time, I was more insulated within higher education than they were in primary and secondary instruction. Calling myself a fellow gay teacher, then, was a slippage of language and meaning not inconsequential to our researcher–research participant dynamic.

Not only was I not a teacher in the same sense as my participants were, but I also did not identify as gay (or lesbian), but rather as queer—a distinction that is perhaps not as irrelevant as it might seem on the surface, given the concerns raised by Rooke (2012). In (mis)representing my sexual identity like this, perhaps I foreclosed the possibility of recognizing similar incoherencies and fluidities in my participants. It may also have led my participants to assume that my political leanings were in line with those of the mainstream gay rights movement, one that identifies coming out as the quintessential political act, even the sacred duty of LGBTQs. The first stirrings of this realization, incited by my encounter with Peter, stopped me in my tracks and created a fundamental theoretical shift in the project that would ultimately come to form the basis of my later book. Queer theory conceptualizes discomfort as a productive tool for challenging the status quo and inciting social change; I would argue that the same is true for queer methods. Dwelling on these moments of possible misrecognition is a step in the queer research process, one that can lead to more profound methodological and analytical insight.

Paying attention to the emotion and affect in an interview is one useful way to hone in on such productive discomforts. Peter's anger and angst, my fear and frustration, the tearfulness at the end of the meeting—without it, this interview might have simply blurred into the next in the midst of a harried summer of data collection. Instead, the emotional impact of our encounter lead me to linger on it, and that pause was enough to allow me to reconsider the project in a new light. (For more on the analytical value of engaging in emotional reflexivity, see Kleinman & Copp 1993; McQueeney & Lavelle 2015).

It became startlingly apparent to me as I processed this exchange not only that gay and lesbian teachers are constrained by the teaching profession, which inhibits all but the most vague and sanitized expression of sexual "diversity" in schools (and even then, only in some select schools), but that contemporary LGBTQ politics was having a similar constraining effect. When I, as one nonheterosexual person to another, pressed teachers on the factors that inhibited them from coming out, I left unexamined the assumption that coming out is the one true path to liberation, one to which we should all aspire. My questioning may have provoked feelings of anger, anxiety, or shame in the participants who were not out in the classroom. It might also have inhibited some from sharing their feelings of resistance to or discomfort with that coming-out imperative, because they thought I might not understand or agree.

That I should do such a thing is powerfully dismaying to me. After all, the queer commitments of my own life stem from frustration with these very same static and identitarian understandings of sexuality. Yet, however dedicated I am to queering my own life, identity, classroom, family, and so forth, I had forgotten to queer my *research*. This is easy to do, given the disciplining power of traditional methods, which urge us to take ourselves—our identities, our politics, our feelings—out of the research process and to avoid confusion and ambiguity at all costs. In contrast, a queer methodology can retain the affective dimension of the research process and all the messiness it may contain.

With this in mind, Peter's irritation with me might have had as much to do with the framing of the project as it was about the breach of his privacy. It could not be dispensed with through reassurances of friendliness, sameness, or confidentiality going forward. In fact, perhaps it was the reassurance of sameness that created so much friction between us: to reread his words in light of this realization is to see an entirely different text than I first imagined. Why did he describe sexuality as a "cross to bear"? Was it because I was making it feel like a heavy burden that "we" should shoulder? Why did it make him sad to think of his lack of gay role models, and more striking, why did he identify role modeling as the "point" of my project? Had I made him feel like a failure in that regard, and is that why our meeting was one of such heightened emotion? It took a deeper examination of this moment of mutual misunderstanding to reveal just how deeply rooted the coming-out mandate is for contemporary LGBTQs. Through my self-presentation, my affect, my interview questions, I had aggravated that tension between his decisions as a teacher and the expectations of the "good" gay citizen. With this realization, my research question moved from asking how gay and lesbian teachers survive their homophobic working conditions to asking how gay and lesbian teachers negotiate this no-win situation of trying to meet the opposing demands of teaching professionalism and of gay pride.

CAN AN INTERVIEW CHANGE A LIFE?

I wish I could say that all subsequent interviews were free from such profound misrecognitions and anxieties, but of course they were not. I rewrote my research questions to be less focused on coming out and more open to the variety of paths a gay or lesbian teacher might take, so that they might not so easily induce anxiety about not meeting the expectations of gay pride. I adjusted my presentation of self to minimize perceptions of approval or disapproval of their answers or experiences; for example, I more carefully monitored my facial expressions and body language to appear neutral about their decisions about managing their sexuality at work. I also tried to be less dogmatic in describing my interest and investments in the project. But of course, true neutrality is a myth; no researcher is a blank slate. Inevitably, respondents made assumptions about me (and I about them) that shaped the data-gathering process. Becoming more keenly aware of this pressure helped me notice and appreciate the moments of ambivalence in their narratives in a new light, but it did not remove them from our encounters.

This became especially apparent in a couple of encounters after I had officially "left" the field. After finishing up in California over the summer, I returned to Texas at the start of the fall semester to conduct another round of interviews there. (My dissertation was a comparative analysis of teachers' experiences across opposing LGBTQ policy climates.) Linda, a special-education teacher in a central Texas middle school, was one of the last participants I interviewed in the project. I spent an afternoon observing her classes and conducted the interview after the students went home for the day. It was a fairly unexceptional afternoon—I was reaching interview saturation at this point, so the conversation was not particularly surprising or remarkable in the moment. Like many in my sample, Linda had not made her sexual identity known on campus, with the exception of a couple of trusted coworkers. At some point in the conversation, she divulged that as a late-in-life lesbian, she also had not disclosed to her twelve-year-old daughter. I asked her to talk a little bit about that, then steered our conversation back to the classroom. Our interview was short compared to earlier ones—about forty-five minutes long. As we concluded, I wished her luck with everything, including the family concerns she'd mentioned, and left.

Two weeks later, I received a follow-up email from Linda. In it, she thanked me for encouraging her to think more about her sexuality and shared that, as a result of our conversation, she had come out not only to a number of colleagues but also to her daughter. My stomach dropped; I hadn't really considered the possibility that this could be a consequence of our interview, and moreover, I didn't want it to be. What if she was fired or otherwise penalized for coming out at work? What if her relationship with her daughter was damaged or her custody arrangement threatened by this turn of events? I didn't want to be responsible for such possibilities. Something felt fundamentally wrong—dangerous, even—about this turn of events. Yet Linda seemed happy that the interview had spurred her to reconsider her decisions and empowered her to change them. I was torn about how I should interpret this unexpected consequence of our interview.

Two years later, I ran into Kenny, another respondent, and we stopped to catch each other up on our post-interview lives. I was, at that point, out of grad school, in my first year as a tenure-track professor, and working on turning the dissertation into a book manuscript. When I told Kenny about this, he grabbed my arm—it's so funny, he laughed, that he'd been so worried about coming out on the job when we last spoke. At the time of our interview, he was considering leaving teaching to enter another job, where he would feel less compelled to separate his sexual and professional selves. Even though his school did have local nondiscrimination protections, he didn't feel safe to come out. "It does bother me," he said in our interview, "knowing that I never like—well, who's to say that I *can't*, or who's stopping me?—but it wouldn't feel comfortable at my school right now, having a picture of me and my boyfriend [in my classroom]." Since the interview, though, he had not only changed his mind about quitting, but he'd also come out to coworkers, administrators, and even his students. "It's so weird to me," he told me in our later conversation, "to think about how nervous I was then, when I think about where I am now. I think in some ways that interview was sort of a first step in helping me relax a little bit about things."

While not as immediately distressing as Linda's email, this conversation still left me feeling a little unnerved. Should I (and really, could I?) prevent such outcomes in my interview process? In one respect, I worried that these outcomes meant that my methods had inadvertently reproduced the "out and proud" mandate of LGBTQ politics that I wished to critique and that put pressure on them to come out. But in another, it was remarkable that these participants had reflected on and made changes to their lives that they saw as beneficial after the interview encounter. As it turns out, perhaps an interview can change a life, and that's not an entirely bad—or an entirely good—thing. Rather, it's a reality of field and interview methods that we should do more to grapple with rather than simply ignore or wish away.

CONCLUSIONS

As qualitative researchers, we tell each other that we should try to leave the field the same or better than we found it. At times in this research process, I worried I'd missed the mark on this basic tenet of ethical research practice. Was my self-presentation or the wording of my interviews creating, or at least exacerbating, a pressure on teachers to come out? What does this mean about the uneven power dynamics between researcher and researched? What does this say about the potentially harmful intrusions of social science research? Most of the methodological ruminations on these sorts of questions have focused on ethnography rather than interview research (e.g., Stacey 1988; Stein 2010). A study like mine, based on discrete, one-time interview encounters, rather than prolonged embeddedness in a field site, seems, at least on its face, a less risky and intrusive method and one with few, if any, long-term effects for the participant. However, as these examples revealed, interviews can sometimes have profound and unanticipated consequences in the "real lives" of our participants long after we say our good-byes.

These moments sensitized me to the fact that interview (and ethnographic) research projects, even longitudinal ones, represent only a sliver of an individual's life or an institution's environment. The pathways I identified as my participants' chosen approaches to the pride-professionalism dilemma are not fixed, stable, or necessarily enduring; they represent a strategy, a response to the conditions of the moment, subject to change, fluidity, and movement as conditions shift. They are, essentially, *queer*, no matter how hard we may struggle to fit them into categories, typologies, heuristics.

In light of all this, what's a queer researcher to do? How do we acknowledge or even cultivate the queerness of the research encounter without abandoning the endeavor of social science entirely? Fortunately, we now have the benefit of a growing body of feminist and queer reflections on method and discipline to draw on; I'll share three here that have been especially helpful in my own pursuit of answers to these questions.

In "Feminist Ethnography: Critique, Conflict, and Ambivalent Observance," Jessica Fields (2013) brings the psychoanalytic concept of ambivalence to bear on the practice of feminist methods. Ambivalence, a simultaneous attraction and repulsion to an object, is a psychological state we often find difficult to tolerate; "our impulse is to resolve the contradiction, to achieve a consistency across our emotional states, to come down on the side of attraction *or* repulsion, love *or* hate" (Fields 2013: 6). Fields recommends that feminist researchers embrace "ambivalent observance" (7) in their methodological approaches, a practice that recognizes—but does not attempt to reconcile—the inherent tensions within feminism's varied political and intellectual commitments.

Ambivalent observance, in this case, might mean recognizing that it's potentially both productive *and* reductive to ask about how gay and lesbian teachers make decisions about disclosure. It might mean both opening *and* foreclosing research possibilities when you claim a sexual or political identity in the interview process. The value of queer or feminist research is being able to tolerate those ambivalent possibilities, to "confront our disappointments and complicities and work within and against a state of ambivalent observance" (Fields 2013: 8).

Also helpful for making sense of these complexities is Jodi O'Brien's "epistemology of contradiction" (O'Brien 2009, 2010). In the field, just as in our own lives, O'Brien writes, "we encounter contradiction, tensions and ambiguity much more than we are trained to acknowledge" (2010: 471). O'Brien's work gives researchers permission to recognize the messiness of social life and social research. "Any seasoned researcher," she says, "knows that the real gems of insight typically come into focus when we are mucking about in terrain that has not been precisely mapped" (O'Brien 2010: 471–72). So why deny the mess? Instead of taking this as a rationale for abandoning the goals of precision and systemization inherent in the social science research process, O'Brien encourages us to lean in to the messiness, to use it to sharpen our analytical insights rather than obscure them.

As I begin a new major interview study, this time with US soldiers about the repeal of "Don't ask, don't tell," I find myself acutely alert to the possibility of repeating my past research "mistakes." I feel an urgency to solve those past dilemmas, to somehow fix my new project so it avoids the pitfalls of the previous one. Yet I try to take heart in Jack Halberstam's meditations (2011) on the queer art of failure. Halberstam encourages us to embrace our failures, to commit to "failing well, failing often and learning . . . how to fail better" (24). Failure provides us the opportunity to evade the limitations of discipline, both the limitations of our academic disciplines and the limitations of discipline in the Foucauldian sense—the regulatory discourses we use to make sense of our selves and our social worlds. When we allow ourselves to fail, Halberstam says, "we will wander, improvise, fall short, and move in circles. We will lose our way . . . but in losing we will find another way of making meaning in which . . . no one gets left behind." And isn't that the ultimate goal for so many of us committed to feminist and queer research? While I do believe it's important to be attuned to ways you can continually improve your research approach, I am encouraged by these reminders that the pursuit of queer research is not the *resolution* of ambivalence, contradiction, or failure in the field, but rather the *recognition*—to tolerate the uncertainty and the vulnerability, the pleasures and the pains of the work, and to keep asking, keep thinking, keep writing, keep fighting in the face of it.

NOTE

1. All names are pseudonyms to protect the confidentiality of my participants.

WORKS CITED

Connell, Catherine. 2014. *School's out: Gay and lesbian teachers in the classroom*. Berkeley: University of California Press.
Fields, Jessica. 2013. "Feminist ethnography: Critique, conflict, and ambivalent observance." *Journal of Contemporary Ethnography* 42(4): 492–500.
Halberstam, Jack. 2011. *The queer art of failure*. Durham, NC: Duke University Press.
Kleinman, Sherryl, and Martha Copp. 1993. *Emotions and fieldwork*. Qualitative Research Methods, vol. 28. Newbury Park, CA: SAGE.
McQueeney, Krista, and Kristen M. Lavelle. 2015. "Emotional labor in critical ethnographic work: In the field and behind the desk." *Journal of Contemporary Ethnography* 46(1): 81–107.
O'Brien, Jodi. 2009. "Sociology as an epistemology of contradiction." *Sociological Perspectives* 52(1): 5–22.
———. 2010. "Seldom told tales from the field: Guest editor's introduction to the special issue." *Journal of Contemporary Ethnography* 39(5): 471–82.
Rooke, Alison. 2012. "Queer in the field: On emotions, temporality and performativity in ethnography." In *Queer methods and methodologies*. Ed. Catherine J. Nash and Kath Browne. New York: Ashgate.
Seidman, Steven. 2002. *Beyond the closet: The transformation of gay and lesbian life*. New York: Routledge.

Stacey, Judith. 1988. "Can there be a feminist ethnography?" *Women's Studies International Forum* 11(1): 21–27.

Stein, Arlene. 2010. "Sex, truths, and audiotape: Anonymity and the ethics of exposure in public ethnography." *Journal of Contemporary Ethnography* 39(5): 554–68.

8 Studying the "Right" Can Feel Wrong

REFLECTIONS ON RESEARCHING ANTI-LGBT MOVEMENTS

Tina Fetner and Melanie Heath

> To conservative Christians, homosexuality was sinful, unnatural, against God and family. To the vast majority [of Americans], who believed that religion—and sex— should be kept private, these words sounded intolerant, overly zealous, even hateful.
>
> Stein 2001: 110

Scholars have studied how conservative Christians who believe homosexuality to be a sin can be fundamentally intolerant and narrow-minded, willing to articulate the worst elements of homophobic society. Over the past forty years, leaders such as Jerry Falwell have disseminated hateful language about the "gay agenda" and God's judgment on a society that tolerates homosexuals. They have mobilized tremendous resources and organized a massive social movement in opposition to lesbian and gay rights and in support of the social exclusion of trans people. How does one, as a queer or queer-supportive scholar, go about studying issues of sexuality among conservative Christians and other anti-LGBT activists? Arlene Stein, quoted above, grappled with this issue in her research on how a small Oregon community dealt with an early-1990s political referendum to prohibit "special rights" for homosexuals. Her book *The Stranger Next Door* (Stein 2001) offers a balanced and sympathetic view of the logic of the conservative Christian perspective, demonstrating the source of the panic about homosexuality as rooted in a weakening economy caused by a slump in the timber industry. Her analysis provides a broader understanding to counter the simplistic impulse to name all conservative Christians as intolerant. She helps us to understand the structural conditions that can motivate anti-LGBT politics. At the same time, her research highlights the ways that studying conservative Christian perspectives takes an intellectual and emotional toll on researchers who might feel themselves implicated in the politics of hate that can spew from the religious right.

As researchers who have studied anti-LGBT movements among conservative Christians in the United States, we have firsthand knowledge of the opportunities and challenges of studying right-wing politics. For Melanie Heath's dissertation research, she left her progressive enclave in California to conduct an in-depth ethnography of the politics of marriage in Oklahoma, one of the first states to use welfare funds to support a statewide marriage initiative. The goal of the initiative, begun in the late 1990s, was to solve the problem of poverty and the economic hardships the state faced by promoting and strengthening heterosexual marriage in order to reduce state expenditures stemming from divorce and single motherhood. During this time, activism was high in Oklahoma to ensure that lesbians and gay men could not legally marry, and Heath sought to understand the tensions and contradictions in efforts to promote marriage for some and ban it for others. As a graduate student, Tina Fetner began researching the anti-LGBT activism of the religious right in the United States. She dug into the historical records of anti-LGBT movement groups, collecting their press releases and organizational data, listening to their broadcasts, and conducting interviews with people in key positions in religious-right organizations. She became an expert on how the religious right movement formed, solidified its ties with the Republican Party, and shaped public policy. She has also studied groups that conduct "ex-gay" reparative therapy, interviewed founders of Tea Party organizations, and researched the religious right in Canada.

In studying the institutional forces of right-wing politics, each of us drew on elements of a "queer methodology" to shine light on the specific power structures that animate anti-LGBT movements. Our empirical and historical methods offered insight into the construction of LGBT people as deviant others, and how conservative religious forces build their power based on the principle that heterosexuality is completely natural and unquestionable. Anti-LGBT activists struggle with the contradiction that their own activism demonstrates the instability of hegemonic ideas about heterosexuality. Studying groups that embrace a politics of disgust for people and practices that anti-LGBT activists view as deviant and sinful presents specific challenges to queer and queer-supportive scholars.

In this chapter, we share insights from our experiences studying anti-LGBT movements among conservative Christians and the religious right. We have organized the chapter to reflect particular concerns we faced during the important steps of entering the field, collecting data, and analyzing findings. First, we consider the complexities of managing self identity in a research environment where participants' views radically diverged from our own. Second, we offer insights about difficult interactions in the field. Finally, we discuss the bleakness of spending extended periods of time analyzing and writing about data that are adverse to our core values. We reflect on the value of studying right-wing activism and offer some thoughts on managing these research projects.

MANAGING IDENTITY IN CONSERVATIVE SPACES

[Fetner] As a graduate student at New York University, I took numerous steps to adjust my appearance to become presentable to the religious-right activists that I had arranged to interview face-to-face. I tried to look less feminist, less urban, and less mistakable for a lesbian. I aspired to mainstream beauty standards for young women. I spent months growing out my hair, I picked out a professional but feminine outfit, and I put on makeup. When I arrived at the offices of a major religious-right organization where I had an interview appointment, the first question that greeted me was, "So, you are from New York City?" The suspicion was thick in the room; it was clear that I had no chance of fitting in here, despite all my hard work to look "normal."

Looking back on my extensive-yet-feeble attempts to manage my appearance as I entered the field of anti-LGBT activists, I have to laugh at my naiveté. *I spent all that time growing out my hair for nothing?* It was clear to these activists that a graduate student from New York doing research on their group was not a friend of theirs no matter what I looked like, and they were right. I am a queer-supportive, straight-identified sociologist who is concerned about the harm done by this major religious-right organization. However, in person, in the field, I had hoped to package and suppress my concerns, my judgments, so that I could conduct a successful interview. I tried to demonstrate my goodwill, and my openness to connecting with the person who agreed to be interviewed, by presenting myself as traditionally feminine, but she saw right through me. And I learned that it is OK to conduct qualitative research in the field even though I didn't fit in. She completed the interview and answered my questions even though she didn't trust me, even though we never did connect.

Qualitative researchers generally recognize the importance of appearance as a methodological tool. By fitting in, investigators become less strange in the eyes of those they study. The challenges to fitting in, however, are multiplied in anti-LGBT settings like the ones I studied, and sometimes efforts to fit in fail. Despite this problem, data collection strategies can succeed. Arlene Stein (2001) found in her study of conservative Christians in Oregon that being a stranger had its advantages. People were willing to share with her the issues dearest to their hearts, precisely because she was an outsider and, more astonishing, because she was viewed as an *exotic* outsider—her Jewishness ultimately facilitated trust. Simultaneously, she recognized the importance of managing which identities she presented in the field. When people asked her about her personal life, she answered in ways that drew on their heteronormative assumptions about family life. Yes, she was married and had a son who was nine months old (there was no need to explain that she was married to a woman). She believed that introducing more than one type of otherness—in this case her sexuality—might pose too much of a threat.

In my case, not only was I an exotic other like Stein, but my participants met me with an active distrust—one I deserved, from their perspective. Rather than make a connection with my participants, then, I had to find another reason for my participants to share their thoughts and interpretations with me. I soon learned how to channel an active and open curiosity. That is, instead of building rapport based on common ground with my participants, I encouraged my participants to explain everything to me precisely because I was not aware of where they were coming from. I cultivated a presentation of self that communicated a curiosity based on my strangeness and my ignorance of participants' everyday lives. While this didn't build the sort of rapport that qualitative texts recommend, it did give my participants an powerful incentive to share their perspectives with me. They sought to fill me in, to let me know what the world looked like from their side, to correct my ignorance of their motivations for making a living by promoting what they would call traditional values. For my part, I was careful not to express or even hint at any judgments or disdain—whether in my questions, my body language, or my tone of voice. Rather, I presented myself as inquisitive, perhaps at times puzzled, about one detail or another that I might follow up on, but always willing to hear whatever my participants had to say.

It is difficult to anticipate how, and even whether, a researcher will be received in the field. Ultimately, fitting in does not have to be the goal. Our experiences, along with those of Stein, highlight the importance of approaching the field with thoughtfulness and a desire to connect with participants. No matter the beliefs or opinions a person carries, she or he wants to be heard and understood. There are many ways to find common ground and manage the messiness of conducting fieldwork with groups who may be hostile to a researcher's political perspective. Stein calls this "critical empathy," or the ability to understand the relationship between personal biography and social context that informs worldviews (2001: 230). Entering the field and managing one's identity mean risking failures and finding solutions. Researchers may have to revise their research design whenever a plan to interview particular people meets with closed doors. Such obstacles may arise more often when one is studying conservative groups like anti-LGBT organizations. At the same time, entering the field with a genuine desire to learn about other people's perspectives in a nonjudgmental fashion can aid in securing institutional support, finding a key informant, or recruiting interview participants.

DIFFICULT INTERACTIONS

[Heath] Interviewing conservative Christians often involved explicit anti-gay language that left little doubt about intentions. I remember one interview with a participant who had attended a marriage workshop that included a lesbian couple. Toward the end of the interview, I asked him how he felt about this couple's attendance. He responded that he hadn't even thought about it. This surprised me, as their presence had seemed to create tensions concerning how to talk about sex and the assumption that sex is always heterosexual. Then seemingly out of context, the participant told the following story that left me speechless.

> I had a homosexual in the eleventh grade. If you think back to that time, if you ever went outside and played sports, you get a lot of butt patting—good shot! [He demonstrates.] I made a move in basketball in the gym, and the guy was known to be gay. . . . I made a good move, and he goes, Good job! [he demonstrates the guy patting him on the butt]. And all I remember was turning around, right-crossing him, watching him hit the ground, and he was unconscious. And I could care less. You violated my privacy, homeboy, because I didn't touch you.

After this confession, I nodded my head and mumbled "ah-huh," trying to cover the intense internal conflict I was experiencing about how to respond. I smiled and moved to the next question.

I responded to this confession as if this man had actually struck me; I had difficulty regaining my composure after hearing these words that, as a queer scholar, left me feeling vulnerable. Yet this visceral response surprised me. When I entered the field, I was prepared to conduct interviews with people whose beliefs and opinions differed fundamentally from my own. A few years earlier, I had conducted interviews with Promise Keepers, a Christian organization that encourages men to be leaders in their families and society (Heath 2003). My own upbringing in a conservative Baptist church aided me in establishing rapport with conservative Christian men in order to learn about how they negotiated masculinity to produce a "soft-boiled" form that allowed them to reinstate their positions of authority in the family and society. Much as in my previous research, I entered the field for this new project with an open mind and a desire to understand the belief systems of actors who embraced heterosexual marriage as the bedrock of society. At the time of the interview described above, I had already conducted many others with actors who used homophobic language, and I had responded by trying to understand their perspective. In this case, the complete incongruence and violence recounted in the story caught me off guard, and I quickly changed the subject to hide my feelings of fear and disgust.

Reflexivity

Feminist and sexuality scholars have recognized the importance of reflexivity for identifying one's own privilege or social location in respect to the people one is studying. Being reflexive is also important to challenging one's own stereotypes and prejudices and understanding the power researchers have over their participants. But how does this concept apply in cases of conservative movements, particularly when the individual being interviewed may have greater institutional power than the research has? After all, we were in a workshop backed by the U.S. government, the state of Oklahoma, and the local church. His homophobic response was affirmed by hegemonic masculinity and heteronormativity. How can we think about our roles as ethnographers at such moments when our impulse is to speak truth to power? Orit Avishai, Lynn Gerber, and Jennifer Randles (2013) propose the idea of a "feminist ethnographer's dilemma" to point out how a commitment to feminist politics can hamper identifying empirical realities that do not conform with feminist expectations. In the case of beliefs that motivate anti-LGBT movements, attending to this kind of dilemma can help in situations where you are caught off guard. Perhaps my reaction would have been less violent if I *had* at this moment set aside the personal beliefs that led me to instinctively judge this man's story as homophobic. It was not my job during the interview to defend the rights of the gay boy who was left unconscious on the floor, a feeling that arose instinctively. This kind of reflexivity needs to guide every stage of the research, not just the moments off the field when one is theorizing, designing research, or analyzing data. The value of this kind of reflexivity can help one to allow a moment of silence in which to recover.

Interviews with and observations of anti-LGBT and other right-wing activists necessarily involve difficult interactions. People with strong anti-

LGBT views often support policies that harm LGBT individuals and families. They hold values that can be understood to be exclusionary and judgmental. Spending time in the field listening to hateful or insensitive remarks that get to the heart of things that you care about can be challenging. It is difficult interactively—how do you respond to these statements? It can also be difficult emotionally—perhaps you feel complicit in an anti-LGBT agenda. We have learned in conducting research on anti-LGBT groups that researchers collecting data from individuals with anti-gay views must expect these sorts of uncomfortable interactions. They cannot be sidestepped by refraining from asking about them directly. Instead, researchers should prepare for them by practicing these kinds of interactions in a supportive space with a friend or colleague who is willing to role-play.

Beliefs versus Values

[Fetner] I was interviewing the communications director of one of the religious right's foremost social movement organizations. I was frustrated that the woman who had agreed to be interviewed would not answer my questions about how their organization selects the wording of their advertisements—this was specifically her job, and it should have been a fairly straightforward set of questions to answer. Marked as an outsider who needed to be convinced of the merits of the organization's anti-LGBT activism, the interviewee kept telling me what she considered to be facts about gay men:

> You know, homosexual couples have way more domestic violence, but the news doesn't report it. . . . They get into the schools—that's what they are trying to do with those rights laws; they want to be teachers! They want to recruit the young boys. They can't have their own [kids], so they have to recruit. . . . [She pulled a clipping from a file.] Here is a news story about one who stabbed his boyfriend.

This seemed to go on for so long. I wanted to leave so badly; I couldn't take listening to this. Plus, I had made a long trip to collect this and a few other interviews, and I was not getting the data I needed for my research. Why wouldn't she just answer my questions?

In my Introduction to Sociology class, I talk about the difference between beliefs and values. Beliefs, I say, are people's understanding of what is, while values are what they think ought to be. As I prepared to conduct these interviews, I had steadied myself for interacting with people whose values were different from mine. I had practiced my interview technique with colleagues who role-played as conservative activists, and I tried to present myself in a neutral, open way during interviews. What I had not prepared for, however, was a difference of beliefs that manifested as a barrage of "facts" that were as dangerous as they were demonstrably false. As I listened to statements about gay men having mental illness, engaging in deviant sexual practices with minors, being prone to domestic violence, I was infuriated. I wanted so badly to correct the record, to set my interviewee straight. I was ready for a disagreement about what ought to be, but our disagreement about what is frustrated me greatly.

I realized later that this encounter with beliefs was something else I should have prepared for as I entered the field. Indeed, to do in-person interviews with anyone, we try to bracket off our understandings of what is so that we may make the space to listen and learn about what our participants' understandings and beliefs are. My purpose in the field was to collect data through observations and interactions, and my impulse to correct my interviewees ran counter to this research objective. It is vital to enter the field with an open mind ready to take in participants' beliefs and opinions. This is especially important for research on anti-LGBT groups and others among which a common knowledge cannot be assumed. I recommend using the same active-listening techniques that work well for qualitative research generally—nodding, making eye contact, and leaving long pauses in the conversation for your research subject to fill.

As social norms about sexuality change, it is not always easy to collect explicit claims that condemn LGBT rights or disparage LGBT people. Most people keep these opinions to themselves. However, like all activists, conservative Christians in the religious right must generate discourse. They are among the few who make explicit anti-LGBT claims that we as researchers can record, collect, and analyze in our research. These uncomfortable interactions in the field are also uniquely rich research opportunities. Only when the talk of right-wing activists is explicit can we accurately capture their discursive strategies, their beliefs, their understanding of the "facts."

That does not mean doing so is easy. The emotional toll of repeated interactions with people who express anti-LGBT beliefs is something to take seriously as a researcher. The toll is compounded for those researchers who, like Heath, pack up their belongings and travel to a conservative setting to live for long stretches of time. It takes a particular kind of openness to take in these data, to silence the voice that wants to respond to the research subject, and to encourage research participants to elaborate, give more details, and dwell on uncomfortable topics. This openness is also a form of vulnerability, and the hurtful words we hear may cause discomfort or even pain. Self-care should be a part of the researcher's data collection plan—time to retreat, to express frustrations to supportive friends or colleagues, and to rest between interactions.

We also think it is OK to take steps that set reasonable limits on our exposure to anti-LGBT beliefs and values. Perhaps some data can be collected through a document search rather than interviews, or perhaps collecting data from some movement groups and not others will provide data without exacting too high a toll. For example, Fetner collected data from large professional organizations on the religious right, but chose not to include activists from a local church in which pastors ritually exorcised the demons out of lesbian and gay people. While this may have been a missed opportunity, the church felt unsafe in a way that the organizations did not. Perhaps another researcher will be better positioned to take on exorcism one day.

SITTING WITH ANTI-LGBT DATA: ANALYSIS AND WRITING

[Heath] I was able to conduct in-depth interviews with individuals at the top of the organizational hierarchy of the marriage initiative in Oklahoma, and one of the final interviews was with Mary Myrick, president of the public relations/affairs firm that managed the initiative. A constitutional amendment that defined marriage as a union between one man and one woman had just passed in Oklahoma in the 2004 election, with

76 percent of voters in favor. I asked Myrick about whether the marriage initiative took a stand on the constitutional ban. Her answer was simple:

> We actually don't deal with it much. We are very clear about our mission. . . . Our position is that we're a marriage initiative designed to encourage activities that lead to marriage, and our state has defined marriage as an act between a man and a woman, and until the state defines it differently, we . . . it's really all defined for us. We don't get into the debate about it.

There were times when my emotional response to data like this got in the way of my analysis. How could Mary Myrick dismiss the issue of same-sex marriage so briskly? Her response initially infuriated me, but sitting with my data after the interview allowed me to see that her words made perfect sense within her worldview. Since the marriage initiative's goal is strengthening marriage in society, involvement with the same-sex marriage debate could muddy the waters. Her words point to the logic that perpetuates heterosexuality's institutionalization in society. Same-sex relationships are marked as other, to be dealt with separately from what she saw as the more important issue of creating stronger marriages that the state defined as heterosexual. This example highlights the particular stakes involved in studying conservative, anti-gay movements and organizations that openly embrace the "institutional embeddedness of normative heterosexuality" (Seidman 2009: 25). While I found Myrick's response infuriating, it was no surprise that it was so easy for conservative actors to dismiss the marital politics that facilitated an easy victory for a state constitutional amendment to ban same-sex marriage. Over and over in my interviews, participants would give this kind of politically savvy response to evade the appearance of homophobia—referencing the state as the decisive actor provided an easy out. The directness of their responses shone a light on ways that heterosexuality is institutionalized to provide cover for those in high-status positions to avoid addressing discrimination and oppression against lesbians and gay men.

Analyzing and writing about these kinds of anti-LGBT actors and spaces was both inspiring and demoralizing. For months, I coded passages from my interviews and field notes that documented how a systematic culture of heteronormativity was reinforced through the marriage initiative in

Oklahoma, involving both state actors who organized free workshops that taught about communication and the importance of marriage, and the individual participants. On the one hand, I was inspired by the opportunity to focus a sociological lens on these processes that support heteronormative social structures. On the other hand, I felt discouraged when immersed in data that uncovered the strength of these movements, state bureaucracies, and social processes, all organized to marginalize queer people and to deny LGBT rights. It is a dark place to occupy on a daily basis.

To deal with the possible pessimism that can arise from studying and writing about movements that challenge our deepest beliefs, we point to the thoughtfulness of other scholars who have conducted research on painful topics. Gloria Anzaldúa conceptualizes such a dark space as "nepantla" (originally a Nahuatl word), an "unstable, unpredictable, precarious, always-in-transition space" that can produce "an uncomfortable, even alarming feeling" (2002: 1). In her research on incest in Mexican society, Gloria Gonzáles-López (2010) builds on Anzaldúa's concept to theorize the "epistemologies of the wound," or the places that enabled her to build knowledge about the sexualized wounds recounted by her participants. Researchers must make an epistemological commitment to deal with the intense emotions that can arise in studying topics that can be painful. This openness and depth produces meaningful analyses by taking seriously perspectives that may seem intolerant and hateful (O'Brien 2009). Studying anti-LGBT movements means facing the contradictions between our own standpoints and those whom we study.

What steps can we take to deeply engage with data that represents hateful perspectives? We recommend writing memos at all stages of the research process to remind ourselves of the humanity of individuals who hold beliefs antithetical to queer and queer-supportive scholars, and to spotlight possibilities for social change. While the study of anti-LGBT institutional structures can expose the hateful underbelly of these movements, there is still hope. In both our research experiences, we found evidence of pro-queer social change: Fetner in the way anti-gay movements energized and shaped lesbian and gay activism; Heath in the ways that increased contact with lesbians and gay men led many to change their opinions. A decade later, we can look back to see that these glimmers of hope actually led to real social change. Keeping an eye on the prize is ultimately the best way to negotiate the dark spaces of studying anti-LGBT activism.

CONCLUSION

Research on subjects who not only are anti-LGBT but are also activists against social inclusion, civil rights, and personal expression of LGBT and queer people is important, valuable work in the social sciences. Without a cogent and accurate understanding of the resources, discourses, strategies, and identities that support anti-LGBT politics, social science will be disadvantaged in its analysis of queer politics and social change. Studying the anti-LGBT right offers unique insights and opportunities for advancing knowledge, but it also poses challenges to researchers, some of which we have discussed here. Difficulty in fitting in, awkward interactions, and the darkness of immersing oneself in a setting or a set of ideas that are antithetical to the researcher's deeply held beliefs are three problems that we expect to grapple with in the field. In some cases, the standard advice found in methods texts is useful: be a good listener, open yourself to your research subject, remain critically reflexive of your own social position and identity. These are all important tools to develop for collecting data from anti-LGBT research subjects. In other cases, however, we need to tailor tools and strategies to deal specifically with our unique research projects.

In this chapter we offer some food for thought about the practices of studying the anti-LGBT right. Like other work that explores painful inequalities and mistreatment of groups and individuals, this research can demand attention to the needs of the researcher. At the same time, the work advances social scientific knowledge in a key understudied area, contributing an important piece of the puzzle of understanding social change, and resistance to it, over time. We want to affirm that this research can also be personally fulfilling. The discovery and careful documentation of right-wing activism give us the opportunity to expand sociological inquiry into less explored territories, chronicle and analyze this worldview, and understand key aspects of resistance to social change. Collecting and analyzing these data help us develop a much richer understanding of the social, cultural, and institutional barriers to LGBT equality, social inclusion, and full citizenship. This research makes unique contributions to sociological knowledge. As Arlene Stein reminds us, the anti-LGBT sentiment at the forefront of people's actions may be connected to and entwined in other social and economic forces that influence ideas and identities. Having a deep understanding of anti-LGBT sentiment gives us insight into its root causes and reveals the path through them to positive social change.

WORKS CITED

Anzaldúa, Gloria E. 2002. "Preface: (Un)natural bridges, (un)safe spaces." In *This bridge we call home: Radical visions for transformation*. Ed. Gloria E. Anzaldúa and AnaLouise Keating. New York: Routledge.

Avishai, Orit, Lynn Gerber, and Jennifer Randles. 2013. "The feminist ethnographer's dilemma: Reconciling progressive research agendas with fieldwork realities." *Journal of Contemporary Ethnography* 42(4): 394–426.

González-López, Gloria. 2010. "Ethnographic lessons: Researching incest in Mexican families." *Journal of Contemporary Ethnography* 39(5): 569–81.

Heath, Melanie. 2003. "Soft-boiled masculinity: Renegotiating gender and racial ideologies in the Promise Keepers movement." *Gender & Society* 17(3): 423–44.

O'Brien, Jodi. 2009. "Sociology as an epistemology of contradiction." *Sociological Perspectives* 52(1): 5–22.

Seidman, Steven. 2009. "Critique of compulsory heterosexuality." *Sexuality Research & Social Policy* 6(1): 18–28.

Stein, Arlene. 2001. *The stranger next door: The story of a small community's battle over sex, faith, and civil rights*. Boston: Beacon Press.

9 The Mess

VULNERABILITY AS ETHNOGRAPHIC PRACTICE

Tey Meadow

The elevator let out onto the fourth floor of the Puck Building in New York City, and I pushed through glass doors into the lobby of New York University's Sociology Department. I made a left, as I did every morning, and ducked into the copy room to check my mailbox. Joan (not her real name), a senior faculty member in the department, was also there checking her mail. Joan and I had a collegial relationship. I had worked as her teaching assistant some years before, and we kept in touch. She checked in now and again to see how my dissertation was progressing. I liked her, and felt she supported me.

After we exchanged hellos, Joan asked me how the job search was going. I told her I had received an invitation to give a talk and that I was obsessively preparing for it every minute I could. She paused, looking at me intently for a moment, and then asked me if I'd like her to take me shopping. Genuinely confused, I asked her what she meant. She replied, "Well, I was thinking that you should go get a nice skirt suit, and it seems like maybe you don't have someone to help you with that." I was stunned. Trying to joke through my discomfort, I replied, "Joan, . . . have you ever seen me wear a skirt? Can you even *imagine* me wearing a skirt?" She thought for a moment and said, "Well, no, but given the topic of your research, it might not be a bad move."

Anyone who has ever met me knows I'm not the kind of female person who wears skirts. Ever. And while my first inclination was to dismiss the conversation as utterly absurd (and, indeed, it has generated a laugh or two from close colleagues at ASA cocktail parties), I found myself scrutinizing my wardrobe, finding ways to subtly soften my "look" for the interview. I left my button-down shirt open at the collar and didn't wear my usual black T-shirt beneath it. I left my hair a bit longer than usual. I wore a pair of my mother's oxfords rather than my lace-up boots. I didn't do this because I was worried the department in question wouldn't hire a masculine woman. I did this because I knew the topic of my dissertation, transgender children, would incite confusion and discomfort, and because I thought it important to embody a professional distance from my subjects. Though it may seem oxymoronic, I've come to think that some of the political impulses that lead us to do politically inflected, emancipatory research also condition us to have an anxious and therefore limited relationship to the very sexualities and genders we seek to liberate.

Sexuality and gender fluidity breed discomfort, tension, and anxiety. These responses on the part of others can form a corrosive force that spreads from our fieldwork encounters into our professional personas, leading us to undertake tremendous emotional and intellectual labor to present sexual and gender material—most notably our own sexualities and genders—in palatable ways to an audience we imagine to be apathetic or even hostile to the material. The story I just told seems to me an apt metaphor for a process of professionalization, one in which we cover or minimize evidence of our gender or sexual dissidence to establish a credible relationship to our data and to minimize our vulnerability to claims of self-interest. This is not merely something we do in the presentation of our work to colleagues; it influences the ways we interpret our fieldwork experiences, leading us to disavow experiences of our sexual and gendered subjectivities in the service of analysis.

This chapter is about two fieldwork moments—one implicating my gender and the other my sexuality—that literature on reflexivity would position as data contaminants, moments I was inclined to sanitize for the sake of disciplinary legitimacy. Both, however, ultimately led me to generative conclusions about the social world. This chapter is about trusting our own queer sensibilities, even in moments when it seems as if everything is going wrong. It's about leaning into rather than away from the complexities of being a sexual and gendered subject in the field. It's about embracing a particular type of vulnerability—the risk of being dismissed as unprofessional, overdetermined, politically motivated, subjective—about being in "the mess" of gender and sexual material with our subjects and, by extension, with our colleagues. This engagement requires unlearning some of the reflexive habits we pick up in our training, and allowing our sexual and gender subjectivities to be queerly messy, unruly, and difficult to affix.

MOMENT ONE: GENDER FIELDS

During the course of my dissertation fieldwork with the families of transgender children, I spent ten days at the most controversial gender clinic for kids in North America. The Centre for Addiction and Mental Health (CAMH) in Toronto was headed by psychologist Kenneth Zucker. In his decades-long career, Zucker had treated hundreds of transgender children and written nearly as many articles and commentaries on associated topics. He was the head of the task force that revised the gender section of the *Diagnostic and Statistical Manual of Mental Disorders*. He was, in short, the leader of the field. Ken himself was a lightning rod for both praise and criticism—respected by many clinicians for being the first in North America to prescribe puberty blockers to children, while being reviled by many trans activists for lagging behind contemporary practice and discouraging some forms of gender atypicality in children. For my part, I was continually surprised by his openness to me and to being researched, his easy invitation to me to enter the clinic, and his ability to withstand disagreement. I was surprised to find that I liked him, even though there were many moments when he did or said things that made me distinctly uncomfortable.

On my last day at CAMH, I invited Ken to dinner to thank him for hosting me and putting me in contact with clinic patients to interview. We sat eating cheeseburgers and drinking beer at a café near the clinic. He told me about his son, the front man for a political punk band called *Fucked Up*, which had recently gained some notoriety and was touring throughout Canada. We chatted about clinic patients, about Ken's affinity for the Toronto Bluejays. Then, for the first time, he asked me about my gender. He asked only a few questions, and he seemed tentative. He first asked about where I grew up, and then about what my parents were like. There was something about the latter question—less its content than its searching tone and the way he watched me as I answered it—that immediately made me ill at ease. I answered honestly but briefly, and attempted to shift the conversation.

As we continued to talk, we discussed a child he was treating whose gender atypicality came bundled with severe social and emotional issues. Ken described his concern that, for this particular child, gender nonconformity might be a coping mechanism for some underlying trauma, for poor body image, for some autistic traits. Perhaps, he thought, her distress might be showing itself in the form of gender, but might not, in fact, be an immutable underlying identity. As he spoke, a question arose in me. If he thought gender atypicality could be an adaptation to trauma or difficulty, did he think it could ever be a positive adaptation? As I spoke the question aloud, I was surprised to feel my eyes brim with tears.

Ken didn't know that I had been a relatively normatively gendered kid. All he saw was the adult standing before him, with short hair, masculine clothing, no makeup. I felt those qualities at the surface of my skin when we spoke. I was acutely aware of the contours of my body, of the way I was holding myself. In many other contexts, my atypical gender presentation felt like a source of strength; in this exchange, it was quite the opposite. I felt a quiet worry, a subtle shame. When I returned home from the trip and friends and colleagues asked me about it, I didn't mention the encounter to anyone. I wondered if I'd somehow made a "mistake" that produced the exchange. I wondered if discussing the encounter with more conservative mentors would expose me as more gender transgressive than they already knew I was or, worse, indistinguishable from my subjects, the ultimate "me-searcher." For a long time, I viewed the encounter as an artifact of my inexperience.

Because I didn't speak about the incident, I also didn't learn much from it for a while. I buried it somewhere behind my anxiety and continued crunching the "real" data. Some months later, I sat at coffee with an anthropologist friend, and we began discussing awkward fieldwork encounters. The conversation was light, and we took turns describing moments we had each "felt like idiots" in conversations with informants. I began describing the scene and interaction with Ken Zucker in a light-hearted way, but as I heard myself talking, I realized I sounded much like my research subjects when they described encounters with mental health practitioners. I realized Ken and I were enacting precisely the social process I was trying to capture in the project. I realized that my discomfort was not inexperience; it was data.

We are always studying each other (Meadow 2013). When Ken asked me about my family, he became not my research subject but a psychologist with an interest in gender. When he posed questions about my family life and my gender, he was trespassing into my psychic life. It was not the condition of our exchange—he was the subject and I was the analyst, not the other way around—but it was easy to lapse into that dynamic. It was well-worn. And it felt invasive. My impulse to evade his questions was my impulse to evade being captured in the clinical discourse. I failed. I suspect that when I asked him about gender as an adaptation, I asked as equal parts sociologist and gender deviant. And Ken knew I did that; in fact, he invited it. During the process of researching my dissertation, I realized that even as I looked into the social world, those I encountered were simultaneously studying me, my gender, my body, my sexuality, even my intellect, to see what of the material of me might be useful to them—useful for cementing a relationship of trust, useful for their own identity projects, useful for their own intellectual projects. As I've begun to piece together the ways these things happened, I've realized that they produced a useful form of data about how identities in a process of iteration take form, and about the forms of relationality that surround them. By understanding this as a moment of "dialectical objectification" (Borneman & Hammoudi 2009: 20), I was able to explain it to others as a kind of gender searching we all engage in, as we become agents in the logics of "assessment" that Candace West and Don Zimmerman (1987) described decades ago. I realized that my own emotional responses, my discomfort, anxieties, desire for privacy, as well as my excitement, urgencies, affections, and investments, at times mirrored those of my subjects. Those responses of mine became data, once I was able to detach from them sufficiently to view them as kinds of ephemeral objects, and to consider what they meant, outside and apart from my concerns with securing good field relationships and access to informants.

I was nervous the evening I prepared to meet Stephanie. She was the executive director of one of the organizations whose work I hoped to study, and a key gatekeeper to research subjects I hoped to interview. I was primed for anxiety by the way her staff fiercely guarded access to her. It had taken me weeks of massaging my way through the organization to arrange the encounter. The night we met, I arrived with one of her staff at a mostly minority, urban charter school where she would conduct a training for parents whose children shared a class with a newly transitioned twelve-year-old transgender boy. We arrived early, as teachers moved diminutive desks into a circle. I hung back, just beside the doorway to the classroom, chatting with an administrator about the school's short history. My field notes contain the following description of our first encounter:

> The door creaked open and in strode Stephanie. She was tall and very thin, dressed in loose-fitting trousers and an untucked, patterned button down shirt. She was older than me. Her face was lined. Her brown and silver hair was cropped close to her head. She wore no makeup. She stood upright and commanded her surroundings. She appeared competent. I quieted an urge to shift my weight. I felt intimidated, but I greeted her with my hand extended. She shook it firmly while making direct, purposeful eye contact. I tightened my grip. She did the same. Neither of us smiled, but it felt like a moment of recognition. I felt like she was thinking, "I'm a butch, and you're a butch too. We are of a kind. This might work." I don't know if that's what she was thinking but something softened. We began to talk.

As I read over my field notes many months later, I understood the moment, which at the time felt like something of a victory, as a particular kind of queer encounter. Something about the exchange felt familiar. It established a foundation upon which we would begin to build something together. As I sat with that feeling, I recalled a similar scene in the classic lesbian novel *Stone Butch Blues,* which took place between the adolescent butch protagonist and an older woman who would become a mentor:

[Butch Al] looked me up and down. I widened my stance. She took that in. Her mouth refused to smile, but it seemed her eyes did. She extended a beefy hand. I took it. The solidness of her handshake caught me by surprised. She tightened her grip. I responded in kind. I was relieved I wasn't wearing a ring. Her clasp tightened. So did mine. Finally, she smiled. [. . .] I guess you could explain away that handshake by calling it bravado. But it meant more to me then, and it still does. It's not just a way of measuring strength. A handshake like that is a challenge. It seeks out power through incremental encouragement. At the point of maximum strength, once equity is established, then you have really met. I had really met Butch Al." (Feinberg 1993: 28).

The particularity of an affective field, the handshake as an introduction, a challenge, and a demonstration of group membership, the ways competent masculinity is established between women who share an unconventional cultural gender frame: it was all there in that moment of greeting, and it formed the backdrop for our subsequent encounters in the field.

This was not, however, a relationship between equals, and Stephanie made that clear from the start. I introduced myself and opened my mouth to ask a preliminary question about how the evening would go, and she interrupted, firing a string of questions at me about how I envision the frame of my project, what sorts of things I'll want to know, what my angle would be, how it fit into the teaching and writing I do. I had immediately and seamlessly lost control of the conversation. Anxiety blossomed inside my chest. I shifted my weight and placed a hand deep inside the pocket of my pants. I described my teaching in gender studies, rather than sociology. I slipped into queer vernacular. "Transgender" became "trans"; "LGBT" became "queer." I was establishing myself as an insider. Stephanie's distrust of me was palpable, but there was also something more than that. It felt as though Stephanie wanted to know she would be in charge.

She was. I spent the better part of a weeklong visit out West trying to nail down a time to sit down with her for a one-on-one conversation. She evaded my attempts, finally sending me a one-line text message on the last day of my trip to offer up an hour-long window. I quickly jumped at the chance, boarded a train, and headed forty minutes outside the city to meet her near her organization's office. She arrived in torn jeans and a gigantic grey hoodie sweatshirt. We drove to a park near the train station and sat at a picnic table. It was the first of many conversations we would have, and at the end of it I presented to her my standard consent form. Stephanie made many changes to the form. She wrote in that she needed to approve anything I wrote about her before it was published. Fearful that I would lose her as an informant, I acceded, something I would not have done with more peripheral research subjects. She made it clear that the discourse was hers, not mine. She didn't trust me with the story. I wondered if I'd be able to use any of it.

Slowly my worry dissolved in the course of many conversations we had at conferences and events I attended sponsored by her organization during the following year. Both early risers, we often found each other in the hotel lobby or at a breakfast table in the hours before conference halls filled and panel discussions began. We discussed the challenges of her work and political issues relevant to communities we shared, and over time, our conversations seeped into the personal. We discussed our primary relationships, our families and personal histories. We talked about our dating histories. Stephanie's partners were typically other butch lesbians; mine were femme. At times, we commented on that difference, and on the connections between gender and sexuality. I admired Stephanie enormously. She was a creative thinker and a pioneer on many issues related to gender and sexual self-determination. I felt I had much to learn from her, both related to my research and outside its confines.

A year after our initial meeting, Stephanie was facilitating a workshop at a conference for transgender adults attached to the one for children I was attending, and I had gone because of a personal interest in the topic, which was unrelated to my research. I shared with the group a personal story that resonated with Stephanie's own life experience, something I would not have told another research informant. I watched her body language soften in a way I recognized from our more personal exchanges. She made eye contact with me as she spoke to the group. As we walked out of the meeting and down the hallway side-by-side, she commented that she was continually surprised that we were more alike than she had earlier realized. Smiling, feeling at ease and familiar, I nudged her and said, jokingly, "Oh yeah? So maybe you'll finally sign a blank consent, like all my other research subjects have?" She paused, looking surprised. "Um . . . okay," she muttered. "I mean, yes. I will." I replied, teasingly, "Good." We walked in silence for a moment, and then she turned to me, the air around us thickening with erotic tension. She seemed to have seen me in a different way in that moment, to have some new appreciation of me. She stepped closer, made direct eye contact, and said, "You know, people don't talk to me that way." She looked humbled and more submissive than I'd ever seen her. There was a silent pause. The field of power surrounding us shifted. Without thinking, I raised an eyebrow and replied, "I'll keep that in mind." I winked at her, smiled, and walked away.

As I walked away, I felt my face flush with embarrassment. *Had I just flirted with a research subject . . . while discussing her consent agreement?* Stephanie was no shrinking violet. I wasn't worried that she would do something she ultimately didn't want to do. And the exchange had been reflexive, had occurred without conscious thought on my part. But something between us changed. I felt her desire to please me. I immediately worried that I had breached some rule of professional etiquette, that I had contaminated the research site—in short, that I had just done something wrong. I spoke to nobody about this encounter, and I have never published a word about it before this volume. It makes me anxious even now. Even as I write this, my mind swirls with questions about why it happened with her and not others, the ways power breeds the erotic and the erotic draws on power as a resource. As I sat with my worry, I began to wonder not whether it was a bad or good thing, but why it had happened at all, what social purpose the tension between us had served.

In the introduction to *Taboo*, the first comprehensive volume of writing on sexual and erotic subjectivity in fieldwork, Don Kulick argues that sex as a domain is overdetermined in Western culture and in our empirical practices. We think about sexuality in a circumscribed way, always in relation to concretized identities or sets of practices, and always with tremendous anxiety. In his view, erotic encounters take on a "special urgency" as we scramble to assess how to respond, armed not with fieldwork training but only with standards we might use at home. We do this with an eye toward enabling, or at the very least not destroying, the rapport we have with subjects. These anxieties blind us to the generative potential of the erotic as an affective experience, as heuristic, as a means of participation in the social worlds we study. "Erotic subjectivity does things. It performs, or rather, can be made to perform, work" (Kulick 1995: 5). It can draw attention to "the conditions of its own production," but it can also be an important interactional facilitator. Amy Tweedy (2016) explored the possible utility of flirtation as a fieldwork strategy among lesbians, its usefulness for elucidating power imbalances and for forging connections between people. As I experienced that moment with Stephanie, and as I looked to the ethnographic literature to help me make sense of it, I began to wonder about all the quotidian ways the erotic enters in to assist in the constitution of social connection. Sometimes what seems particular to a research site, unrelated to our data, tells us something greater about the sexual culture in which we live.

I didn't see Stephanie for several months after that, and we had no other moment of erotic tension like that during my fieldwork period. She did eventually send me a signed, unedited consent form. In retrospect, I now understand our encounter to have been a moment of harmless flirtation, scaffolded by our evolving understanding of each other as butch lesbians with some flexibility about our gender presentations. The moment aided my understanding of the erotic as a resource that, in this context, generated a feeling of familiarity, commonality, and of trust. It helped Stephanie hand me her story, and solidified my investment in holding that story carefully. In some small way, that moment of erotic tension was productive of a different form of relationality. It was another way we "met" each other, a more ephemeral form of a handshake.

Kulick writes that "desire in the field seems to be one especially poignant means through which anthropologists become aware of themselves as positioned, partial, knowing selves" (1995: 18). I think it also allows others to feel they know us more deeply. Perhaps it even has a particular currency among queers, lends itself to being used to cement group membership, to thwart the presumption of heterosexuality that attends most standard interactions. Perhaps an ability to catch the pitch of homoeroticism is a way to prove oneself to be conversant in a common language, unafraid of its affective resonances, willing to be bodily invested. Perhaps it is a way of forging intimacy through the shared risk that the other will drop the thread, leaving us vulnerable and exposed. The erotic is always around us, often beyond our volition. But in the moments we engage in it, we are doing a particular form of productive work; namely, work to forge connection, to open a relational space that might otherwise remain narrow.

MAKING SENSE FROM VULNERABILITY

There were times in the field when I felt as if I was negotiating treacherous terrain, when the orthodoxies I'd learned in graduate school didn't feel helpful, and when I worried I had made consequential mistakes. The field is messier than many of us are prepared for, and when working with complex gender and sexual material, that messiness can provoke anxiety. Remaining open and undefended in moments when our own subjectivities interact with our empirical practices, and defending the usefulness of those overlaps and interactions to colleagues, requires embracing a kind of vulnerability that seems antithetical to professionalism. It's not antithetical, but it is oppositional. We might think of it as a "queer vulnerability" in that way.

If, as Matt Brim and Amin Ghaziani write, "to queer empiricism means to embrace multiplicity, misalignments and silences," and to come to terms with the fact that "gender and sexual[ity] are not empirically stable," (2016: 17) then we must attune to the ways our own sexual and gendered subjectivities are used by others in the field and the ways we ourselves use them. In this way, queer ethnographic work replaces "the uninterrogated critic with accounts of relationality that situate and destabilize the self that is written and the self that writes" (Morgensen 2015: 311). In moments when we confront, sometimes with discomfort, the ways our identities are relational, the ways we and our subjects coconstruct each other, the observer-observed boundary breaks down. In moments when affect gets messy, when we feel affection that exceeds scholarly regard, or when we find ourselves attracted to inappropriate objects, it's natural to move quickly to shut down the interaction. In both cases, it feels risky to leave open the potential for ambiguity, for messy data. It is in these moments that queer theory can offer us some useful insights.

Queer theory can inform ethnographic practice in several ways. First, it confronts the multidimensionality of both identity and the erotic. In *Cruising Utopia,* José Muñoz writes that "there is often a gatekeeper, representing a straight present," who adjudicates claims to knowledge (2009: 65). The gatekeeping system relegates to the periphery knowledge it considers unverifiable or unreplicable. Studies of social categories in formation, subjects whose identities and practices elide the categorical systems that undergird social research, dispersed and invisible communities of practice—all of these pose unique dilemmas for the researcher employing conventional methodological approaches. In truth, "queer" practices involve a certain unreliability; they fluctuate, resist normative assessment, are in some cases designed to be covert. "The key to queering evidence, and by that I mean the ways in which we prove queerness," Muñoz writes, "is by suturing it to the concept of ephemera" (2009: 65). Queer phenomena, by definition, stand at the limits of cognizable experience and in opposition to what we already know and can describe. Queer phenomena are those that reveal themselves in "the trace, the remains, the things that are left hanging in the air like a rumor" (65). Further, Muñoz observes, "ephemeral evidence is rarely obvious.... Ephemera are the remains that are often embedded in queer acts, in both stories we tell one another and communicative gestures such as the cool look of a street cruise, a lingering handshake among recent acquaintances, or the mannish strut of a particularly confident woman" (65). The question is how we identify and describe the ineffable traces of affective residue, the subtle suggestion of a queer aesthetic, the shifting gaze of recognition that fuels a moment of trusted verbal exchange. All of these are endemic to the practice of ethnographic work in queer contexts, and, I argue, attunement to them requires a particular form of erotic subjectivity seldom explored in fieldwork theory.

Once able to tune into the ephemeral frequency on which gender and sexuality vibrate (in both its normative and nonnormative forms), we can better comprehend sexuality as an affective conduit through which social relations are carried out. In some cases, it is possible to externalize these processes (most typically in sexualized spaces where one can observe erotic interactions made explicitly public); in many others, however, the researcher is herself implicated in the erotic field. As such, we must find some way to manage our anxiety about our erotic subjectivity sufficiently to absorb and reflect the ways it constructs our access to data. If we fail to do so, if we relegate the messy data to the margins of our notebooks, we unwittingly reproduce a heteronormative, hegemonic approach to knowledge that renders our very selves unrepresentable (Tweedy 2016).

The modalities of conducting qualitative research "are messy, emotional, complicated and embodied" (Tweedy 2016). This chapter is a provocation to accept the messiness of gender and sexual material. By the time I began studying "transgender children," I had read enough queer theory to expect the category to be unruly. And I knew enough from reading the work of other ethnographers to know that my identity would matter. What I didn't know was that the two would interact with such nuance, that my self-understanding would matter less for access to subjects than for the evolving sense-making my subjects were doing of their own lives. I most certainly didn't expect to learn things about sexuality and the erotic from fieldwork on parents and children. But when I reformulated moments of discomfort, anxiety, and perceived failure into opportunities for analysis, they proved uniquely generative. Perhaps the very anxiety that leads us to take a professionally imposed distance from gender and sexual material is precisely the place to pause and look deeply for the most hidden meanings. Once I could build theory from the messiness of the data, my sexuality and the contours of my gender stood, not apart from the empirical validity of my work, but in intimate relation to it.

WORKS CITED

Borneman, John, and Abdellah Hammoudi (eds.). 2009. *Being there: The fieldwork encounter and the making of truth.* Berkeley: University of California Press.

Brim, Matt, and Amin Ghaziani. 2016. "Introduction: Queer methods." *Women's Studies Quarterly* 44(3–4): 14–27.

Feinberg, Leslie. 1993. *Stone butch blues.* Ithaca, NY: Firebrand Press.

Kulick, Don. 1995. "The sexual life of anthropologists: Erotic subjectivity and ethnographic work." In *Taboo: Sex, identity, and erotic subjectivity in anthropological fieldwork.* Ed. Don Kulick and Margaret Wilson, 1–21. New York: Routledge.

Meadow, Tey. 2013. "Studying each other: On agency, constraint, and positionality in the field." *Journal of Contemporary Ethnography* 42(4): 466–81.

Morgensen, Scott L. 2015. "A politic not yet known: Imagining relationality within solidarity." *American Quarterly* 67(2): 309–15.

Muñoz, José Esteban. 2009. *Cruising utopia: The then and there of queer futurity.* New York: New York University Press.

Tweedy, Amy. 2016. "Openings, obstacles, and disruptions: Desire as a portable queer method." *Women's Studies Quarterly* 44(3–4): 208–23.

West, Candace, and Don Zimmerman. 1987. "Doing gender." *Gender & Society* 1(2): 125–51.

PART III   Strategies

10 Challenges, Triumphs, and Praxis

COLLECTING QUALITATIVE DATA ON LESS
VISIBLE AND MARGINALIZED POPULATIONS

Mignon R. Moore

In the winter of 2002, while living and working in New York City, I met a black, working-class lesbian couple (a billing receptionist and a part-time dental assistant) who invited me to their apartment on the Grand Concourse in the Bronx for a game of cards. I accepted their invitation. As a family sociologist and urban poverty researcher, I found this couple sociologically interesting. One of the women had two children from a prior heterosexual relationship with an incarcerated drug dealer. Her partner was divorced and had a son whose primary residence was with his father, but who spent weekends at his mother's home. I wanted to know how this family fit into their Bronx community. Would anyone have identified them as a "two mom" family? How did the children relate to each mother? And what were their relationships like with the fathers of their children? I also wanted to know how their experiences related to the existing literature on lesbian families—a body of work that largely drew from the experiences of white, middle-class, college-educated women who held particular feminist ideologies and who mainly lived in predominantly white neighborhoods.

The observations I recorded during my encounter at this couple's home were the initial entry in my field notes for what would eventually become my first book, *Invisible Families: Gay Identities, Relationships, and*

Motherhood among Black Women (2011). As I continued to spend time in the LGBTQ social spaces of New York City, I met more and more working- and middle-class African American and Latina women who were "in the life" and building families in predominantly black and Latino neighborhoods. I was invited to dinner parties, book salons, and game nights in peoples' homes, but just as often, I attended cocktail hours, dance parties, and after-hours kickbacks at nightclubs, bars, performance spaces, and other public venues throughout the five boroughs and New Jersey. This was before the expansion of social media outlets, so my invitations to these activities came through flyers passed out at similar events or by word of mouth. Many of these occasions drew hundreds of participants, and the spaces were largely racially segregated and age and class integrated. During my time in the field I continually marveled at the array of women I saw. Descriptions of the different ethnicities, socioeconomic backgrounds, hues, ages, hair textures, and gender presentations fill my field notes. It wasn't until I was well into writing the book that I realized the same question kept coming up when I discussed and presented my work: how did you find all of these racial minority gay women? Other (primarily white) researchers had experienced difficulty recruiting black and Latina sexual minorities in their studies of family formation, lesbian identity, and other related topics. Indeed, in much of the literature in these areas there were very few nonwhites in study designs.

In this chapter I share some of the insights I gained in the process of collecting data on this hard-to-reach and marginalized population. I present the creative approaches I used to address the methodological challenges I encountered throughout my time in the field, as well as some of the issues I continue to experience as I collect interview and archival data for my current project on a related population: African American LGBTQ elders. I focus my comments on three areas: gaining entry into diffuse and elusive populations, building relationships and trust while negotiating insider and outsider status, and exiting the field after becoming part of a community. My hope is that the reader will draw from the particular case of black sexual-minority women to think more generally about the various methodological approaches to qualitative study design and data collection on other less visible and stigmatized groups.

GAINING ENTRY: THE INVERTED ORDER
OF THE GATEKEEPER

Never is a gatekeeper or key informant more critical to a researcher's entry into a community than when one is attempting to locate populations who lack geographic boundaries, have porous boundaries, or who are culturally marginalized. In qualitative research designs, scholars often locate a "key informant" who brings them into a community that they study. The expectation is to first develop a research question and then search for a gatekeeper to facilitate access to the group that one wants to observe. However, my approach has deviated from this structure. While I have used several methods to locate informants that would help me reach my study populations, the relationships I have managed to build with the gatekeepers in each of my qualitative research projects have all come about as a result of my *first* frequenting a range of physical spaces where members of the group are thought to spend time. I located a group to study, then found an informant who would introduce me to key people who would help me make inroads into the community and learn the ins and outs of the group under study. In each case my gatekeeper did not start out as an informant. They gradually took on that role as I began to develop a research question and move from general ethnographic observation of a group that was sociologically interesting, to fieldwork that was specifically intended to address the principal components of a study that I designed after spending time with members of the population. The research question came *after* I had begun participating in the general community of interest.

For example, in my ongoing study of African American sexual-minority elders, I met my West Coast informants through a series of invitations I accepted to a variety of LGBTQ events throughout the city, including entertainment industry parties, political action group meetings, LGBTQ pride receptions, and private parties or informal get-togethers in peoples' homes. When I moved to Los Angeles in the fall of 2006, the only black lesbian I knew was the woman who had allowed me to sublet her house the previous summer while I searched for a home to purchase. This person was a well-known writer and filmmaker, and she introduced me to different groups of her friends and acquaintances. My lesbian identity was an open part of my field identity, and because of that one of these people invited me to a Christmas party, where I met others in the LGBTQ community. A few months later some of these women invited me to a wine bar in downtown LA that was owned by an older black lesbian couple. This couple became my gatekeepers. After some months of talking to them and getting to know people in their social networks, I developed an initial set of research questions about the social histories of black sexual-minority people who came of age during the 1950s, 1960s, and 1970s, and their current experiences with social support and access to health care as they approached retirement. These questions crystallized over a period of months as I spent time at the wine bar and continued to get to know their social group of retired or semi-retired friends. I found them and their experiences sociologically interesting and sought to learn more about the lives of people in their age and race cohort—how they understood race, gender, and sexual orientation in the context of the various social movements taking place as they entered adulthood. The couple introduced me to different groups of baby boomers and seniors. These were largely people who were very reserved and private about their sexual orientation and sexual identities.

Without my gatekeepers I would not have known how to find these individuals or identify them as LGBTQ. As I attended barbeques, retirement parties, and milestone birthdays, various members of the group would share colorful stories about their coming-of-age experiences (many during the pre-Stonewall era), the parties they used to host or attend, tricks they employed to create an appearance of heterosexuality in social spaces, and their experiences in the "paddy wagon" when police would figure out the true nature of these events, raid the parties, and arrest those women who "did not have on three items of women's apparel." The racialized context of South Los Angeles, as well as other places where they were raised, including Detroit, Chicago and Brooklyn, added an important layer of meaning to their interactions with police and the necessity of portraying a particular type of heterosexuality.

When I moved to Los Angeles, I had not planned to conduct research on sexual-minority elders, but as I engaged in conversations with them, I would return to my computer and try to connect what I had heard with what the literature had to say about lesbian and gay history. There was a notable absence of historical information on racial-minority lesbians in their own ethnic and cultural communities, and this made my research seem more urgent to analyze and develop. So in this case, I came across a facet of LGBTQ life that was sociologically interesting, and the people I met became informants because I decided to try to learn more about some of the experiences members of their group have had, situating those practices in existing bodies of academic research. This chain of events differs from what a primer on methods might prescribe, but in my experience, once one figures out a general population of interest, spending time in the physical space where members of the group are known to frequent can help one clarify and develop a study agenda.

GAINING ENTRY: CREATING AN ACTIVITY THAT BRINGS PEOPLE TOGETHER

Sometimes one meets individuals who claim membership in a community, but cannot find public spaces where group members gather. This can make it difficult to conduct ethnographic research or to locate people to interview. In my research on LGBTQ populations, I have learned the value of designing opportunities for members of the group to come together. The creation of social spaces can serve multiple purposes, particularly for groups who are in some way bounded by a social stigma. Returning to the example of the older black lesbian couple in Los Angeles, my then partner (now spouse) and I decided to host a monthly activity for women at the wine bar the couple owned. My partner was a disc jockey and had been spinning music at various events throughout the city. Prior to moving to Los Angeles, we lived in Manhattan, where we hosted weekly events for the women's community. By 2008 we had been living in LA for more than a year and during that time had noticed that there were not many social activities that catered to the musical tastes and cultural interests of lesbian and bisexual women of color. We began to develop an email list from attendees at these occasions to build a social network. We had gotten to know many different communities of LGBTQ people. We participated in, and my partner provided music for, receptions for Outfest, a film festival for LGBTQ-themed movies and filmmakers, and Fusion, a festival for LGBTQ-themed films and filmmakers of color. I had been giving talks on my research on lesbian-headed families and had entered various queer scholarly communities. We also signed folks up at the gatherings we attended in peoples' homes.

We approached the owners of the wine bar and offered to host a monthly event for "women who love women and their friends." We did this to center the experiences of sexual-minority women of color while remaining inclusive to others. We decided on an open-mic theme where singers, poets, and musicians would perform two or three sets. This would fit a place like Los Angeles, which attracts individuals with artistic talent that they would want to showcase. Each of these "sets" of artistic expression was followed by a music set that the DJ played, and altogether the night offered a space for dancing, networking, and friendship building.

A WORD ON PRAXIS AND RECIPROCITY

We hosted this activity every month for the following two years, receiving no monetary compensation, just food and drink for our time. Everyone benefited: the community looked forward to the chance to come together for socialization and fun, the wine bar gained new clientele, my partner got other DJ gigs from people who attended, and I developed my relationship with the owners and gained access to their social networks. The events grew in size. In 2010 the wine bar closed, and we moved the social activities to hotels and other, larger venues across Los Angeles, where we continued hosting about ten events each year until the end of 2014. We expanded beyond the open mic to provide happy hours, dance parties, brunches, wine tastings, speed dating (which resulted in one marriage proposal), a fitness club, an intermural women's basketball team (which won the championship held in the Los Angeles Staples Center), and a party bus to an LGBTQ event in Las Vegas. We also brought in speakers and organized a free workshop for women and trans men who wanted to expand their families through assisted reproduction or adoption. The average size of the dance parties ranged between 150 and 200 people, with more than 300 during special events such as Christmas parties and gay pride weekends.

These were joyous events! I found great pleasure in watching everyone have a good time and creating positive experiences for a community that was often a location for stigma. Hosting these events was a highlight of my life and time in Los Angeles. But fulfilling the community's expectations that we host a monthly event was a stressful and time-consuming endeavor. There were months when I did not want to host an event—when I wanted to focus solely on my writing, teaching, and other duties as a faculty member and scholar. Hunting for venues took time, and they exposed me to financial risk—I had to leave large deposits of my own money and hope to recoup those funds with a successful event. There were times when the venue owners acted in unscrupulous ways. In one instance we had contracted to bring an A-list celebrity to guest-host a special party at a well-known venue in West Hollywood. She was supposed to come by, say hello to the audience, and take a few photos with those who paid an extra fee. Instead, the club owners directed her to perform for a crowd of about fifteen hundred white gay men in a different room and never brought her downstairs to our smaller party, which had about five hundred people in attendance. We had to refund the money of those who paid for the private meet-and-greet (the venue did not compensate us for this mishap).

But these pitfalls and stressors were outweighed by the fulfillment we experienced in engaging in this type of reciprocity. We found that by creating an openly LGBTQ presence in public venues that centered the experiences and interests of black and Latina women, our events helped reduce individuals' feelings of shame relating to sexual-minority status. So in addition to creating a research site, we provided a needed creative and social space for LGBTQ people of color. I did not take field notes or collect data on what happened at these gatherings. I constructed an activity so that my population of interest would find me. But the work was also motivated by my own personal goals and ideologies. I wanted to help promote a sense of community for women of color, who were often marginalized by the very white, very male West Hollywood, which is the center of gay life in Los Angeles. We were able to break into this area and host events at popular nightclubs there. The events also and importantly helped my partner and me integrate ourselves into this new environment. In 2013 we received awards from a Southern California African American trans men's group and a local black lesbian political group for our efforts at community inclusion. In 2014 we were honored with the Los Angeles City Council

LGBT Heritage Award for our outreach to LGBTQ communities of color in Southern California.

Feminist epistemology recommends a tight link between research and social change and transformation (Hesse-Biber 2012). One of the expressed intentions of feminist ethnography is to "excavate subjugated knowledge on women's lives and the lives of other marginalized groups" in order to achieve empowerment and social change (2012: x). While I did not purposefully seek to utilize research perspectives that were specifically feminist, throughout my career my approach to data collection has been consistent with goals that frame this perspective. Feminist approaches to research methods attend to "relationships, reciprocity, representation, and voice" (Pillow & Mayo 2012, 199). They stress the importance of *praxis,* or social action. Praxis is about the way we carry out our research and the actions behind the work, rather than merely what we think or theorize. Karl Marx used the term to refer to all purposeful action, or the process through which people act upon one another and the world. The underlying belief is that what we theorize is important only to the extent that it shapes and gives purpose to action. The social events I organized for LGBTQ women's communities in the process of conducting research on that population might be considered a form of praxis. In this case, racialized sexual minorities have a history of being treated poorly in society. In my opinion, it becomes especially important and ethical to provide something tangible to the group to counteract past efforts by researchers to take from marginalized populations through their data collection while offering little of substance in return.

While not everyone will have the opportunity or networks to create the types of social spaces I developed to facilitate my research, anyone can think about how to create an activity that brings potential research subjects together. The event should be mutually beneficial for all parties and grounded in reciprocity and ethics. For example, if one wanted to study the ways parents socialize young children, one might bring parents of young children together for a family activity, such as a story time or movement class. In this way all participants gain something from the research experience.

In the process of carrying out social events while in the field, I developed other research questions, collected data to answer those questions, and wrote and published the results. For example, in 2009, as a result of my interactions with those actively working against the Proposition 8 anti–gay marriage campaign, I began conducting fieldwork on the political activities of black LGBTQ people in Los Angeles as they lived, worshipped, and socialized in their racial and ethnic communities. That work resulted in several published papers about black LGBTQ political work (Moore 2010a, 2010b). I met some of the informants for this work from the monthly happy hour I hosted from 2008 to 2010.

BUILDING RELATIONSHIPS AND TRUST WHILE NEGOTIATING INSIDER AND OUTSIDER STATUS

When studying marginalized groups, one should always be mindful of the power dynamics between the researcher and those being "studied." Once a level of comfort is developed, or if the researcher perceives herself as having a personal tie to the group under study, it is easy to minimize the power differentials that may exist because of race, income, education, position as an academic, or various other statuses that create a social ordering. I have always tried to strike a balance between acknowledging my education, occupation, and income privileges and deemphasizing in my data collection interactions that might be experienced as evaluations of how others measure up relative to my status. For example, "So, what kind of work do you do?" might seem a straightforward query. But demographic questions about occupation or education really ask individuals where they fit into the American hierarchy. They are used to evaluate social status. Those who are satisfied with how well they have done in the US stratification system are happy to answer these questions and often look for ways to volunteer this information. Others who are less satisfied with where they lie in the class hierarchy or who do not want to be evaluated by the type of work they do or the income they have may experience this question negatively. Asking demographic questions early on in the introductory process can immediately create social distance and distrust between the researcher and the group.

To highlight the commonalities between researcher and subjects, one must be ever cognizant of the many ways one's position as a scholar and representative of the academy can be understood by different members of the community. In her paper on negotiating an insider or outsider status in research, Nancy Naples (2003) makes three points relevant to my work. She observes that we are never fully outside or inside the community, that our relationship to the community is constantly being negotiated and renegotiated in everyday interactions, and that these interactions are located in shifting relationships among community members. I found all of these assertions to be true when looking back on my experience conducting research for my 2011 book on black, lesbian-headed families.

While I might have been an insider because of my racial and sexual identity, there are many ways I was an outsider in lesbian communities of color. First of all, many of the "regulars" in the nightlife scene had come of age sneaking into bars and clubs in their late teens, whereas I had spent my teen years in a conservative Pentecostal church, and all of my twenties in graduate school. I had very few experiences in sexual-minority spaces. I did not know the proper way to dress when going out to a bar or dance party, and I was naive about the undercurrent of activities, legal and otherwise, that might take place in the nightlife scene. My work to promote social events was motivated by my desire to create community and also to locate individuals in a hard-to-reach population; I did not use it as a consistent source of income. This difference kept me from being perceived as a legitimate party promoter by the more seasoned in that field, or by individuals who earned a sizable portion of their incomes through event promotions. Fortunately, sexual-minority communities are quite porous. New people are continually joining them as they "come into the life," and people leave them when they move away, form monogamous relationships, change work shifts, or the like. This porosity allowed me to quickly stake a claim in that social world.

Another way I experienced the permeability of insider-outsider status was through my ethnicity as a black American woman in a city with an ethnically diverse population of black people. During the first decade of the 2000s when I was conducting my fieldwork for *Invisible Families*, Caribbean and African women constituted about 35 percent of the black population in New York City. As a black American woman with familial roots in North and South Carolina, my history and experiences were different from those of the immigrant and first-generation Caribbean and

African women who were part of sexual-minority communities. This difference became acute at times, and redefined my role as insider or outsider, depending on the circumstances. For example, in an interview with Sifa Brody, a Jamaican-born woman who migrated to the United States as a young adult, I sought to learn whether there were differences between the characteristics that were primary for individuals when defining a self-identity, and characteristics that were primary when defining themselves as a member of a group. In my reasoning, a person may look in the mirror and primarily define themselves through a gendered lens, but when asked to organize with another group around social injustice, may regard race as the identity around which the most salient boundary making for them occurs (Moore 2011). Sifa had just finished telling me how connected she felt to her Jamaican culture and people, but when I asked how comfortable she felt with black American women, her first response was "Oh, that's a tough question," followed by a short laugh. When I repeated the question, she again laughed uncomfortably, this time having no response. Here is what followed:

MIGNON: If you can't answer [the question], just tell me why and that would be fine, too. That's an answer, too.

SIFA: [more uncomfortable laughter]

MIGNON: You don't feel you have much in common with black American women?

SIFA: No. Because as far as culture, we're totally different. I'll date women that are American black women, and we'd have a relationship, but the culture part of it is going to be a problem because we're from two different backgrounds. So that's it.

I believe that if I were Jamaican or perhaps of Caribbean descent, Sifa would have had more to say on the subject. She might have gone into the ways she feels different from "American black women," including perceptions of behaviors or interests that involved negative or positive stereotyping of black Americans and Jamaicans. While throughout the interview there was much positive rapport between us, and in fact we are still quite friendly today, in that moment I became an outsider and a barrier was erected that affected my ability to connect with the respondent.

I could provide examples regarding my movement into and out of the insider position while studying a population for which I feel a personal connection. The general thinking about this issue in the literature is that in the process of conducting research we are constantly negotiating an insider-outsider status because of the many identities and variables involved in the creation and maintenance of boundaries around group identity. The problems that racial-, ethnic-, or sexual-minority group members may experience include issues common to all researchers, as well as dilemmas imposed by the minority-group membership (Baca Zinn 1979).

Sometimes, as a result of feeling connected to or protective of the group under study, researchers may, consciously or unconsciously, deemphasize behaviors or attributes that might be perceived as negative by outsiders. They might omit examples of "bad behavior" they observe in the field; they might fail to analyze a situation that places their respondent in a negative light. In *Invisible Families*, for example, I provide a detailed, qualitative analysis of five families each of which represents different pathways to parenthood. In one of those families there is a mother named Jackie whose personal history includes a period of time when she abused drugs. Her own mother suffered from addiction and was not available to parent during Jackie's childhood. The primary arc of Jackie's story was how she came to adopt her biological nephew at birth, and since her drug use occurred before she became a parent to her son, I might have eliminated this aspect of her life history. But doing that would signify, if only to myself, that I had a negative opinion of the drug use and wanted to hide it from my readers. I concluded that omitting that part of her history would be an attempt to sanitize her life. The drug use was an important part of the larger story of Jackie's development and maturity that would allow her to eventually become a parent. Sometimes the researcher, in perceiving herself to be an insider or outsider, brings a judgment to the behaviors of the individuals she is studying. When researching marginalized groups, the "do-gooder" researcher may want to present people in a "positive" light to change the way the group is perceived by society. The researcher should avoid this inclination. It carries more than a whiff of paternalism. Just tell the story and focus on finding and analyzing the sociology in the experience or interaction.

LEAVING THE FIELD

A host of complicated issues arise in exiting a field that one has played a part in creating. What is the relationship between building or crafting a space that one must eventually leave, and what will be lost by the researcher and by the community in that departure? In my experience, exiting the field has had multiple meanings because my participation in my study communities was so multidimensional. Outside the actual interviews I conducted and surveys I asked others to complete, there is no doubt that my presence in the communities I have studied altered those spaces in some concrete way. I created events that would not otherwise have taken place. Those events caused people to meet one another under certain conditions. They were important in the formation and development of business, personal, marital, and other types of relationships. The events produced experiences that became part of individuals' life stories. They are a contribution to LGBTQ histories in New York and Los Angeles.

In both of my major ethnographic sites my fieldwork had a concrete ending point. The events I hosted in New York as part of the data collection for *Invisible Families* came to an end when I moved to Los Angeles. Although the interview, ethnographic, and survey data collection for that project ended in December 2005, I continued to host parties with my business partners and my romantic partner until we moved in the fall of 2006. I could have stepped away from the activities once my fieldwork was concluded so that I could focus on my writing (indeed one of the promoters I worked with quit after a few months to return to graduate school). It had become taxing to continue with the events when I was trying to organize, analyze, and publish my work. But I thought it would be bad praxis to stop hosting LGBTQ events just because I no longer needed a space to collect data. The community appreciated the social networking our weekly lounge party provided, and it felt selfish for me to end it just because the site no longer served its purpose for my research. The job offer at UCLA required us to relocate, and a cross-country move was a reason the community could legitimately accept for why the events had to end.

In Los Angeles, my exit from the community occurred in stages. I had finished the first round of interviews for my study of black sexual-minority elders, but I still needed to collect archival data, and to do that, I had to continue to develop my relationships with LGBTQ activists and with people who were connected to archives that were potential sources of material I needed. In 2012, my partner and I married, and we began hosting fewer events as we started working more concretely on building our family. We were invited to participate in the marriage equality campaign, which made our relationship particularly visible to the LGBTQ community. We had our daughter in 2013, and people followed us on our journey to parenthood through social media and our activist work on lesbian family building. These activities further reduced our ability to host parties, though we also began to host other types of events for the community, such as a forum on alternative insemination and adoption. LGBTQ people recognized and appreciated this work, so even though we hosted fewer purely social activities, they did not see us as removing ourselves from the community. Once we had our son in 2014, it really became difficult to host events, but again people seemed to understand this constraint. Many in the community had children or wanted to grow their own families, so they could relate to why we had less time available. In January 2015 we moved back to New York; our last event was a farewell brunch in December 2014. The move effectively ended my time in the field, though I have remained in contact with folks through social media. I hope and believe that most people did not view our exit as abandonment.

I recognize that it is not possible to end all community fieldwork in a gradual way. If data collection takes place in a location far removed from home or in a space you have agreed to occupy temporarily, one suggestion is to begin the exit before your period of data collection ends. Although my experience was somewhat unconventional, there are some lessons to be gleamed. It can be less jarring, both for the researcher and for the community being observed, to leave the field in stages. After primary interviews have been completed, one can step back, listen to the recordings while reading through field notes, and see if there are loose ends that need to be addressed. Points of clarification from respondents or exit interviews with venue owners can provide a reason to return to field sites, but with less frequency. And once official data collection has ended, it is nice to return periodically to say hello.

CONCLUDING THOUGHTS

Qualitative approaches to research focus on the creation of meaning and experiences of everyday life. In an essay on the study of sexualities in qualitative research, Joshua Gamson (2000) argues that the development of the field of lesbian and gay studies in the 1970s and 1980s stemmed in part from the historical and ethnographic approaches of African American, ethnic, and women's studies, as well as work emerging from outside the academy in which "personal narratives and experiential truths were used to reclaim a gay or lesbian subjectivity that had been historically denied" (2000: 351). Researchers who were also members of the groups they began to study were concerned with "telling our own stories," a problematic standpoint because of the supposed absence of the "outsider" (read white, heterosexual male) who is thought to lend objectivity to the research.

The tensions in evaluating and validating "minority group research" conducted by minority group members persist today, though the study of sexualities has gained legitimacy over time as societal attitudes toward sexual-minority populations have jolted forward by fits and starts. Norman Denzin and Yvonna Lincoln (2000) liken the work of the qualitative researcher to that of a "bricoleur" or "quilt maker" who fashions together approaches, methods, and empirical materials to produce a set of representations tailored to the specifics of a complex condition or location (4). As sociologists, and social scientists more generally, continue to make progress in the acknowledgement of and serious inquiry into the lives and meaning making of marginalized populations, we must challenge ourselves to do this work with an open-mindedness to alternative strategies and research designs that will help us arrive at the most complete understanding of the phenomenon or population in question.

WORKS CITED

Baca Zinn, Maxine. 1979. "Insider field research in minority communities." *Social Problems* 27(2): 209–19.
Denzin, Norman K., and Yvonna S. Lincoln (eds.). 2000. "Introduction: The discipline and practice of qualitative research." In *Handbook of qualitative*

research, 2nd ed. Ed. Norman K. Denzin and Yvonna S. Lincoln. Thousand Oaks, CA: SAGE.

Hesse-Biber, Sharlene Nagy (ed.). 2012. *The handbook of feminist research: Theory and praxis, 2nd ed.* Thousand Oaks, CA: SAGE.

Gamson, Joshua. 2000. "Sexualities, queer theory, and qualitative research." In *Handbook of qualitative research,* 2nd ed. Ed. Norman K. Denzin and Yvonna S. Lincoln. Thousand Oaks, CA: SAGE.

Moore, Mignon R. 2010a. "Articulating a politics of (multiple) identities: Sexuality and inclusion in black community life." *DuBois Review: Social Science Research on Race* 7(2): 1–20.

———. 2010b. "Black and gay in LA: The relationships lesbians and gay men have with their religious and racial communities." In *Black Los Angeles: American dreams and racial realities.* Ed. Darnell Hunt and A. Christina Ramon. New York: New York University Press.

———. 2011. *Invisible families: Gay identities, relationships, and motherhood among black women.* Berkeley: University of California Press.

Naples, Nancy A. 2003. *Feminism and method: Ethnography, discourse analysis, and activist research.* New York: Routledge.

Pillow, Wanda, and Cris Mayo. 2012. "Feminist ethnography: Histories, challenges, and possibilities." In *Handbook of feminist research: Theory and praxis.* Ed. Sharlene Nagy Hesse-Biber. Thousand Oaks, CA: SAGE.

11 How Many (Queer) Cases Do I Need?

THINKING THROUGH RESEARCH DESIGN

D'Lane R. Compton

When I was in graduate school at Texas A&M University in the early 2000s, the sociological methods courses I took emphasized empirical research and the notion that our questions should determine our methods. By this point, I had had a number of methods courses from a diverse group of professors during my undergraduate career and more qualitatively focused MA program. However, throughout this time, while I was taught to respect both quantitative and qualitative research and methodologies, empirical research was upheld as a clear gold standard. The research that received the rewards—the (fast) publications and grant monies—held the positivist triple crown: random sampling or assignment, replicability, and generalizability. I soon discovered that quantitative studies of large populations were more likely to be received in the discipline as "good" sociology. And, as a former engineering student who was often identified as a "quant person," I may never have questioned this standard—though my mentors encouraged me to pursue my interests and follow my questions. The 2000 census data drop, which included data on unmarried cross- and same-sex partners, became public and changed everything.

As I started to think how we could use this data and how to incorporate LGBTQ people into demographic methods, I realized that one barrier to this research was the assumption many scholars held: LGBTQ populations could not meet the gold standard of sociological research design, and, thus, such research could not produce significant results—an assumption, I was even more surprised to learn, that demographers and queer studies scholars alike held. Encouraged by allies like Dudley L. Poston Jr., I marshaled the queer determination that had led me, early in my graduate school years, to present a lecture on the queer history of Texas A&M to the Corps of Cadets (who, once they got over their shock, really got into it), and began working to challenge the assumptions that queer populations were too "messy" for demography.

Following my questions has led me to do both quantitative and qualitative queer research. Working across the methods divide has taught me a great deal about the challenges of queer research design in a discipline that values a particular understanding of "good" research. Don't get me wrong—I love positivism (perhaps a controversial statement in a volume about queer methods). What I don't love is how methodological critiques are levied at qualitatively driven queer research methods in ways that seek to dismiss them as insignificant. While methodological critiques are applicable to all social science research, it is my experience—and that of my peers and students—that queer research is more likely to get dismissed by journals on the basis of methodological critiques because of the heteronormative assumptions, practices, and biases embedded in the discipline's conventions (see also Ward, this volume).

In this chapter I focus on research design as it specifically applies to studying LGBTQ populations. Playing off of Mario Small's influential critique (2009) of the tendency in sociology to privilege evidence that stems from the quantitative social sciences when evaluating any piece of research regardless of method or question, I explore the question, How many (queer) cases do I need? As we learn in graduate school, design choices made during the early stages of research impact our outcomes. But when we are studying groups with a short history of sociological research behind them, such as the LGBTQ population, our choices and outcomes potentially impact the field as a whole and can, if we are creating a new area of research, shape what becomes the standard procedure for this type of work. At the simplest and most idealistic level, the goal of much LGBTQ research in sociology is knowledge production and solution building—which, for me, necessitates a strong research design. We may want to use our research to solve problems, engage in advocacy, and offer solutions for policy. To work through these issues, I draw on my experiences designing multimethod LGBTQ research projects and what I have learned from my colleagues and students. Oh, and don't worry—I will tell you how many queer cases you need (a preview—the answer is "probably less than you think").

QUEER RESEARCH, STRAIGHT METHODS

When I was starting graduate school in the 2000s, the idea of demographic research with LGBTQ people seemed impossible to many demographers I met, because they were a "hidden," marginalized population (see Moore, this volume). Hidden populations put demographers on edge because by definition they have no preexisting sampling frames, making population size and group boundaries unknown. Sociologists also consider hidden populations to be relatively rare. Moreover, due to the social stigma often associated with revealing membership in a marginalized population, it can be hard to recruit individuals into a study. The lack of definition of the size of the LGBTQ population and the inability to gather a random sample mean that those who manage generic social science survey instruments have historically been reluctant to include LGBTQ-related questions or to collect information on sexual identity. Aside from producing a huge gap in our sociological knowledge, this lack of inclusion creates a self-fulfilling prophecy: we can't estimate the size of the LGBTQ population or build measures for reliability and validity, because we don't collect demographic information on the LGBTQ population. And, while some of these methodological issues do stem from the long history of social stigma that LGTBQ population continue to face, some demographers also resist studying a population they have dismissed or imagined to be too small to matter statistically. In attempting to overcome this resistance to queer demography, I have run into a series of quandaries around research design that I discuss in this section.

Sampling

Let's begin with sampling—the starting point for most research design. Traditionally, sociologists have thought about sampling in the statistical sense, with random probability sampling being the gold standard we are trained to strive for (Small 2009). Yet, as I note above, this requirement for random sampling can be challenging for research with the LGBTQ community. First, LGBTQ people are not evenly dispersed across the country. Recent census data show us that 35 percent of same-sex unmarried partners live in the South, 17 percent in the Pacific region, and 19 percent in the North. Among US regions, the South holds the largest population of same-sex partners (Williams Institute 2016). And most same-sex households with children present are located across the Bible Belt (Baumle & Compton 2015). Second, the long history of social stigma and, until fairly recently, criminalization of homosexuality and gender nonconformity makes LGBTQ people a marginalized population. These two factors—the lack of random dispersion and social stigma—created a feeling among demographers that it was impossible (and, until the mid-2000s, improper) to track LGBTQ identities in large, nationally representative surveys. Further, researchers who always have limited funds assumed most respondents would be cisgender and heterosexual, and therefore worried about the expense of including LGBTQ-specific identity categories and questions. Buried in this resistance is also a concern about alienating the straight-cis majority.

This lack of inclusion of LGBTQ populations in large-scale, national surveys means we have had (until quite recently) no way to estimate the size of the LGBTQ population in the United States. While most social science disciplines are beginning to build strategies for addressing this knowledge gap, there is no unified idea about which estimates are best. This confusion has contributed to a lack of confidence in enumeration in the few cases where it was attempted or estimated (see Gates & Herman, this volume). Consequently, researchers intent on creating generalizable research about LGBTQ populations face problems in generating sampling plans and research designs. The gold standard for sampling and research design would be to have measures related to the LGBTQ population added to a variety of social surveys (including, among others, the General Social

Survey [GSS], American National Election Survey [ANES], and the US Census). And, happily, as more measures are added across surveys, we will converge on reliable population estimates.

While all of this may sound like "quant people problems," including more measures on nationally representative surveys will also benefit qualitative research. For example, if we wanted to do an interview study with queer Hispanic families, we could use the census data to plan our study. In looking at where to find our respondents, we could decide that our study should take place in San Antonio, Texas, based on the size of the Hispanic-headed same-sex households with children in that locale compared to the rest of the country. Here, then, is an example of how these quantitative measures can help researchers of all kinds develop greater efficiency in accessing and recruiting their population of interest.

Access and Recruitment

Let's say you have a sampling design. How do you recruit LGBTQ people? It is important at this stage to think through any preconceived notions about where to find LGBTQ people. Stereotypes affect not only consumers of LGBTQ research but researchers as well (yes, even queer researchers). Our assumptions, coupled with research strategies we see used in prior work, can lead us to create recruitment strategies that unknowingly leave out certain subpopulations of LGBTQ people. For example, usage of the word *queer* in a recruitment call may prompt some individuals to volunteer for the study but push others away, particularly older gay and lesbian people and southerners, many of whom may still experience that word as an insult. Such recruiting strategies would continue to support what is already known and expected. Consequently, we may also miss hearing and thereby recognizing less visible or newly emerging voices.

Here is a classic example of this problem: researchers looking for LGBTQ populations historically started at gay bars. While at one time this recruitment strategy may have been the best from a design standpoint—as bars were for many people the epicenter of visible gay life—it was less effective for recruiting lesbian and queer women (Compton & Baumle 2012). Most cities lacked a host of lesbian-specific bars to choose from; rather, it was more typical that gay bars hosted a "lesbian night" once a month. The time that women spent in gay bars, then, may have been experienced as more of a "special occasion," making women less willing to take time away from their evening to fill out a survey. Further, then as now, gay bars may lack racial and class diversity—whether it be the result of who patronizes the bars or their location (Greene 2014). Thus, bars may be more or less useful in recruitment strategies, depending on the population of interest and study aims. Further, due to the forms of social change we often push for in our research, what is deemed as an appropriate and effective venue or site for recruitment changes over time—as evidenced by the growth in virtual LGBTQ spaces and the increased visibility of queer communities in the South and Midwest.

One strategy recognizes the power of drawing on a variety of entry points to recruit samples in order to diversify the pool of respondents. I learned this the hard way when I was finding LGBTQ parents for a study I did with Amanda Baumle (Baumle & Compton 2015). At first, our recruitment plan drew on prior LGBTQ research and our own prior work of recruiting subjects. We looked for what we believed to be relevant list serves and organizational networks that could reach into the LGBTQ community at large; we hoped to find LGBTQ parents within those spaces. Ideally, we would have had access to an LGBTQ parenting group or list serve in each area, but at that time, such groups were quite rare. As our study was multisited, we reached out to local researchers for their insight into the location and the best way to reach the LGBTQ community and LGBTQ parents in that specific place. What we learned eventually was that we should look for general parenting groups rather than LGBTQ-specific groups. In retrospect, our initial approach seems quite naive, but it's easy to get stuck in a mindset that we recruit LGBTQ people through LGBTQ venues and communities. Recognizing both LGBTQ venues and parenting venues as recruitment sites greatly extended the reach of our calls for participation. And, in fact, many of our referrals came from heterosexual parents and allies who had seen our call and shared it with their LGBTQ parent friends or with community or school parent email lists. In the end, this multipronged approach contributed to efficiency in the data collection process. But, more important, it also challenged our presumptions and expectations for various locales and contexts.

Sample Representativeness

Once you have a solid strategy for recruitment that involves many avenues of inquiry, how can you get a diverse sample, and how can you know if your sample is representative of the LGBTQ population? Representativeness, or the degree to which a subgroup (sample) reflects a larger group (the population), allows a researcher to reliably describe the population.[1] The logic of sampling assumes that no matter what your population entails, you have an exact knowledge of its size and characteristics so that you can speak to representativeness. Even if you are not aiming for the sociological gold standard and you purposively design a small, qualitative study, you will likely be faced with questions of representativeness from reviewers. Here, the lack of ability to enumerate and describe the LGBTQ population and its demographic characteristics, combined with the desire to get an intersectional sample that gives visibility to the diversity in the LGBTQ community, can present a challenge.

I faced such questions of representativeness when I attempted to publish research findings that I developed from an analysis of the same-sex partner data in the 2000 US Census. Reviewers wanted to know whether these families reflected the general gay and lesbian population. The answer to this question (the lack of existing data) was evident to me as someone doing queer work—but it was not to people from other subfields who were evaluating my work. Eventually, I added a footnote to all my articles that explicitly stated that my data could not speak to patterns among unpartnered LGBTQ people—but also, and more important for me, that the answer to this question about the general LGBTQ population was beyond the scope of my research question about same-sex, partnered households. The big takeaway here is that research drawing on survey data is generally concerned with generalizing to a *particular* empirical population—in my case, same-sex partnered households. When working with populations in which the representativeness is unknown, you can face critiques from reviewers who want your study to do more than it can within the limits of your data and the boundaries of your research question.

Qualitative research can confront a similar set of issues. In the case of my work with Amanda Baumle (2015), we wanted to use in-depth interviews to investigate the different routes to parenthood that LGBTQ individuals take. We started by asking how they became parents (a process that can take many routes for queer people). The responses we received included having children in previous heterosexual relationships, insemination, surrogacy, and formal and informal adoption. Here, we got what we wanted—a range of routes to LGBTQ parenthood by a range of parents, single and partnered. Surrogacy and adoption, particularly private and international adoption, however, are more costly and require greater resources related to income and wealth. As we wanted to speak to *all* of the common routes to parenthood, we included these options even though they skewed the average (and potentially the median) household income of our respondents from what census data would suggest is the average household income of same-sex parents. In other words, in seeking to represent a broad range of responses, the economically privileged families in our sample that had access to surrogacy and could cover the costs of international or private adoption drove up the sample's average household income. These families were also more likely to be headed by white parents, because it typically takes LGBTQ individuals more resources to intentionally become parents (as compared, for example, to families with same-sex parents in the census, who may have children from previous heterosexual relations). Yet in originally designing our research, it was the range of routes to parenthood that we sought. So, while our interview sample did not directly align with the larger body of census data on the economic demographics of same-sex parents, it did reflect a range of formal and informal routes to parenthood from a range of parents, including single parents and partnered, and those with resources and those without.

Reception

You have done your study and now you are in the home stretch—introducing your work to the broader discipline. Like many people doing queer work whom I know, you may face questions about the "believability" or "validity" of your findings, particularly from reviewers with little knowledge of LGBTQ populations. While the believability problem emerges in quantitative research with LGBTQ people due to the enumeration problem I discussed earlier, it is particularly thorny for qualitative research because we can't counter with the statistical findings that often help in sociology. Rather, we may find that we have to debunk assumptions and stereotypes about the LGBTQ community held by our colleagues that are preventing them from evaluating our research findings on their own terms.

As an early-career researcher, I gave numerous demographic and sociological presentations on issues of sexual orientation. A majority of the conversations following these presentations, however, were not directly about their content, but rather about my experience as a white, queer, gender-nonconforming person living and working in first Texas and then Louisiana. To learn that there were queer people in Texas, that I wasn't the only one, and that some of us had a deep love for our state (enough to tattoo it on my arm) challenged many stereotypes within academia—among them that queer people born and raised in rural, conservative, or southern cities move to New York or San Francisco as soon as they turn eighteen. The idea that queer people could build community and family in these places is, oddly, hard to reconcile with such stereotypes—even for many queer sociologists who prioritize living on the coasts in big cities.

Colleagues and reviewers frequently did not know what to do with this work. They complimented me for my sample sizes (which, over double digits, exceeded people's expectations about how many queer people lived in Texas) and asked skeptical questions of disbelief. Often, the two responses were intertwined. My most effective defense at the time was to show how the 2000 census data had revealed Texas to be the "third gayest state" (knocked down to fourth by Florida with the 2010 data) in regard to the population of same-sex partners. I addressed this finding by showing how it was "sensical" (as we say in Texas) if you think about absolute population across states. The stereotype that LGBTQ people reside only in urban spaces had to be debunked before my work with southern populations could be considered "believable." To this extent, the demographic data bolstered my qualitative work in a way that validated and legitimated my findings. And I was lucky to have census data (gold-standard data for quant people) to draw on. A great deal of qualitative work on queer populations is likely not so lucky.

SIZE MATTERS AND THE LORE AND LURE OF 30

Most of the issues that I address above are what I faced as an early-career researcher in the 2000s. In a rapidly changing social landscape with increased LGBTQ visibility and momentum, it is now far less sensational to think about LGBTQ people living in rural or conservative spaces than it was even five years ago. And, with the growth of queer research that embraces poststructuralist critiques of positivism, we have created a little more space for scholars who are not seeking to be legitimated by the sociology gold standard. But, if we want a career in sociology, we often have to market our work to the broader discipline. For qualitative researchers, this can require adopting the statistical language of "outcomes," emulating quantitative research designs and write-ups, undertaking mixed-method approaches, and trying to beef up sample sizes so that we can run some descriptive statistics and insert tables in our articles. I get the impulse. In a discipline focused on statistical significance, more numbers and cases seem better (and safer for people doing "edgy" work). In setting out to write this chapter, I intended to make a grand statement about the state of queer work in the field related to sociological respectability politics. I wanted to say boldly, "Queer folks—you are potentially being overresponsible in research designs and sampling. You can calm down now!" However, returning to my love of positivism, I don't really think that being too rigorous is ever a problem for academic research. And, taking stock of the field, I think queer sociological research overall is doing just fine without my bold statement and concern for efficiency. Nevertheless, it is important to learn where our anxieties about sample size are coming from, how they are supported—and how we might challenge them collectively. So let's take seriously the question "How many (queer) cases do I need?"

Two decades ago, to have more than fifteen interviews from an LGBTQ population would have been seen by most people in the discipline as a major accomplishment. People may even have wondered how a researcher could have "found" that many people. I still remember the first study I read that drew on 40 interviews with queer people. We read the article in a graduate course, and the class discussion centered mainly on this impressive sample size. Yet now, with the LGBTQ population becoming more visible on- and offline, we have more avenues through which to tap into this population. These new avenues, however, raise expectations regarding what is a reasonable sample size—meaning, really, what convinces the field as an appropriate sample size. But, before I work through this question, I want to state clearly that assessments of how to draw a sample and what size the sample should be cannot be evaluated outside the context of a particular study and its goals. I believe that we can learn a great deal from small samples. Size matters, yes, but only in relation to research design and its application to the questions we want to address in our particular study. This means that the logic behind assessing samples and issues related to size holds across methodologies—quantitative, qualitative, or experimental.

Practically speaking, there is a threshold to what is deemed an acceptable or appropriate sample size by our discipline and colleagues. Within sociology, many consider p-values (which are determined by sample size) to be objective standards that determine whether or not a finding is statistically significant. Reaching a p <0.05 threshold is technically a field agreed-upon benchmark. But why? Consider a recent statement from the other ASA, the American Statistical Association, regarding p-values:

> In February, 2014, George Cobb, Professor Emeritus of Mathematics and Statistics at Mount Holyoke College, posed these questions to an ASA discussion forum:
> Q: Why do so many colleges and grad schools teach p = 0.05?
> A: Because that's still what the scientific community and journal editors use.
> Q: Why do so many people still use p = .05?
> A: Because that's what they were taught in college or grad school

Evaluating this question, the authors of the piece noted that this concern spoke to "*a long-worrisome circularity in the sociology of science based on the use of bright lines such as p <.05*" (Wasserstein & Lazar 2016: 129; emphasis mine). While not arbitrary, this response shows that the idea of how many cases we need to generate a significant finding with a p-value <0.05 is socially constructed by the discipline.

So quantitative researchers have a benchmark for sample size and statistical significance. But the issue becomes thornier with qualitative work. Consider the common question "How many interviews do I need?" I tell my students, the correct answer should be "It depends." It depends on study aims, areas of concern, development of theory, and prior evidence. While we don't like to sully our pure research design with material matters, the answer also often depends on resources available to the researcher, including money, but also time and availability of participants to interview. And, even when we realize we are not generating any new information from additional interviews, whether we should stop at that point also depends on what is acceptable to our colleagues and discipline. Combining these three features—the ideal, the practical, and the acceptable—further increases the difficulties of qualitative research.

Mario Small's influential article "How Many Cases Do I Need?" (2009) gave qualitative researchers key citational support for staking a claim with the answer "Enough to get saturation" (see also Charmaz 2006; Mason 2010). While there is no established metric for saturation, the academic lore and best practices passed down by my mentors over time suggests about 30 interviews. I have never read anything that addresses this lore, but I have read a number of articles that continue its assertion—making it, in disciplinary terms, a social fact. It is likely related to probabilistic logic: we know that we can usually see a normal distribution develop at around 30 observations whether it is students' grades, coin tosses, or some other variable of interest. We also know (from our basic stats course in grad school) that the t turns into the Z around 30. Again this is all tied back to the sampling distribution and its ability to act as a bridge between a sample and its population—and we are really talking about variation.

These are statistical examples, but the same general logic applies to qualitative work whose purpose is to include as many observations as required for the variation to be decreased. In other words, you interview until unique responses no longer occur. Less variation and greater homogeneity in responses leads more quickly to saturation, and thus we require fewer observations. What I mean to show here is that the logic behind drawing statistical samples is related to the logic of saturation. However, where these logics of inquiry differ returns us to p-values. There is no similar 0.05 standard for qualitative work—no verifiable measure to prove we have hit saturation. This means it is unlikely we can answer the question

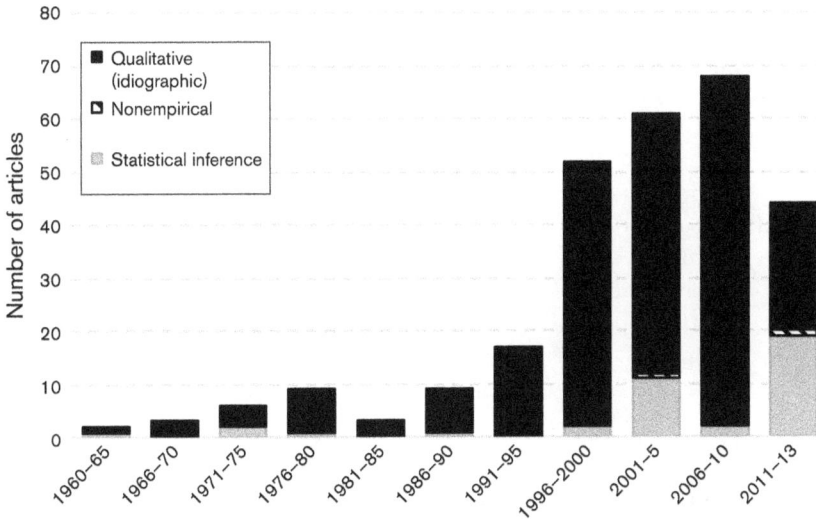

Figure 1. Frequency of Articles in JSTOR on LGBTQ Research, by Methology, 1960–2013.

of how many cases we need before undertaking a qualitative study, because saturation relies on a combination of accumulation of evidence and expertise.

So how does this play out for queer research? To answer this, I did a crude analysis of the 274 LGBTQ research articles published between 1960 and 2013 and housed online at JStor.org as a proxy for queer sociology.[2] As figure 1 shows, the number of research articles published each year that center on LGBTQ topics has steadily increased, with more than half of these articles published in the last nine years of the sample period (2004–13). The knowledge base and research productivity in the field have grown tremendously over the past decade. This indicates an extreme growth period for the discipline. Thirty-nine of these articles (14%) seek to address statistical inferences, while 233 articles (85%) are idiographic and draw on qualitative methods, and 2 articles (0.73%) are theoretical or literature reviews.

This analysis shows that in LGBTQ research, the lore of 30, or perhaps more accurately the allure of 30, may be that it seems to be accepted

Table 1   Sample Sizes of LGBTQ Qualitative Studies Published on
JSTOR, 1960–2013

		N	Average	Median	Minimum	Maximum
Interviews only	pre-2004	46	36	29.5	1	150
	post-2004	57	38	30	6	111
	All interview-only studies	103 (44.2%)	37	30	1	150
	All qualitative studies	233 (100%)	52	30	1	150

within the field. The largest proportion of the LGBTQ scholarship published in JStor.org (37.6%) is based on interview data alone. The median
number of interviews utilized by LGBTQ articles in JStor.org continues to
hold at 30 across data collection and qualitative methodologies through
2013 (see table 1). This number also holds across time. If we look across
the latter nine years of research in the sample, we see that the average
number of interviews per study increased by 2.

Overall, then, it seems that in queer work we feel we can draw sound
conclusions with 30 cases or observations and get our work published in
an atmosphere that privileges the use of "statistical language" (Small
2009). But, while 30 can be a worthy aspirational goal, I reiterate that
sample size should depend on the number of variables of interest and the
number of categories within those variables—not on what other researchers have done or some imagined standard of "what you have to have."
Further, the increasing visibility of a diverse LGBTQ population means we
should expect variation in research trends: sample sizes for qualitative
work are likely to increase as we begin to look more across the diversity of
the LGBTQ population but, at the same time, are likely to remain small in
studies that seek only to compare across a few categories of interest, such
as parenthood status or region. With all these new possibilities, I see it as
vital in queer research design to clarify the research aims and their association with sample size—to match our research questions with our
research design and sampling strategies.

CONCLUSION

Sampling is a paramount part of empirical research. It has enormous implications for the quality of our findings and their reception. The established literature on sampling clearly indicates that if the sample size is too small, the confidence in the findings is low. At the same time, large sample sizes can be expensive to gather and can offer superfluous information. Studying an entire population is impractical and often unnecessary. Research is expensive and demands other resources, including our time, energy, and funding, all of which are finite. What I hope to show in this chapter is that we need to reexamine our anxiety about how many queer cases we need to earn sociological respectability, because there is often a point of diminishing returns to expanding our samples. Collecting more cases does not necessarily mean we garner more information. Likewise, not all observations are equal. Within idiographic qualitative work, we are typically looking for meaning and seeking to understand specific processes. The concern in qualitative work should be that we have enough cases to contain and yield the full range of perceptions on a subject, and the goal should be saturation—sampling until no new information is being generated. In all research, we should remember that how many cases we need depends on what we seek to understand. There are certainly methodological guidelines, but in the end, research design is a matter of the question being asked and the history of that question.

So, rather than a grand statement, I end with a call that might sound mundane but that I think is important to scholars doing queer sociology in particular: from start to finish, we need to be conscientious in our methodological decision making. It is important to continually recognize and assess how decisions are being made, and to keep in mind that they are being driven by research questions and study goals. This goal is, of course, important to most social scientists regardless of area of study. But researchers doing queer work are more likely to get dismissive methodological critiques that reflect the heteronormative assumptions, practices, and biases deeply embedded in our discipline. While not all queer sociologists embrace positivism (as this volume shows), we do have to think about publication if we seek to build a career in sociology. I have found it helpful to have a well-formed rationale to artfully defend my choices when responding to editors and reviewers, and this is how I now train my students. Even if we reject the sociology gold standard, it is useful to be able to articulate what we reject about it and why we can have confidence in how many queer cases we have.

NOTES

1. Most often we think of populations as sets of people or cases, but they can also be forged through theory-driven sampling, such as with experimental work.

2. Articles were found by doing individual keyword searches for *lesbian, gay, homosexual, homosexuality, bisexual, bisexuality, transgender, transsexual, transsexuality, same-sex partners,* and *queer.* Book reviews and editorials were excluded.

WORKS CITED

Baumle, Amanda K., and D'Lane R. Compton. 2015. *Legalizing LGBT families: How the law shapes parenthood.* New York: New York University Press.

Charmaz, Kathy. 2006. *Constructing grounded theory: A practical guide through qualitative analysis.* Thousand Oaks, CA: SAGE.

Compton, D'Lane R., and Amanda K. Baumle. 2012. "Beyond the Castro: The role of demographics in the selection of gay and lesbian enclaves." *Journal of Homosexuality* 59(10): 1327–55.

Greene, Theodore. 2014. "Gay neighborhoods and the rights of the vicarious citizen." *City & Community* 13(2): 99–118.

Mason, Mark. 2010. "Sample size and saturation in PhD studies using qualitative interviews." *Forum: Qualitative Social Research* 11(3): art. 8.

Small, Mario. 2009. "How many cases do I need? On science and the logic of case selection in field-based research." *Ethnography* 10(1): 5–38.

Wasserstein, Ronald L., and Nicole A. Lazar. 2016. "The ASA's statement on *p*-values: Context, process, and purpose." *American Statistician* 70(2): 129–33.

Williams Institute. 2016. "LGBT in the South," The Williams Institute, UCLA School of Law, March. Retrieved, July 2017. https://williamsinstitute.law.ucla.edu/research/census-lgbt-demographics-studies/lgbt-in-the-south/.

12 Queer Spatial Analysis

Amin Ghaziani

In 1990, Consumer Affairs reported that the US gay and lesbian population clustered in coastal cities. By 2014, unexpected new hubs had emerged in Salt Lake City, Louisville, Norfolk, Indianapolis, and other places in conservative states, while traditional strongholds like Los Angeles, Atlanta, New York City, Miami and Washington, DC, had fallen in the rankings of top residential locations.[1] As individuals make similar decisions about where to live (or where not to live), and as those patterns change over time, we redraw the cultural cartography of cities. Seattle provides a stark example. Between the 2000 and 2010 U.S. Census collections, the number of same-sex households increased in every single neighborhood—with one notable exception: the city's most visible gay district, Capitol Hill. There, the number of male and female same-sex households plummeted by 23 percent (Balk & Potts 2014). Zoom next onto the streets of San Francisco. A 2015 survey shows that 77 percent of people who have lived in the Castro for ten years or more self-identify as gay or lesbian. The percentage falls to 66 for those who have inhabited the area for five years or less, 61 percent for those who moved in during the previous two years, and 55 percent for those who arrived in the previous year (Staver 2015). Such migrations are inciting a "new turmoil" across the country, the *New*

Yorker notes, as more straights select gay neighborhoods as their home while queer people fan out to other parts of the city, the suburbs, and even into rural areas (Greenspan 2014).

What can we learn from gayborhoods? Rather than ask why they first formed or explain why they have been changing in recent years, as I have done elsewhere, in this chapter I use my experience with studying them as an opportunity to reflect on five methodological problems: (1) how to sample hidden populations; (2) how to interview in ways that capture the interactional tone of life on city streets; (3) how to position demographic statistics in a cultural context; (4) how to move beyond binary conceptions of urban spaces as gay or straight; and (5) how to identify indicators of sexual geographies. For me, these inquiries collectively capture the spirit of "queer methods" (Brim & Ghaziani 2016), and I use them to offer advice to future researchers: once you embrace fluidity, multiplicity, and silences, you will realize that the systematic and the chaotic are beautifully compatible in queer spatial analysis.

CENSUS CONVENTIONS

Gayborhoods are not tightly sealed districts; their boundaries are fuzzy. Existing studies in a number of disciplines have managed this problem by relying on census data to infer the size of the gay and lesbian population and to identify the density of same-sex households in specific geographic regions. One common strategy is to create an "index of dissimilarity." The statistic represents the proportion of minority group members (same-sex partner households, in this case) who would have to exchange places, usually census tracts, with majority group members (different-sex households) to achieve an even residential distribution: a neighborhood that replicates the sexual composition of the city overall. The index measures residential segregation and spatial isolation. Its values range from 0 to 100, where 0 represents total integration and 100 signifies conditions of extreme segregation. Research shows that male and female same-sex households became less segregated from all different-sex households between the 2000 and 2010 census counts.

Scholars also use census data to create a "gay index" that ranks regions based on their density of same-sex households. Developed by Gary Gates, the index is expressed as a ratio of the concentration of same-sex couples in a geographic area relative to the overall population. A value of 1.0 indicates that a same-sex couple is just as likely as a randomly selected household to live in the particular area. A value of 2.0 means that couples are twice as likely to locate in the area, while values less than 1.0 indicate that they are less likely to do so than a randomly selected household. Studies that use the gay index show that same-sex couples are much more likely to live in cities like San Francisco, Seattle, Austin, and Portland, along with smaller towns like Provincetown and Northampton, Massachusetts; Wilton Manors, Florida; and Palm Springs. City officials have taken a keen interest in this index because scholars who are visible beyond the academy, including Richard Florida, argue that it predicts economic competitiveness in a globalizing world.

The 2010 census was the first in which government officials allowed respondents to identify themselves as married to a person of the same sex (Massachusetts pioneered legal same-sex marriage in 2005). Studies that use data from that particular census still produce low estimates of the gay and lesbian population because the survey counts only *coupled* households. It excludes those who are not partnered (about a fourth of gay men and two-fifths of lesbians are in relationships at any given time). Those who do not live with their partner, those who are unwilling to self-identify as gay or lesbian, those who self-identify as bisexual, and those who self-identify as transgender also remain uncounted. These limitations raise questions: What does it mean that same-sex marriage makes some of us measurable while concealing others? If we know where same-sex couples live, does that tell us where *all* queer people live? That the census renders an incomplete portrait is not up for debate—the survey still doesn't ask about individual sexual orientation, sexual behavior, or sexual attraction, after all—yet it remains one of the few probability samples that we have about the gay and lesbian population.

Having considered two common techniques that scholars use to describe the gay and lesbian population and its geographic expressions, let's now think about possibilities for methodological innovation. The advice that follows is organized around a series of problems that I encountered as I was researching and writing my book *There Goes the Gayborhood?* (Ghaziani 2014b). I should note that these districts are generally white, male, and middle-class in composition. It goes without saying, therefore, that we can generate yet other principles based on the study of lesbian spaces and those crafted by people of color, ball and drag cultures, queer youth, and suburban and rural migrations. What I offer here is an incitement to further discourse for queer spatial analysis.

MISALIGNMENTS, MUTABILITY, DIVERSITY

Gays and lesbians are a hidden population, and thus they are impossible to randomly sample. You can address this problem in three ways. First, remember that sexual orientation is a composite concept; what you learn depends on what you ask. Your options include questions about attraction or arousal (the desire to have sex or be in a romantic relationship with one or both sexes); about behavior, acts, and contact (any mutual and voluntary activity that involves genital or bodily contact, even if an orgasm does not occur); or about identity (socially and historically meaningful labels that guide how we think about sexuality). Here's why measurement matters: if you define homosexuality by same-sex behavior, then you will omit gay virgins while including self-identified straight men who have sex with other men. If instead you define homosexuality by an identity label like *gay* or *lesbian,* you will exclude those people who experience same-sex arousal or behavior but do not identify as such. You'll also overlook those who identify as bisexual or queer, along with individuals who use language not tied to mainstream terms (e.g., "aggressive," "in the life," or "same-gender loving"). Did you know that in the biological and health sciences, a single instance of same-sex behavior automatically places an individual in the "homosexual" category regardless of the frequency of sex and whether the person enjoyed it (Savin-Williams 2006)? If we follow queer theoretic commitments to misalignments, the corresponding principle of queer methods is to be mindful of the components of sexual orientation—do not ignore, conflate, or reify them—and to draw conclusions based on the type of data you gather.

My second item of advice is to use sampling strategies that approximate probability theory. I adapted a technique, developed by Matthew Salganik and his colleagues, called respondent-driven sampling (RDS). This method of data collection uses a variation on chain referral, a snowball mechanism that is sensitive to community structure, geographic clusters, and social networks. Krista Gile, Lisa Johnston, and Salganik (2015) explain how it works:

> RDS data collection begins when researchers select, in an ad hoc manner, typically 5–10 members of the target population to serve as "seeds." Each seed is interviewed and provided a fixed number of coupons (usually three) that they use to recruit other members of the target population. These recruits are in turn provided with coupons that they use to recruit others. In this way, the sample can grow through many waves, resulting in recruitment trees. . . . The fact that the majority of participants are recruited by other respondents and not by researchers makes RDS a successful method of data collection. (242)

RDS is useful if your inferential objective is to understand how people who are connected assign meaning to their lives in specific spatial contexts, rather than to calculate central tendencies that you hope to generalize. The logic of this approach to data collection is to study networks within a population, each of which is heterogeneous in its contacts yet still geographically clustered. The chain of friends and acquaintances in each network should be large enough to generate ongoing recruitment efforts, even if some seeds prove fruitless for you as you seek additional referrals. Multiple waves provide access to parts of the network that you otherwise may have missed, and they avoid the small-world problem of short network distance between any two people.

I started with twenty seeds. This number is larger than what Gile, Johnston, and Salganik advise, but I wanted to cap the upper end of my sample to around one hundred people rather than the thousands common in big data studies. Four of the seeds did not produce additional waves of recruitment. The other sixteen snowballed into a total of 125 interviews with gay and straight residents and business owners of two neighborhoods in Chicago. I lived in the city for ten years before I did my fieldwork, yet I knew only one out of the twenty-five straight residents of Boystown; six out of the twenty-five lesbians and gay men in Boystown; two out of the twenty-five straights in Andersonville; and seven out of the twenty-five lesbians and gay men who lived in Andersonville. Thus, I encourage you not to get preoccupied with random sampling, since the procedure assumes that a given population is fixed and unchanging. Chain referral techniques are compatible with an understanding of queerness as mutable and group membership as fluctuating.

A third strategy is to maximize your efforts at representation by not relying exclusively on the census as your primary source of data. Andrew Whittemore and Michael Smart (2016) examined the street addresses of rental and for-sale properties advertised over twenty-six years in a weekly LGBTQ newspaper in Dallas. This type of data has its own limitations— "not all of this population can express their preferences in a capitalist land market," the authors acknowledge (2016: 193)—but it can track change over time, provide more precise data points than the decennial census, diversify your data beyond business listings, widen your analytic scope beyond traditional enclaves, and dismantle the tyranny of the couple that the census promotes. If you decide to use this method, keep in mind that property listings are skewed toward trendy and profitable areas, and these often attract heterosexuals. If you rely too heavily on advertisements as a proxy for queer people, you will underrepresent racial and ethnic minorities, women, people with lower levels of education, and economic variation. The more you can diversify your data and methods the better.

INTERVIEW LIKE AN ETHNOGRAPHER

Instead of conventional accounts that rely on demographic data and statistical techniques, I exploited the unique strengths of qualitative approaches, especially interviews, to explain why queer spaces are changing and to predict what will happen to them in the future. My decision was controversial. Some scholars argue that interviews capture ex post facto explanations for what people have already thought or done (Vaisey 2008). Others decry an attitudinal fallacy: what people say is a poor predictor of what they will do (Jerolmack & Khan 2014). Surveys can capture the prevalence of an attitude or a snap judgment—in, for example, a feelings thermometer about sexual integration—but these data exist at an individual level and are abstracted from lived experiences. When ethnographers encounter interview data like mine, they wonder about the situated nature of social life. What does it actually feel like to be a straight person living next door to a lesbian or gay man? Or to walk along rainbow-lined streets next to same-sex couples who are holding hands?

Interviews can capture interactional tones if we ask questions about specific groups of people and the situations in which they interact, even if we weren't around when the action occurred. For instance, I organized my conversations around a set of newspaper articles that presented scenarios in gayborhoods across the country. One story from the *San Francisco Chronicle* was entitled "SF's Castro District Faces An Identity Crisis: As Straights Move In, Some Fear Loss of the Area's Character" (February 25, 2007). The article includes a photograph of a woman, whom the reader assumes is straight, pushing a baby carriage on Castro Street with a rainbow flag visible behind her. Sitting next to my interviewee, I read aloud the following passage:

> To walk down San Francisco's Castro street—where men casually embrace on sidewalks in the shadow of an enormous rainbow flag—the neighborhood's status as a "gay Mecca" seems obvious. But up and down the enclave that has been a symbol of gay culture for more than three decades, heterosexuals are moving in. They have come to enjoy some of the same amenities that have attracted the neighborhood's many gay and lesbian residents: charming houses, convenient public transportation, safe streets and nice weather.

I then asked open-endedly, "What are your reactions to this headline, this photograph, or this story?" The question always generated a rich exchange.

I followed the same procedure with a second article. This one, published in the *New York Times*, was entitled "Turf: Edged Out by the Stroller Set" (May 27, 2004). The piece also included a photograph of a woman pushing a baby stroller, whom we again are to assume is straight, with two presumably gay men on either side of her who have been wedged apart by her stroller. I read this passage out loud:

> It was supposed to be a kind of homecoming. Last year, Chris Skroupa and John Wilson sold their apartment in Hudson Heights, in northern Manhattan, and moved to Chelsea, where, as a gay couple, they already spent most of their time socializing. But they soon discovered that the neighborhood was changing faster than they expected. Home prices were

rising, and many of their friends were moving to Hell's Kitchen, a few blocks west of Times Square. In restaurants that used to be almost exclusively gay, they noticed an influx of straight customers, often with children in strollers. On a recent Saturday, Mr. Skroupa and Mr. Wilson went out for brunch and "literally less than one-third of the restaurant was gay," Mr. Skroupa said last week, pausing between bench presses at a New York Sports Club on Eighth Avenue.

The final story that I used to structure my interviews came from the *Huffington Post* and was entitled "Boystown Gay Bar Bans Bachelorette Parties" (2009):

> Bar owner Geno Zaharakis sat one busy evening at the window of his gay nightclub, watching as groups of straight women celebrating bachelorette parties made their way along a strip of bars in Chicago's gay-friendly "Boystown" neighborhood. That's when he made a decision now posted for all to see: "No Bachelorette Parties." Though the small sign has been there for years, it's suddenly making a big statement amid the national debate over gay marriage. While most gay bars continue to welcome the raucous brides to be, Zaharakis's bar Cocktail is fighting for what he sees as a fundamental right, and his patrons—along with some peeved bachelorettes—are taking notice. "I'm totally losing money because of it, but I don't want the money," Zaharakis said. "I would rather not have the money than host an event I didn't believe in." Gay bars are popular with bachelorettes, both for the over-the-top drag shows that some offer and for the ability to let loose in a place where women are unlikely to be groped or ogled.

I would encourage you, as a researcher, to harness the unique power of interviews. Unlike observations alone, interviews will allow you to learn about the subtleties of queerness in three ways: you can identify specific actors, situations, and symbols; you can ask respondents about their meaning; and you can focus your conversations on how symbols, in particular, structure the interactional tone of city life. Using media documents is an innovative approach in that it reduces the threat of social desirability bias. Respondents can offer comments about the characters in a story without implicating themselves personally. Be careful, though, about which vignettes you select. Although queerness can challenge reproductive logics, remember that many same-sex couples also have children. You need to acknowledge that symbols acquire significance in particular places and times and for certain groups of people. In the passages that I read aloud during my interviews, strollers and bachelorette parties were symbols that journalists regularly used as anathema to queer space. They were meaningful, richly resonant, and emic cultural codes that Chicagoans, gay and straight alike, shared in the 2010s.

STATISTICAL SILENCES, CULTURAL MEANINGS

Most research, as I mention earlier, uses census data to create an index of dissimilarity. As a qualitative researcher, I knew that statistical scores were silent about attitudes and motivation. What is behind the drop that demographers and geographers have documented in sexual segregation? A bird's-eye view of statistical desegregation is a fine place to start, but it will leave you with little more than a numerical description of a phenomenon that demands an explanation. If people believe something is real, then it is real in its consequences. As sociologists, we know this, and so perceptions about sexuality should matter in queer spatial analysis. In my book, I developed a qualitative counterpart to the dissimilarity index—a "dissimilarity meanings measure"—that I used to explain why lesbians, gay men, and even straight people choose to live in an area of the city widely recognized as a gayborhood. What a neighborhood means is more than the sum of the bodies that inhabit it or the central tendencies that describe it.

In addition to thinking about the cultural meanings of sexuality and space, rather than just the statistical distribution of same-sex households across census tracts, I would also encourage you to broaden your vision of the city beyond a binary conception of gay or straight spaces. Consider that gay neighborhoods formed in North America after World War II. Many gays and lesbians were discharged from the military at this time for their real or perceived homosexuality, and rather than return home disgraced, some remained behind in major port cities. These spatial clusters grew rapidly in the 1970s and 1980s. Gays and lesbians perceived their emerging concentrations as havens of tolerance that offered reprieve from heterosexual hostilities. Today, there is an emerging concensus among academics, journalists, and even residents that the significance of gayborhoods is changing. The wisdom connecting these observations that span several decades is as follows: gayborhoods are "a spatial response to a historically specific form of oppression" (Lauria & Knopp 1985: 152). When the nature of oppression changes, so too should the spatial response.

Making this move will permit you to unhinge sexuality from specific places, since gayborhoods, along with queer-friendly areas and queered straight districts, can exist anywhere in and even beyond the city. One surprising finding from my research is that cities with the highest percentage of same-sex couples who are raising children include Albuquerque, Salt Lake City, and Bismarck, North Dakota. This outcome should remind you of arguments from queer theory. Power operates through the imposition of binaries like gay or straight, male or female, and masculine or feminine. These binaries have always inadequately mapped onto people's lives. In early-twentieth-century New York, a man could have sex with another man without anyone questioning whether he was "normal." A world of "trade," "husbands," and "wolves" existed in a highly gender-segregated bachelor subculture alongside "fairies," "third-sexers," and "punks" (Chauncey 1994). The same thing is happening today with the rise of "dude sex" between straight-identified white men (Ward 2015) and "sexual fluidity" among women (Diamond 2008). When we apply this framework from sexuality studies to the city, we can see what I call "cultural archipelagos." Queer geographies have plural expressions.

INDICATORS OF QUEER SPACE

If the phrase "queer culture" denotes the ways of life of sexual minorities, and if those ways of life are merging with the mainstream as society embraces increasingly liberal attitudes toward homosexuality, then how can we detect distinct urban sexual cultures? The very idea of measuring queer cultures is thwarted in an era of acceptance, inclusion, and integration. What can indicate the presence of queer ways of life in a historical moment characterized by the dilution of cultural distinctions? What does queerness mean in a context of "cultural sameness" or being "post-gay," as I have called it elsewhere? How can we think about the gayborhood as an observable analytic unit in a time when same-sex households are dispersing across the city?

My final bit of advice is to be creative about the indicators that you use to identify queer spaces. Urban sexual cultures are observable, despite the integration of gayborhoods, through placeholders like anchor institutions and commemorations (Ghaziani 2014a). Anchors are organizations such as bookstores, bars, and community centers that have a special resonance among queer communities. They are the primary engines of community building since they locate the material culture of queer people in a symbolically charged place. One resident told me, "Businesses are an important part of anchoring the gay neighborhood and defining it in the same way that ethnic businesses would help define an ethnic neighborhood." Another added, "As long as those businesses are still here, that's a big thing that keeps the perception in people's head that Lakeview is still gay."

Commemorations are a second analytic device that researchers can use to identify queer spaces. These range from municipal markers like rainbow crosswalks to recurring ritual events such as gay pride parades and dyke marches. In a nationally unprecedented move, the city of Chicago in 1997 installed tax-funded rainbow pylons along North Halsted Street to celebrate the area's queer character. Bernard Cherksov, who was once the CEO of Equality Illinois, explained why this was a historic decision: "With these pylons we're saying, 'This is our community space.' People move in and out of this neighborhood for different reasons, but the community isn't moving. Boystown is still here." A professor at a local university agreed with this image of territoriality: "It is a political victory, an urban political victory to have any metropolitan or municipal authority allow you to fix identity to space. So many struggles are really about contestations of space. So, when you are allowed to plant your flag anywhere, I think it's a victory for lesbigay identity politics because it says we are here or we were here: this is an important dimension of the city."

Chicago is not alone in its efforts to install commemorative markers. In 1999, the Newcastle City Council became the first in the United Kingdom to announce that it wanted to actively build a gayborhood by designating a section as the "Pink Triangle." In April 2007, Philadelphia became the second American city to mark one of its neighborhoods as gay by renaming a portion of the Washington Square West district in Center City as "the Gayborhood." The city added thirty-six rainbow flags underneath street signs that bordered the area, which extends from 11th to Broad and from Pine to Locust streets. Finally, in 2013, Vancouver installed permanent rainbow-colored crosswalks in the Davie Village gayborhood. This was the first such permanent installation in Canada. Other North American cities that have installed rainbow crosswalks to mark and celebrate their local gayborhood include Austin; Key West, Florida; Long Beach, California; Northampton, Massachusetts; San Francisco; Sacramento; Seattle; Philadelphia; Toronto; Victoria, British Columbia; and West Hollywood.

Compared to racial and ethnic groups, queer communities lack a clear sense of ancestral linearity. The absence of awareness—who are my people?—induces collective amnesia about our lives. This is one of the most insidious forms of homophobia. During my third year of undergraduate study, I remember feeling astonished when I learned that the History Department was offering the course "Gay and Lesbian History." I had never imagined that such a class could exist. The narrowness of my world-view reflected the burden of queer communities in that historical moment. Anchors and commemorative devices protect against the temptation or coercion to forget. They, like other preservation strategies (renaming city streets to honor queer activists, for example, or building LGBTQ museums), fossilize the culture of a group in space and enable a sense of permanence amid the inevitable realities of migrations and urban change. That said, even those queer cultures that are based in a gayborhood involve more than a collection of organizations, businesses, and municipally sanctioned installations. Sexual ways of life also encompass the symbolic meanings associated with the closet; genres of television, music, and literature; ritual events like pride parades; the iconography of drag; camp; diverse family forms; and countless other measures that show unique subjectivities, aesthetics, and styles of socialization. None of this trivializes the analytic power that inheres in anchor institutions and commemorations. No single mechanism can explain the full range of variation in urban sexual cultures. What we need to do is to expand our methodological portfolio in ways that increase the degree of precision in our observations about sexuality and the city.

AN INTELLECTUAL MOVEMENT IS BORN

Queer studies is in the midst of a methodological renaissance. David Halperin's books *How to Do the History of Homosexuality* (2002) and *How to Be Gay* (2014), along with the fall 2010 *Queer Methods and Methodologies* volume by Kath Browne and Catherine J. Nash, indexed this shift toward methods by reframing the by-now-fatigued question *"What* is queer theory?" to the fresh inquiry *"How* is queer theory done?" The principles that I share in this chapter offer several insights about queer spatial analysis. First, we need to organize our skepticism as we respectfully question the concepts and categories of conventional social science. The dissimilarity index and the gay index are valuable but not without inferential limits. An effort to "queer" existing protocols requires us to embrace misalignments, mutability, diversity, interactions, and silences. Remember that sexual orientation is a composite concept; use chain-referral sampling techniques; access multiple data sources; and study sexual meanings alongside demographic statistics. Second, queer methods are powerful because they clarify the conditions that make life livable. In this regard, I offer innovative ways of interviewing that can capture the interactional tones of city life. Finally, queer methods create space for the coherent and the chaotic. Concepts like cultural archipelagos, anchors, and commemorations will enable you to conceptualize gayborhoods as analytically observable entities without naively denying the realities of residential and commercial change.

The volume in which this chapter appears births in the social sciences an intellectual movement that has been brewing in the humanities as well (Brim & Ghaziani 2016). A new generation of scholars like you is interested in identifying research protocols and practices that have been eclipsed by advances in queer theory. We are all concerned with how to link an account of a situation (what I would call a theory) with a set of guidelines on how to gather evidence about it (what I would call methods). The resulting notion of "queer methods" is paradoxical and provocative. While the queer ethic is deconstructive and anti-positivist, an emphasis on methods invokes a curious sense of order and patterns. The genius of this volume is in its demonstration of the many ways in which research methods, like sociological theory, can be freed from the shackles of a clean and tidy, either-or binary.

NOTE

1. The census first asked about same-sex households in 1990, offering hope for a revolution in how we study the gay and lesbian population. Unfortunately, the data suffered from validity problems because government officials recoded it. When a same-sex household identified as being married, the bureau changed the gender of the spouse to force it into the framework of a heterosexual married couple. Therefore, we need to be careful about how we interpret statistical data that uses the 1990 census. For more on changes between 1990 and 2014, see Allen 2016.

WORKS CITED

Allen, Samantha. 2016. "Why LGBT people are moving to red states." *Daily Beast,* March 9. http://www.thedailybeast.com/articles/2016/03/09/why-lgbt-people-are-moving-to-red-states.html.

Balk, Gene, and Garland Potts. 2014. "Seattle's 'gayborhood' is becoming less gay." *Seattle Times,* July 31. http://old.seattletimes.com/html/localpages/2024202935_seattle-gayborhood-becoming-less-gay.html.

Brim, Matt, and Amin Ghaziani. 2016. "Introduction: Queer methods." *WSQ: Women's Studies Quarterly* 44(3–4): 14–27.

Browne, Kath, and Catherine J. Nash. 2010. *Queer Methods and Methodologies.* New York: Routledge.

Chauncey, George. 1994. *Gay New York: Gender, urban culture, and the making of the gay male world, 1890–1940.* New York: Basic Books.

Diamond, Lisa. 2008. *Sexual fluidity: Understanding women's love and desire.* Cambridge, MA: Harvard University Press.

Ghaziani, Amin. 2014a. "Measuring urban sexual cultures." *Theory and Society* 43(3–4): 371–93.

———. 2014b. *There goes the gayborhood?* Princeton, NJ: Princeton University Press.

Greenspan, Elizabeth. 2014. "It's a new day in the gayborhood." *New Yorker,* August 8. http://www.newyorker.com/business/currency/new-day-gayborhood.

Gile, Krista J., Lisa G. Johnston, and Matthew J. Salganik. 2015. "Diagnostics for respondent-driven sampling." *Journal of the Royal Statistical Society: Series A (Statistics in Society)* 178: 241–69.

Halperin, David. 2002. *How to do the history of homosexuality.* Chicago: University of Chicago Press.

———. 2014. *How to be gay.* Cambridge, MA: Harvard University Press.

Jerolmack, Colin, and Shamus Khan. 2014. "Talk is cheap: Ethnography and the attitudinal fallacy." *Sociological Methods and Research* 43(2): 178–209.

Lauria, Mickey, and Lawrence Knopp. 1985. "Toward an analysis of the role of gay communities in the urban renaissance." *Urban Geography* 6(2): 152–69.

Savin-Williams, Ritch C. 2006. "Who's gay? Does it matter?" *Current Directions in Psychological Science* 15(1): 40–44.

Staver, Sari. 2015. "Castro retail survey shows neighborhood could be getting less gay." *Hoodline,* May 21. http://hoodline.com/2015/05/castro-retail-survey-shows-neighborhood-could-be-getting-less-gay.

Vaisey, Steven. 2008. "Socrates, Skinner, and Aristotle: Three ways of thinking about culture in action." *Sociological Forum* 23(3): 603–13.

Ward, Jane. 2015. *Not gay: Sex between straight white men.* New York: New York University Press.

Whittemore, Andrew H., and Michael J. Smart. 2016. "Mapping gay and lesbian neighborhoods using home advertisements: Change and continuity in the Dallas–Fort Worth metropolitan statistical area over three decades." *Environment and Planning A* 48(1): 192–210.

13 Queer Persistence in the Archive

Amy L. Stone

I am unaccustomed to being in the closet.

But there is room for only one person in this closet, tucked under the concrete stairs of the local theater company in San Antonio, Texas, just a few blocks from my home. The narrow space is crammed with sagging cardboard boxes stacked from the floor to the height of my shoulders. I'm wearing an air mask that I brought from home because of mold issues. My two undergraduate research assistants stand outside waiting for me to pass them boxes. Years ago a disgruntled theater employee dumped all the office files haphazardly into boxes, such that nothing was in alphabetical or logical order. We sort through each box, at times taking pictures of items with my iPad camera on a folding table. I'm looking for something specific—a set of scripts and programs from the 1950s and 1960s written by gay men who put on a mock debutante pageant called Cornyation for a public audience. I have been obsessively looking for these scripts all summer, pursuing all leads with a persistent fervor.

I startle my students when I begin yelling. I'm holding a manila envelope labeled with the name of the show that I have just found in a disintegrating cardboard box. Holding the thick and glorious envelope, I marvel at this archival pay-dirt moment. We all rush to our folding table, my assistants hovering over me as I pull a stack of folders out of the envelope. I randomly open a folder labeled "1953" and find multiple copies of the script from that year on thin typewriter paper. Sitting underneath the concrete theater stairs, covered in dust, I feel chills running up and down my arms as I touch documents written and handled by the men who ran the show in the 1950s.

I never thought archival research would feel this way.

This moment reminds me of the most important thing I have learned about archival research, the value of queer persistence. To find archival pay dirt as researchers, we have to literally dig for it. To persist, we have to follow leads relentlessly, research in unexpected places, make alliances, and push through self-doubt. For me, an Anglo genderqueer researcher studying the South, research is profoundly embodied and affective: the process of discovery is rich with emotion that has revealed my own deep investments in queer history.

The necessity for persistence in queer archival research emerges from the challenges of queer historical research. The structural forces that marginalized queer communities historically have also hidden and obscured queer history, leading to omissions or obfuscations of historical documents in established archives. In my research, geography informs the availability of archives on local queer history, leading to the importance of persistence and serendipity in research outside the queer geographic center. My archival research has frequently involved finding sources in attics and closets. I've developed a rapport with informants so that they trust me to handle their emotionally dense materials safely. Archival research can be just as embodied, emotional, and relational as qualitative methods like ethnography and interviewing.

This chapter focuses on queer geographies, persistence, relations, emotions, and investments as complex parts of the archival research process. My insights come from a major current project, a four-city comparison of LGBT participation in citywide festivals in the Southwest and Gulf South. I have been studying the celebration of the Carnival season or Mardi Gras in Baton Rouge, Louisiana, and Mobile, Alabama; I compare these festivities to the southwestern historical pageantry of Fiesta in San Antonio, Texas, and Santa Fe, New Mexico. My central question concerns whether or not these festivals are sites in which LGBT people assert themselves as valued members of the city as a form of cultural citizenship. Many of my archival insights come from researching a San Antonio Fiesta event called Cornyation, a mock debutante pageant started by gay men in the 1950s that turned into a major HIV-AIDS fund-raiser in the 1990s. This project began with my fascination with this show and its prominence during my city's annual festival. The project combines interview, ethnographic, and archival research to capture the history and contemporary nature of festival life in two understudied regions. The geography of this project, in the urban South and Southwest, shapes the availability of archival materials.

FROM THE CENTER TO THE MARGINS: QUEER GEOGRAPHIES

In his germinal work on the history of gay life in prewar New York City, George Chauncey described the methodological problems of studying gay history as "unusually daunting" (1994: 365) because of the dispersion of relevant sources across the city and lack of cataloguing. Many established archives—government repositories, university collections, public libraries— have historically neglected the intentional collection and cataloguing of items pertaining to LGBT history. To complicate things further, some types of queer history—that which is publicly visible, white, and male—tend to be privileged within archival materials. To compensate for this imbalance, LGBT activists founded counterarchives (Cvetkovich 2003), creating such institutions as the Lesbian Herstory Archives, ONE Archives, and the GLBT Historical Society, along with specialized collections at established institutions such as the Cornell University Human Sexuality Collection. These archives collect materials about LGBT history across the United States and abroad, but the strength of their focus is typically regional history. Most of these counterarchives and specialized collections are located in the major metropolitan areas in the US West or Northeast. There are some exceptions, including excellent collections on queer history at the Tulane University and Duke University archives, and counterarchives in Houston and San Antonio. Many of the counterarchives are not institutionalized and are run by a devoted person or couple with no training in preservation or archives. This archival geography shapes my research experience. Due to the topics I study and the places where I study them, most of my archival research involves sitting in strangers' dining rooms sifting through dusty boxes or climbing into closets with a hazard mask on to find materials.

My research on LGBT history and community has focused on the urban Midwest, South, and Southwest. I'm less interested in exceptionally tolerant cities than "normal cities," the urban experience that typifies where most LGBT people live. I think studying these normal cities provides more-generalizable insight into how LGBT people negotiate urban spaces and communities. Thus, I've spent more time in Baton Rouge than New Orleans; more time in Mobile, Alabama, than Atlanta, Georgia. Scholars have critiqued LGBT history for being metronormative; to that I would add that a few "vanguard" cities—New York, San Francisco, Los Angeles, Chicago—get the majority of this metronormative academic attention. The detailed historical research from vanguard cities can be instructive. For example, George Chauncey's *Gay New York* (1994) informed my research on the YMCA and bars in majority-black neighborhoods as sites of Cold War queer community building.

This emphasis on vanguard cities can also lead, however, to epistemological and methodological blind spots. Scholarly teleology of queer historical development relies on vanguard cities, inadvertently positioning other cities and places as on the same developmental trajectory yet lagging behind. Not even all vanguard cities follow the same pattern of development; Timothy Stewart-Winter's (2015) work on gay and lesbian organizing in Chicago challenges existing narratives of racial coalition building and the gay liberation movement, which are based almost exclusively on New York City movement organizing.

Studying outside the vanguard requires us as scholars to identify new patterns of community formation, question timelines of cultural and political development, and investigate new cultural forms. Ultimately, this research challenges existing narratives of urban LGBT life. First, while studying 1950s and 1960s gay and lesbian history in San Antonio, I noticed that a few bars were located outside the city limits as a way to evade police oversight. The country became a place of privacy and escape where gay men and lesbians retreated for the weekend to dance, play softball, or swim in the pool. The image of New York bars, which were in the city center and run by the Mafia, and entrenched understandings of the city as a gay haven do not adequately capture the experience of gay men and lesbians leaving the city to go to bars. This creative use of rural spaces by urban queers challenges existing metronormative narratives that emerge from studying the vanguard.

Second, while conducting my research, I became acutely aware that not all queer cultural innovation originates in the vanguard and spreads to the margins. In San Antonio, Cornyation, a show replete with campy style, was performed for a public audience of thousands in the 1950s and early 1960s—before similar events were staged in New York or San Francisco. Third, some indigenous cultural forms may never have existed in vanguard cities but may nevertheless be central to the study of queer life. The oldest queer organizations in both Baton Rouge and Mobile are, respectively, a chapter of the Metropolitan Community Church and a Carnival organization ("krewe" or "mystic society"). In Mobile, mystic societies for gay men began as early as the late 1950s. These societies are definitely a southern cultural form, though they are similar to secret societies and fraternities. Instead of viewing carnival participation as temporary or just the carnivalesque, I see these cultural events as embedded in the regional and local history of carnival and the way carnival as a cultural structure shapes city life. Even queer cultural forms that seem rooted in vanguard-city culture are shaped by regional and local cultures; drag in the South is shaped by southern traditions of pageantry and debutantes (Thompson 2010).

Queer geographies shape my ability to access archived collections, the kinds of questions I ask, and the social forms I study. Archival research in normal cities also requires pushing past epistemological assumptions and engaging in creative discovery of materials.

JUST KEEP SWIMMING: QUEER PERSISTENCE

As a graduate student I pictured archival research as the contemplative experience of working in an archival reading room surrounded by other researchers and connected to an archivist who catalogued the materials. I have spent hundreds of hours in universities, libraries, and counterarchives across the country. However, most of my research has involved finding sources buried within conventional archives or, more often, connecting with individuals who own historical documents. I've developed what I call *queer persistence*—relentlessly following leads, researching in unexpected places, pushing past self-doubt—a practice that has proved overwhelmingly productive.

I'm not the first person to think of queer research or, indeed, queer life as requiring persistence. Many queer scholars have persisted within homophobic and transphobic institutional settings; in her eulogy for theorist José Esteban Muñoz after his sudden death, Lauren Berlant (2014) remarked on his persistence as a scholar, defying odds, seeking the elusive future. Queer archival persistence combines doggedness and serendipity in order to find queer history in unusual places, the researcher believing that queer archives could be anywhere and anything. Jack Halberstam describes the archive that scholars doggedly assembled on the life of Brandon Teena as "simultaneously a resource, a productive narrative, a set of representations, a history, a memorial, and a time capsule" (2005: 23).

Such doggedness entails not letting our research be squashed by fear, homophobia, or erasure, and that requires quelling that voice inside us that discourages inquiry and exploration. I encounter self-doubt and hesitation when I contact archivists and individuals about queer history. Yet I push myself to look for explicit or potential collections on queer history at all existing archives in a given city. Hidden within museums, public libraries, rare-book collections, university archives, and collections on festival history, archival gems are to be found. I never know if I'm going to run into a homophobic dismissal or the enthusiastic support of archivists at places such as the library on the site of the Alamo. Sometimes, archives have unexpected queer collections; I have pored over albums of men in drag at public libraries in the Deep South.

At other times, I've had to convince myself that archival materials stubbornly persist, which is how I ended up in a theater closet looking for scripts that had eluded me all summer. I knew that the Cornyation show had been organized in the 1950s by a theater company that still exists. The company donated many of its files from this time period to a theater collection that was part of a defunct circus and performing arts archive. I spent weeks emailing and calling archivists before I found the theater archive in the genealogy collection at the downtown public library. Buried in those files were a few pictures and programs, but no scripts. My students tracked down the one scriptwriter who was still alive, an Anglo woman in her seventies named Squeaky, who remembered that the theater had asked her to mail her copy of the script in the 1960s. I spent two months getting ahold of the theater's executive director, who said I could look through its closet of "old stuff." I set my two competent undergraduate researchers to work digging through the closet of boxes. I ended up with scans and copies of scripts, office files, budgets, and cast lists for shows from the 1950s and 1960s. The scripts were full of campy, coded, transgressive language. My analysis of the script mobilized both my childhood experience of discerning coded queer references in movies and television and my scholarly knowledge of Cold War gay culture in the United States.

Finding these scripts would not have been possible without a growing social network of supportive individuals. It takes a proverbial village to study history, and I quickly began to imagine my project as a web of people, documents, stories, and knowledge extending throughout the city. Persistence, then, is having the bravery to ask everyone about my project, from my next-door neighbor to the cashier at the grocery store. Some of my most insightful interviews about San Antonio gay life in the fifties and sixties came from an octogenarian Anglo man who had been a hairdresser in the 1950s, and an Anglo heterosexual woman who was a member of the social elite; I got in touch with them through my retired gay Latino neighbor, whom I told about the project while walking my dogs.

My rule of thumb in this sort of historical research is to follow all leads, regardless of how dubious they may appear. I would rather waste my time on a dead end than miss an unexpected opportunity. When an interviewee asked if he could bring his closeted octogenarian friend to the interview, I learned the most astonishing information about gay involvement in elite Mardi Gras organizations. When someone suggested that I talk to the gay son of a Cornyation participant from the 1950s, I unexpectedly left the meeting with a stack of 18 mm home movies, which included the only recorded footage of the 1960s show. Making a historical project visible to the broader public increases your chances of finding information. Early in the project I gave talks about Cornyation at the public library and a museum, presentations that were advertised in the city newspapers. After these events I received emails from former participants in the show.

My interviews have taught me to be more attentive to personal archives. I bring several devices for scanning or photographing materials—often a tablet, camera, and wand scanner—because archival materials, such as programs from early political meetings or the flag from the first Pride march, are often casually pulled out during interviews. Use of these documents involves complex negotiation. Sometimes I facilitate the transfer of private materials to local archives. During one interview, the minute I walked in the door, the informant handed me a box full of records that he had painstakingly collected showing police entrapment of men in local parks in the 1990s. He didn't know what to do with them, and he expressed relief at giving them to me, as though pleased that his child was finally going to a good foster home. More often, I negotiate the scanning or other use of materials without removing them from people's homes. Negotiations about confidentiality, secrecy, and trust that happen during interviews are critical for handling these documents, which often have full names and revealing details about individuals.

This queer persistence is challenging on multiple levels. At times this work reminds me of ethnographic research: the challenge I feel as an introvert pushing myself to connect with strangers, ask for favors, and negotiate complex social relationships is inherent in both forms of research. These interactions are replete with my own emotions and my informants' affective connections to the past.

QUEER RELATIONS AND EMOTIONS

The entire archival experience for me is an embodied and affective one. In *Bodies of Evidence: The Practice of Queer Oral History,* editors Nan Boyd and Horacio Ramírez (2012) argue that the body is central to queer history practice and the production of queer historical knowledge. Heather Love (2009) and Ann Cvetkovich (2003) have argued that the project of queer history is affective. My own research has felt exhilarating, saddening, frustrating, and uplifting at different moments. The pay-dirt moment of archival discovery feels like the endorphin high of riding a roller coaster or the excitement of college graduation. The frustration of a missed connection makes me question the endeavor entirely.

This affective experience is related to handling documents, which "carry with them an aggregate, temporal stickiness that accrues through each reading and interpretation" (Stone & Cantrell 2015: 11). Informants often have deep sentimental attachments to their queer memorabilia, which contain experiences of coming out, shame, discovery, joy, transgression, death, and transformation. Navigating the owners' emotional attachment to objects is critical to building trust. I felt this acutely when I sifted through a remarkable collection of early gay and lesbian historical documents at the home of an elderly Latina *lesbiana* in San Antonio. She allowed me to scan the documents on-site. However, when I broached the subject of donating them to the university archives, she touched the folder I was holding gingerly, looked me in the eyes, and said, "I'm not ready to let go of them yet." And indeed letting go is the hardest part.

In the Gulf South one summer, I spent a long afternoon in a storage unit thinking about anxiety, grief, and letting go. My student and I were meeting with Dawn, a white lesbian in her late sixties and longtime member of an LGBT Mardi Gras mystic society who was also the group's historian on its board. Mystic societies frequently have rules about secrecy, including wearing masks at public events, never using full names, and having no pictures taken by guests. I waited until I had been attending events for over a year before I asked the board for access to the archives, with promises of security and confidentiality. While I was in town, I met with Dawn in the archives, the aforementioned storage unit, packed floor to ceiling on one side with cases of alcohol and the other side with plastic and cardboard boxes of material: shirts, old posters, photograph albums, engraved plastic cups with ball themes, and piles of beads. Dawn was open and generous with some of the materials; my research assistant and I received ephemera from old events, including a poster from the 1990s. But other materials evoked anxiety about the process. Whenever we sort through old photo albums of ball costuming in the 1980s, I'm cautious about photographing them, asking constantly, "Can I take a picture of this one? He's wearing a mask," After the meeting with Dawn, I left somewhat dissatisfied, as there were important materials that she dismissed as insignificant or asked me not to photograph as too revealing. But I was also acutely aware while working with Dawn that for her, each picture from the 1980s was one of a suddenly departed friend. In the 1980s and 1990s most festival organizations were run by gay men, and these organizations were devastated by the HIV-AIDS pandemic. Archival research was always rife with memories of the dead. The specter of HIV-AIDS hung over us, unspoken, as we sifted through the documents haphazardly.

I think of this affective attachment months later while sitting in José's home in San Antonio. I have been in José's living room before, watching him smoke a pack of Marlboros and drink vodka while he waxed poetic about doing drag makeup and dresses in the 1970s. During this visit, he tearfully tells me about his brother, a well-known drag queen in South Texas who was brutally stabbed to death decades ago. José learned how to do his brother's hair and makeup at a drag bar called the Ponderosa, a club with a predominately Latino clientele located on the outskirts of San Antonio. I'm drawn in by his narrative about the bar. I mention briefly that I wish I could have gone to the Ponderosa to see the drag show, and his face lights up. "I have pictures, honey," he says, which makes my skin tingle. He tells me a complex story of a man with the nickname "Mother" who took pictures of the drag acts at the bars. When Mother died, he gave the pictures and negatives to a trans woman named Crystal, who then gave them to José. José gave away many of the best pictures and admits that he threw some away out of regret and sadness for the dead. "Why am I alive and they're not?" he asks. But he pulls out three photo albums full of rich photographs of the bar, its inhabitants, and various drag shows, including a Queen of Soul pageant that drew black drag queens from across Texas. Negotiating the scanning of the photographs takes several months, and donating them to an archive is unthinkable. The photographs are indelibly connected to José's brother, his artistry, and potential financial remuneration. What facilitates the use of the photos is having an undergraduate research assistant interview him and write an article about the Ponderosa for a local magazine. When the magazine came out, José called me in tears. "You made me look so good," he said. I wondered if the magazine article symbolized an acknowledgment of the importance of both his and his brother's queer artistry.

As an archival researcher, I'm constantly aware that even in the present, the dead are with us. There are moments in doing archival research when the process feels infused with a queer form of grief, bringing tears to my eyes as I leaf through documents and touch people's private belongings. These feelings are not just present mindfulness, but also feeling backward into a past that is relevant to me. Archival research has included wrangling with my investments in a queer past.

FINDING MYSELF TOO: QUEER INVESTMENTS

I once burst into tears at a meeting with a key informant, a Latino gay man, when he told me I was too focused on the gay aspects of festival events. "It doesn't really matter," he told me. "What does being gay have to do with anything anyway?" My tears were partly due to personal turmoil, but they were also fed by the disavowal of the importance of queerness. Queer archival research involves both interpretive challenges to studying the past and the challenge of our own investments.

Initially, queer historical studies was profoundly concerned with interpretive issues, about how to decipher a historical figure as bisexual, homosexual, or heterosexual, a debate that continues today. I experienced this interpretive challenge when researching the designers of Cornyation in the 1950s and 1960s. I dug through genealogy documents to figure out where they were born, lived, and died; whether they served in World War II or the Korean War; and how old they were when they participated in the show. I found that most of them were middle-aged, unmarried veterans who had extensive experience traveling and living in other parts of the country. They were self-employed or worked in gay ghetto occupations like window dressing or hairstyling. They fit easily into tropes of the sophisticated, artistic white gay man of this era studied by other scholars.

However, a second question has become more critical to queer history: why do we care so much about finding a queer past? My queer investments were most acute in my own city, San Antonio. When I first went to see the show Cornyation, I was surprised by the "royalty" at the event: the King Anchovy that year was the city manager, dressed up in a superhero costume, stiletto boots, a cape, and a wig. I wondered immediately how the gay and lesbian community had enough political power to convince the city manager to perform on stage with them to raise money for HIV-AIDS and other causes. Intellectually I was intrigued, but watching the show was also my first moment of ecstatic queer connection with the San Antonio queer community.

I had just transplanted to Texas. As a California native, I had never imagined that I could feel at home in Texas. But having moved to San Antonio, I immediately loved much about my new hometown: the comfort of living in a Hispanic-majority city again, the variety of art and cultural activities, delicious food, the affordable housing. I had not yet found a place in the local LGBT community for my transgressive queer self. I felt too politically exhausted to join the fierce Latina *lesbiana* political community; too transgressive for the gay and lesbian community; too genderqueer for the transgender community. And I didn't even try to fit into the butch-femme dating scene. Watching the Cornyation show, I felt connected for the first time to a transgressive, irreverent queer subculture. When exploring the show's deep roots going back to the 1950s, I felt an irrevocable connection to all that came before me, a sense of my own history. It brought into my life a profound respect for celebration and playfulness. I think the search for queer history is often driven by our desire to feel part of something larger than ourselves, and this research served that need for me. I cried in front of my informant, because I wanted that history to be queer; I needed queerness to matter.

Just as reflexivity is critical for all other sociological methods, so is it for archival methods. Pinpointing our investments allows scholars to be reflexive about our epistemological approach and assumptions. Whether we are invested in a queer past or not, our assumptions of what we want to find shape our endeavor.

RETHINKING THE ARCHIVE

Archival research on queer history is itself queer. It evokes older meanings of the word *queer* in the sense that archival experiences can be odd or troubling or can spoil existing understandings of history and the archive (Stone & Cantrell 2015). Archival research is shaped by the structural conditions of queer life—by a history of erasure, coded language, and closeting that at times renders queer history illegible on paper. These structures influence the geography of queer research as well as our emotions, relations, and investments.

Yet despite these troubling structures, queer archival research unfolds itself to us in a delightful adventure. When I speak to students about queer archival research, I spout aphorisms of encouragement that make me feel like an overenthusiastic yoga teacher. Breathe into it. You can do it. Hang in there. Enthusiasm aside, my experience lends itself to a few key suggestions about how to pursue archival research on queer history.

First, where you are matters. Be aware of the ways your geography shapes your research, not just in the availability of materials but also in the epistemological approach you take to understanding queer history.

Second, *be* where you are. I encourage fellow scholars using queer archival materials to experience the archive fully, with awareness of the site's embodied and emotional aspects. Reading documents full of anger, grief, shame, and joy can evoke complex feelings in ourselves as well. The journey taken to find these documents may feel like an experience in which queer history and your own scholarship is delegitimated. Sometimes this affective experience is more akin to emotional labor than to the delight of discovery. With this self-awareness should come awareness of your own positionality. What is comprehensible to you as queer is shaped by your own social location. Be aware of yourself and your own investments in the project.

Third, be aware that archival research can be profoundly social, which breaks up some of this method's isolation. You are not alone in this endeavor. Also, these social relations can be complicated as you negotiate access to emotionally complex documents and stories.

Last but not least, to summarize my advice about archival research succinctly: "Don't be afraid to ask." Being aware of your own emotions and investments allows you to push through the places where research is profoundly uncomfortable; on the other side of this discomfort, there may be the delight of discovery. Be persistent.

WORKS CITED

Berlant, Lauren. 2014. "On persistence." *Social Text* 32(4): 33–37.

Boyd, Nan Alamilla, and Horacio N. Roque Ramírez (eds.). 2012. *Bodies of evidence: The practice of queer oral history.* New York: Oxford University Press.

Chauncey, George. 1994. *Gay New York: Gender, urban culture, and the making of the gay male world, 1890–1940*. New York: Basic Books.

Cvetkovich, Ann. 2003. *An archive of feelings: Trauma, sexuality, and lesbian public cultures*. Durham, NC: Duke University Press.

Halberstam, Jack. 2005. *In a queer time and place: Transgender bodies, subcultural lives*. New York: New York University Press.

Love, Heather. 2009. *Feeling backward*. Cambridge, MA: Harvard University Press.

Stewart-Winter, Timothy. 2015. *Queer clout: Chicago and the rise of gay politics*. Philadelphia: University of Pennsylvania Press.

Stone, Amy L., and Jaime Cantrell. 2015. "Introduction: Something queer at the archive." In *Out of the closet, into the archives: Researching sexual histories*. Ed. Amy L. Stone and Jaime Cantrell. Albany: State University of New York Press.

Thompson, Brock. *The un-natural state: Arkansas and the queer South*. Fayetteville: University of Arkansas Press, 2010.

14 Gendering Carnal Ethnography

A QUEER RECEPTION

Kimberly Kay Hoang

Loïc Wacquant's (1995, 2011) concept "carnal sociology" refers to the practice of putting one's self and body at the epicenter of an array of material and symbolic forces in order to understand and theorize a social phenomenon. Carnal ethnography takes seriously the embodied practice in ethnography in order to theorize social phenomena. It is "a sociology not of the body but from the body" (Wacquant 2005: 446). However, carnal ethnographies are articulated mostly on masculine terms and with hyperattention to violence (Collins 2015; Small 2015). Male scholars who trained as a boxer (Wacquant 1995) or performed or posed as a swing dancer (Hancock 2007), gang member (Venkatesh 2008), firefighter (Desmond 2009), or drug robber (Contreras 2013, 2015) draw out their masculinity to demonstrate access, prowess, and legitimacy in their respective field sites. But what happens when a researcher occupies a gendered site where the body is not valorized as psychologically affirming or culturally appropriate via academic or wider normative standards?

For some feminine-centered research, carnal ethnography is a destabilizing enterprise. Scholars who take on an abject gendered position must negotiate the boundaries around their participation in the field and their presentation of self to the wider academy. Scholars of carnal sociology have not engaged with parallel feminist writings on the body, and for the most part, they ignore carnal sociology's relationship to feminist thought (Cobb & Hoang 2015; Hoang 2015; Pitts-Taylor 2015). Drawing inspiration from Pierre Bourdieu's idea of symbolic force, this chapter focuses on how carnal ethnography's association with hypermasculinity obscures some of the complexities of carnal ethnographies gendered as feminine. Though intensely embodied, neither Ashley Mears's ethnography on the modeling industry (2011) nor Katherine Frank's ethnography of strip clubs (2002) have been included in a conversation on carnal ethnography.

In this chapter, I describe the gendered practice of carnal sociology for my book, *Dealing in Desire: Asian Ascendancy, Western Decline, and the Hidden Currencies of Global Sex Work* (2015). My commitment to feminine embodied transformations provides insight into gendered relations of desire that affected me as a researcher in the field. I begin by describing the practicalities of fieldwork that led me to embrace a carnal method of ethnography and the daily rituals involved in my carnal experience. I then describe how my research subjects and I actively subjected ourselves to *symbolic violence* in order to make ourselves desirable under various male gazes. Drawing on Bourdieu, I consider symbolic violence as a gendered relation of subordination and domination often between men and women that reproduces a gendered hierarchy both consciously and unconsciously (Bourdieu 2004: 33). In short, while masculine-centered and feminine-centered ethnographies require the researcher to inhabit space differently, we must unpack the ways that men work to draw out hypermasculinity by gaining strength, becoming a leader, or becoming someone to reckon with in the field, while women must do the opposite; they must learn to subtract by losing weight, eating less, talking less, taking up less space, and being less assertive. These gendered divisions in turn bring about different tensions, struggles, and trade-offs when stepping out of the field and into an academic setting.

DEALING IN DESIRE

Dealing in Desire (Hoang 2015) examines the relationship between gender and global capital flows in four different hostess bars in Ho Chi Minh City, Vietnam. Hostess bars are part of a nightlife industry that primarily employs female workers to cater to males seeking drinks, attentive conversations, and in the case of these bars, sexual activity. I conducted twenty-two months of ethnographic research for this project in two main phases, 2006–7 and 2009–10. In the first phase, I conducted seven months of field research in which I was more of an *observer* from the outside than a participant. I identified myself as a researcher and, with the bar owners' and workers' consent, I took careful notes on the interactions between clients and sex workers, enabling me to examine the complexities of their relationships. This allowed for a kind of in-depth analysis that would otherwise be lost in interviews that were often one-sided and focused on sex workers.

I first spent time in local bars and on the streets to meet and develop rapport with various sex workers, clients, and bar owners in order to map out the different kinds of bars within this field. Being an overseas Vietnamese woman helped me gain access to female sex workers, because many of them saw me as nonthreatening compared to local Vietnamese; if any of the latter arrived and began asking questions, many workers would assume they were either undercover police or local journalists. All of the women knew that I was a researcher from the United States but did not seem to find it important; they cared more about my family history and my life overseas—information that would help them situate me in their mental universe. However, as an outside observer, I did not have access to the interactions backstage (Goffman 1959) where hostess workers could relax and break out of character from the performance they put on for clients during their service interactions. While I was able to gather rich information about the intimate relationships between clients and sex workers, I was unable to examine the organizational structure within the bar or the complex set of relationships among sex workers, bar owners, madams (locally referred to as mommies) who ran the bars, police, mafia, and clients. At times, I felt that I was only skimming the surface.

To dig deeper, I moved from participant *observation* to conducting a carnal ethnography that involved subjecting my body to the daily work rituals of the women in my study. Carnal ethnography transforms the habitus of the researcher. As Wacquant writes, "So many facets of the phenomenon can best be revealed by the body, in the very enactment of [the research] . . . in the cast of the investigator—because they are woven into the very fabric of *urgent yet banal action*" (2015: 6; emphasis in original). Putting one's body into the research process involves an *enactive ethnography*, or an "immersive fieldwork based on 'performing the phenomenon' [in order to theorize] the cosmos under investigation"(2). In other words, I gained much deeper insights into the embodied experiences of my research participants when I subjected my own body to similar demands. In my experience, carnal ethnography involved gendered relations of *symbolic force*, "a form of power that is exerted on bodies, directly and as if by magic, without any physical constraint; but this magic works only on the basis of the dispositions deposited ... at the deepest level of the body" (Bourdieu 1998: 38). In a feminine-centered carnal ethnography with such hyperattention to female bodies as objects of desire for men, I subjected myself to the daily rituals of symbolic violence in order to gain deep access to my field sites.

DAILY RITUALS OF CARNAL ETHNOGRAPHY

As an ethnographer navigating intimate and highly gendered social spaces, I needed to find a way to position myself differently in relation to the multiple actors who operated in these spaces. In embracing carnal ethnography, I spent twelve hours a day for two to three months in each bar, and I wrote my field notes every morning before returning to the bar. I was not paid a wage by any of the bar owners. However, I earned $100 to $500 a month through client tips. This amount was much less than the other women earned, because I spent a significant amount of time interviewing women backstage.

In the bars, my duties included serving drinks, sitting with clients, singing karaoke, and standing in the line-up as men chose the women to invite to their tables. As a Vietnamese American woman born in the United States, I could never pass as a local Vietnamese, but I learned how to adjust my gait, serve, take orders, smile when people criticized my weight, and remain silent when men inhabited my personal bodily space. I was also ten years older than most of the sex workers and overweight according to local standards, which made me nonthreatening to the women and enabled my rapport with them. My acts of public subordination to the men and my secondary role in support of the women and the establishment were crucial in opening doors to workers' and clients' intimate feelings and secrets.

Although I expected to adapt to the rituals and styles of each bar, I could not have anticipated how throwing myself into these social worlds would change my body and myself. Drawing inspiration from Wacquant, I expected to gain deeper insights from carnal ethnography. However, the literature did not quite capture my experience of taking on a devalued role rather than an expansive masculine role that garners credibility and a sense of toughness in the field. Like any new worker starting out in the bars, I could count on no one to teach me the rules of the game. I had to put myself into the work and watch, learn, and manage myself to figure out how to survive.

On my first night of work in Lavender, I had no idea what to wear. I put on a pink dress with a high neck and an open back and a pair of black, three-inch high heels. I arranged my makeup and hair as I would to go out to a bar or club in the United States, but the other workers quickly informed me that I did not embody this bar's appropriate aesthetic. As a favor to the bar owner, Dung, one of the workers, helped me pick out another dress, style my hair, and apply my makeup. After this initial hiccup, I paid makeup artists to teach me how to apply cosmetics properly for the first two weeks in each bar. Moreover, each of the four bars had a different aesthetic ideal that I had to quickly adopt. In the bars that cater to Asian businessmen and overseas Vietnamese, the workers taught me how embrace a pan-Asian ideal. I learned to apply foundation, contour my face to make it look less round and more chiseled, draw on thicker eyebrows for a youthful look, apply eye shadow, eyeliner, and fake eyelashes, and outline my lips with multiple shades of lip-liner and then fill them in with different colors of lipstick. This aesthetic was shaped by new ideals of beauty imported from South Korea. In the bars that catered to Western men, in contrast, I spent hours learning how to darken my complexion and work with various shades of eye shadow to create a smoky effect. As the makeup artists took on my face, a hair stylist taught me how to blow-dry, curl, and style my hair so that it would accentuate my cheekbones and add two inches of height to my short stature. Essentially, I learned how to embody and perform *Third World dependence.* The practice of putting my face on each day forced me to position myself in relationship to local ideals of desire that were foreign to me.

In the field, when I looked in the dressing room mirror at each bar, I saw a woman who did not reflect the image of myself that I had in my head. As Yen-Vy, an eighteen-year-old sex worker in Khong Sao Bar (which catered to wealthy local Vietnamese men), explained to me, "For the first few days you will see a different person in the mirror [pointing to the reflection of my newly made-up face]. You should get to know *that girl*." It took me several weeks to get used to "that girl." This embodied process enabled me to learn the transformation undertaken by apprentice workers and see much that I would otherwise have overlooked. For example, for many of the shy, reserved, and quiet sex workers I interviewed, the practice of getting to know "that girl" was the first step to feeling free, more outgoing, and able to entertain outside the boundaries of "proper femininity." The makeup was also a cloak that allowed them to embrace an external beauty that affected their inner confidence. Hanh, the head madam at Khong Sao Bar, explained, "People are attracted to beautiful people with positive energy. When you look good, you feel good about yourself and people will want to be around that."

Once my hair and makeup were complete, my co-workers taught me how to dress in the appropriate undergarments, anew in each bar. At Khong Sao and Lavender, every bra was carefully fitted to accentuate workers' breasts. Women who weighed more than one hundred pounds were taught to buy tight corsets to pull in their waists. The uncomfortable corset served as a constant reminder that I needed to carefully monitor my diet and eat less in order to lose weight. While I did not wear the tight corsets in Secrets (another of the bars), across all four of the bars the women all sat around in their undergarments while we ate lunch together before the start of the workday. Lunch generally consisted of one of three choices: a small bowl of noodles, a papaya salad, or chicken with rice. These meals were hand-delivered to the back room by local street vendors. The unspoken norm in the bar was to eat only enough to absorb the alcohol that we would consume over a twelve-hour workday.

Following lunch, the women gathered the outfits they had either packed in their bags or had delivered from a tailor through the back door. At both Khong Sao Bar and Lavender, the most elite of the bars I studied, the women adorned themselves in tailored, red carpet–ready dresses. These garments were far from comfortable as the tailors purposely made them extremely tightfitting in the waist; the only way to breathe was to sit perfectly straight. Each day after putting on my dress, I walked from the front to the back of the dressing room several times to check my posture and become comfortable with the dress's movement. I learned to do this after the back seam of a dress ripped one afternoon and a madam scolded me for my bad posture. My own embodied transformation made me far more attuned to the different ways that hostess workers across the four bars embodied specific kinds of class-based femininities, conveying either pan-Asian modernity or Third World dependence. Hostess workers in bars that catered to elite Vietnamese and Asian businessmen were to embody high-status luxury, and their job was to evoke a celebrity-like feeling for their clients. In bars that catered to Westerners, tailors handmade sexy versions of the traditional Vietnamese *ao dai* dress, while in Naughty Girls (the fourth bar), workers wore shorts and tank tops that were far more comfortable, conveying a sense of Third World dependence.

Clients typically started to arrive at the bars at 2:00 P.M., beginning the daily ritual of drinking and entertaining. In Khong Sao and Lavender, once the clients were seated in their karaoke room or at a table, Hanh (the madam) called the women to line up in front of the clients' tables. Standing in the lineup, we watched as the men deliberated among themselves about which hostess to sit with for the night. The most aesthetically desirable women were selected first. The madam then worked to sell to the men at the tables the charismatic qualities of the women not yet chosen. I was never chosen in the first round, so Hanh, Xinh, and Hong (the three mommies in Khong Sao Bar) tried to help me find a place at a table by telling clients, "She can sing American songs with a perfect [American] accent, and she is very good at *su ngau* [a Chinese-Vietnamese drinking game]."

As the least-attractive hostess worker in the bars that catered to Western men, I had to rely a great deal on my abilities to pour drinks and to speak and sing in English. Male clients told me that they invited me to their tables because they were curious to see how far a Vietnamese American was willing to go in sacrificing a respectable femininity to make it in this underground economy. I went from wearing conservative clothes that covered most of my body to adopting short dresses and skirts that made me feel far more exposed. The carnal transformations I underwent in the bars drew me into a set of objectifying and sexualizing rituals under the male clients' powerful gaze. I became a part of the very gendered processes I was studying, exposing my body to judgment every time a group of men came into the bar. This work required a deep form of emotional labor. I watched as women smiled away tears as men ridiculed their bodies. I learned to bow my head and cover my face to hide facial expressions of embarrassment or shame. Such subtle moments repeated over and over again made me feel unattractive, invisible, and insecure. I was not a powerful boxer in this ring; rather, I was someone who took invisible punches, often without much resistance.

In the four bars where I worked, my body and, in particular, my weight were subjected to intense scrutiny. The task of balancing twelve to fourteen working hours of heavy drinking with a strict exercise and diet routine pushed me into a frenzied mental state. I worked frantically to drop ten pounds by eating very small meals throughout the day and by attending the gym four days a week to run for an hour or take a ninety-minute hot yoga class. These practices opened my eyes to the extensive ways that women labored over their bodies backstage to achieve the desirable aesthetics on the frontstage that kept them employed.

The work of entertaining took other physical tolls. Hostess workers built a high tolerance for whiskey by lining their stomach with ginger and drinking a host of herbal supplements. When clients mixed whiskey with beer, we made sure to vomit at the end of the evening to avoid a severe hangover the next day. After spending twelve to fourteen hours a day for nine months in rooms filled with cigarette smoke, I developed bronchitis and pneumonia, which forced me to scale back my research so that in the last bar I studied, Naughty Girls, I visited only three or four days a week.

To manage the grueling rituals of drinking alongside the demands of ethnography, I spent a great deal of time in the bars on my phone writing short field notes about important moments and conversations to jog my memory the next morning. My daily routine was deeply embedded in my field site. Aside from the few friends I made in the sex industry, my personal relationships were all put on hold. For nearly fifteen months, I got to know Ho Chi Minh City's nightlife very intimately. As I went deeper into this transformative embodied experience, I forced myself to adhere to a strict daily morning routine. I woke up every morning between 7:00 and 8:00 to have a light breakfast, drink ginger tea, and begin writing field notes on the previous day. The process of writing these notes was cathartic because it was the one place where I could check in with my sociologist self and reflect on the kind of data that I was generating as well as new questions that emerged during my evenings in the field.

SYMBOLIC VIOLENCE

The bars were all spaces where "men bond over their ability to objectify hostesses with no admonishment" (Parrenas 2011). It is easy to imagine these bars as spaces where women might be vulnerable to sexual assault, rape, or coerced sexual transactions arranged by madams or pimps. Outside the bars, hostesses were not entirely immune from sexual or physical violence from male clients. However, overt violence was extremely rare inside these bars because the bar owners and mommies worked within a strict moral economy tied to a labor structure that depended on workers' consent. Far more prevalent—and I would argue even more powerful—than the threat of physical or sexual violence was the *symbolic violence* I and other women were subjected to. The *body* is the product of a social labor of construction in which "male desire [is] the desire for possession, eroticized domination, and female desire [is] is the desire for masculine domination, . . . the eroticized recognition of domination" (Bourdieu 1998: 21).

Across all four bars, men's access to women's bodies was guided by informal norms and boundaries. On the acceptable end of the continuum, clients could expect to wrap their arms around women's shoulders, hug them, kiss their cheeks, and touch various parts of a hostess's body where they suspected she had had plastic surgery. At the other end, it was unacceptable for men to touch any body part covered by clothes. When men crossed this clear boundary, the other workers in the bar or the madams quickly distracted them with a song, a drink, or a drinking game. The *symbolic violence* often occurred in the middle of this continuum—as women accepted subtle uncomfortable advances from men and succumbed to the pressure to drink.

In addition to learning to deflect sexual advances, women also had to learn to completely alter the way they carried their bodies in relation to the male clients. As a highly educated woman born and raised in the United States, I came to Vietnam with the habit of crossing my arms, leaning back, and looking men straight in the eyes when I talked with them. This subconscious body language signaled my equal status to men. Both the clients and my fellow hostess workers trained me to drop my arms, avert my gaze, and sit with a more demure posture. These bodily adjustments obviously signaled submission, but more importantly, following Vietnamese and Asian customs, they also were gestures that made clients (particularly older men) feel respected. On two occasions, I was disciplined by the clients and asked to leave the table because I treated an important official as an equal by looking him directly in the eyes when talking to him. Respect was so crucial in this culturally gendered space that over time, I grew to feel uncomfortable if I mistakenly looked a client in his eyes. In moments where I slipped, I immediately tried to compensate for my social faux pas by dropping my gaze and serving the client some of the food on the table.

In this cultural context, implicit rules around drinking also signified deference. When sitting at a table, it was considered rude for me to drink from my glass without first toasting the client I was hosting and the other men at the table. I always used two hands to serve a client a drink, keeping my head slightly lowered to the side or looking down toward the floor. Most important, it was always the rule to clink my glass below the client's glass. For clients who were particularly respected in the bar, I clinked my glass toward the bottom of the man's glass, if not completely underneath it, so that the bottom of the clients' glass sat literally over the rim of my glass.

My diligence in learning these bodily transformations helped me blend into the space and to develop trusting relationships with a handful of powerful elites. As I spent more time around these men, they began to talk far more openly with me about their business relationships. At first, I believed that my job in these spaces was simply to provide men with emotional labor, comforting them as they relieved their stress. However, as our conversations developed into deeper discussions, I learned that the performances women provided helped male clients to establish informal social relationship of trust with other Asian businessmen in order to secure multimillion-dollar business deals, transactions that often involved thin contracts and a strong handshake.

This carnal experience taught me how women cultivated desire by disciplining their bodies in ways that often involved tough choices. I came to understand why almost all of the women chose to make permanent alterations to their bodies through plastic surgery. I also learned what men found desirable or aesthetically pleasing, and how those desires varied across the four different bars I inhabited.

THE SYMBOLIC FORCE OF MALE DESIRE

One evening, the makeup artist who normally came to Khong Sao Bar to help with my makeup did not show up, so a co-worker helped draw my eyebrows for me. She was inexperienced working on a face other than her own, and she drew my eyebrows too thick. Over the course of the entire evening, the clients made fun of me, telling me that I reminded them of princesses from Chinese movies. At the end of the night, Hanh, the madam who ran the bar, insisted that I visit a local beautician to get semipermanent makeup tattooed on my face. I ignored her demand for a month, so one Sunday afternoon, Hanh invited a local dermatologist to visit the bar to convince me to get a "3D eyebrow tattoo," for which the stylist uses a machine to mimic real hair. Afraid of permanently altering my face, I was able to deflect these requests, but only because I earned an income outside the sex industry. Yet throughout the time of my fieldwork, I remained terribly worried that I would lose access to my field site because I was unwilling to undergo various procedures to alter my body and did not embody the desired aesthetic in the bars where I worked.

Although I could never fully be an insider in the bars, the daily rituals of entrusting my body to other hostesses, clients, madams, tailors, and beauticians helped me find a "fleshy companionship" (Wacquant 2005) with the hostesses. By subjecting myself to similar kinds of symbolic violence they faced in their daily work, I developed carnal connections that provided a much deeper understanding of the embodied *labor* behind hostess work. Women's subtle embodied transformations were rooted in relationships of *masculine domination*. These transformations became so deeply normative over time that they were "imperceptible and even invisible ... exerted for the most part through the symbolic channels of ... (mis-recognition), recognition, or even feeling" (Bourdieu 1998: 1–2). In the thick of research, I almost caved to the pressure to modify my body in more permanent ways. But I justified my decision not to purchase plastic surgery or permanent makeup by reminding everyone around me that my time working as a hostess would soon come to an end.

I was able to draw emotional boundaries in the field through institutional support from biweekly Skype meetings with fellow graduate students and monthly meetings with my advisor. These meetings were personally cathartic, and were crucial in helping me to refine my central research questions and my ultimate objective in the field. However, the splintering of the academic self from the ethnographic self distinguishes the experiences of ethnographers in research sites that involve feminine labors from those undertaking Wacquant's carnal sociology.

For male ethnographers becoming a skilled wrestler or firefighter, the transformative process they experience shores up their dominant masculinity in the field. By contrast, when ethnographers become skilled in feminized spaces, they become complicit in their own symbolic violence. To be clear, I am not arguing that this difference comes from male and female *ethnographers*. Rather, I am suggesting that carnal *ethnographies* associated with femininity often involve making oneself smaller, taking up less space, and becoming deferential, while masculine ethnographies involve bodily expansion as men learn to take up more space and become stronger in the field. Men get rewarded for their dedication in going out "on the line," while women's dedication makes them sexually suspect— the opposite of the dedicated researcher. When giving a talk about ethnographic methods, one male scholar made a joke in reference to his relationship with his research subjects, saying, "I ate with them, worked with them, and even slept with them." The audience laughed while I shuddered, knowing I could never dare to joke around like that. One audience member praised him for his charisma and ability to take on dangerous field research. This is very different from the reaction that I have received when returning from the field; a number of male colleagues, for example, have pressured me to take them on a voyeuristic journey of my fieldwork.

STEPPING OUT OF THE FIELD

My ethnographic work was physically and mentally challenging. After leaving the field, it was important to me to rest and rebuild my body. I talked through my embodied processes with an excellent therapist, but I ultimately found the process of writing to be far more therapeutic. Depending on how far one is willing to go in adjusting one's body and lifestyle to one's field site, carnal ethnography can take years to unlearn. Sometimes we live with the embodied transformations forever. I often find myself serving other people at a dinner table or clicking my glass below the other guests' at the table, albeit as a sign of care and respect, rather than simple deference. For some men the bodily discipline, physical strength, and confidence might actually benefit them in their academic settings, adding much to their real lives.

The habitus I developed in the field is deeply inflected with other parts of my social life. After undergoing the embodied transformations necessary for hostess work, I learned to observe norms of desire in different spaces and to adjust my body to avoid unwanted attention. Since leaving the field, I have adopted a conservative look, wearing less makeup, glasses, long-sleeved tops, and skirts that fall below the knee, or pants. I've wanted to avoid attention because it drew me into a set of objectifying gazes that require emotional and physical labor to manage. The research required an important kind of code-switching between the field and the ivory tower. I witnessed several instances when colleagues ridiculed both men and women who failed to switch off their street code behind closed doors, and in a number of instances it meant that the researcher did not receive a job offer.

Following Loïc Wacquant's call "that we can and should work to become 'vulnerable observers' in our practice of fieldwork—and not on paper" (Wacquant 2015: 5), I did not write *Dealing in Desire* as a book about my practice as a researcher. Instead, I purposefully chose to avoid academic voyeurism in a concerted effort to build social theory from my carnal ethnography that is, to paraphrase Wacquant (2015), *from* the body rather than *of* the body. Ironically, my efforts to focus on theorizing in what I call *protagonist-driven ethnography* (Cobb & Hoang 2015) were often countered with questions from male scholars about my positionality and whether or not I engaged in sex work as part of my ethnography. Stepping out of the field, I encountered scholars who had a difficult time separating my ethnographic self from my scholarly self. Although these two selves are indeed related, my carnal ethnographies involved a kind of gendered labor that was subject to a particular form of symbolic violence in the academy.

Standing before an audience at talks or at dinners, I was accosted by men and women alike with questions about whether I "slipped into sex work." I refuse to answer these questions, because they are unrelated to my argument and demeaning to the women I study. At one talk, several members of the audience very publicly analyzed my facial features to debate whether I had undergone plastic surgery. Although I had left bar lineups behind, my body was once again subject to scrutiny, this time as a professor. In academic settings, I was again expected to adjust my gait and smile through criticism, only here I was to serve up an academically "appropriate" answer or remain silent. Finally, in the writing process, reviewers used feminist epistemology to critique my efforts to place my research participants at the center of my work, with comments such as, "You have such a sexy topic but we don't see you anywhere in these pages . . . where are you?"

As I straddled the halls of academia and the space I had inhabited in the field, I felt an "eerie sense of the familiar colluding with the bizarre" (Blee 2002: 2). To write my book, I crossed a boundary that divides the sexist underground from the mainstream. This experience was very different from the way my body was disciplined to inhabit a professional academic space where makeup is devalued and where I had to adopt a more conservative appearance. Gendering carnal ethnography requires us to grapple with the contradictions of feminist-standpoint work and carnal ethnography that call on researchers to be reflexive of their own subject position in relation to their research subjects. Men who take on masculine-centered carnal ethnographies and who are reflexive ethnographers emerge as heroes who survived treacherous field sites. Feminine-centered ethnographers, on the other hand, subject themselves to a different set of *embodied costs* (Hoang 2015), objectifying gazes, and disciplining practices both in the field and in the broader academy. These experiences raise important questions about the process of gendering carnal ethnography. Who really benefits from standpoint theory, feminist epistemology, and carnal connections? What can we learn from our inability as researchers to master the embodied practices in the field? What can we learn from vulnerable observers who do not fight fires or people in the field?

NOTE

I thank Loïc Wacquant for suggesting the title of this chapter. Many thanks to Jessica Cobb, Jennifer Jones, Carla Pfeffer, Laurence Ralph, Kristen Schilt, Forrest Stuart, and Robert Vargas for their critical feedback on this chapter.

WORKS CITED

Blee, Kathleen. 2002. *Inside organized racism: Women in the hate movement.* Berkeley: University of California Press.

Bourdieu, Pierre. 1998. *Masculine domination.* Stanford, CA: Stanford University Press.

———. 2004. "Gender and symbolic violence." In *Violence in war and peace: An anthology.* Ed. Nancy Scheper-Hughes and Philippe Bourgois. Malden, MA: Blackwell.

Cobb, Jessica Shannon, and Kimberly Kay Hoang. 2015. "Protagonist-Driven Urban Ethnography." *City & Community* 14 (4):348–351.

Collins, Randall. 2015. "Visual micro-sociology and the sociology of flesh and blood: Comment on Wacquant." *Qualitative Sociology* 38(1): 13–17.

Contreras, Randol. 2013. *The stickup kids: Race, drugs, violence, and the American dream.* Berkeley: University of California Press.

———. 2015. "The need for more 'carnal.'" *Qualitative Sociology* 38(1): 27–31.

Desmond, Matthew. 2009. *On the fireline: Living and dying with wildland firefighters.* Chicago: University of Chicago Press.

Frank, Katherine. 2002. *G-strings and sympathy: Strip club regulars and male desire.* Durham, NC: Duke University Press.

Goffman, Erving. 1959. *The presentation of self in everyday life.* New York: Doubleday.

Hancock, Black Hawk. 2007. "Learning how to make life swing." *Qualitative Sociology* 30(2): 113–33.

Hoang, Kimberly Kay. 2015. *Dealing in desire: Asian ascendancy, Western decline, and the hidden currencies of global sex work.* Oakland: University of California Press.

Mears, Ashley. 2011. *Pricing beauty: The making of a fashion model.* Berkeley: University of California Press.

Parrenas, Rhacel Salazar. 2011. "What I learned by being a migrant sex worker (Part 2)." *Bloomberg View,* October 13. https://www.bloomberg.com/view /articles/2011-10-14/ what-i-learned-by-being-a-migrant-sex-worker-part-2-parrenas.

Pitts-Taylor, Victoria. 2015. "A feminist carnal sociology? Embodiment in sociology, feminism, and naturalized philosophy." *Qualitative Sociology* 38(1): 19–25.

Small, Mario Luis. 2015. "De-exoticizing ghetto poverty: On the ethics of representation in urban ethnography." *City & Community* 14(4): 352–58.

Venkatesh, Sudhir. 2008. *Gang leader for a day: A rogue sociologists takes to the streets.* New York: Penguin Press.

Wacquant, Loïc. 1995. "Pugs at work: Bodily capital and bodily labour among professional boxers." *Body and Society* 1:65–93.

———. 2005. "Carnal connections: On embodiment, apprenticeship, and membership." *Qualitative Sociology* 38(4): 445–74.

———. 2011. "Habitus as topic and tool: Reflections on becoming a prizefighter." *Qualitative Research in Psychology* 8(1): 81–92.

———. 2015. "For a sociology of flesh and blood." *Qualitative Sociology* 38(1): 1–11.

PART IV Epistemologies

15 Translation as Queer Methodology

Evren Savci

How should we understand global sexual politics without falling into easy binaries of culturally authentic versus colonized sexualities—in other words, without reproducing the ideology of anthropological difference? This is an epistemological and, therefore, a methodological question that has preoccupied scholars of transnational sexualities for some time now, without yielding easy answers (Boellstorff 2003). For those of us located in US and Western European academic institutions who are interested in studying transnational sexual formations considered to lie outside "the West," this question gets even muddier because of the political and historical conditions of global knowledge production. Those conditions include, but are not limited to, the fact that knowledge production about "the Other," which has often relied on ethnographic methods, has been a direct tool of imperial domination (Said 1979), and the fact that the Global South has historically been seen as a place to mine "data" and produce theory about (the latter also understood to be an extension of cultural imperialism). In my own work, where I set out to study "queer politics" in contemporary Turkey, I inevitably entered the same minefield. While being born and raised in Turkey indeed made a difference in how "acceptable" my interest was in producing knowledge about a place that falls outside the "Global North," I nevertheless faced epistemological issues resulting from being trained in qualitative sociology and queer studies in the United States.

I was attuned to the importance of categories of thought we operate with (Ferguson 2003) and to the dangers of imposing ready-made intellectual frameworks onto the "field" in the name of knowledge production. And while sociology encouraged me to pay attention to social and political practices, and queer theory to the power of language, knowledge, and meaning making, I was ultimately interested in undoing this binary between practice and discourse. My interests in the interplay of language, knowledge, and political practice led me to ethnographically investigate the effects produced by new concepts being introduced into both everyday and political vocabularies on the ground. Idioms that were increasingly used in public discussions and among queer activists in Turkey, such as *gender identity, sexual orientation, hate crimes, LGBT rights,* and *homophobia* suggested frames for how to think about gender and sexuality, the entitlements that should, and the violence that does, surround nonnormative subjects; these frames therefore informed and shaped the epistemology and practice of sexual politics. Instead of approaching this as a colonization of "authentic" Turkish sexuality or sexual politics, I was interested in understanding what tangible effects might be produced by these concepts, whether everyone had equal access to employing such language, and what conversations might be opened up, and foreclosed, by the frames they offered. It was through this attention to the interplay between language and practice in the context of transnationally traveling terminology that I arrived at translation as a key concept that I also understand as a methodology.

Two terms are critical to my work that are not commonly encountered in sociological research: *language* and *translation.* Cultural sociology has long emphasized that the very thing that sociology is interested in studying, "the social," needs to be understood as deeply intertwined with the cultural. Given this emphasis, and the amount of debate that has occurred over the place of culture within the field, it is quite surprising that sociology would pay so little attention to language itself. While my work is deeply interdisciplinary, and while I could thus have relied on queer studies to understand and theorize the role of language in sexual politics, I was not satisfied with how language was treated in queer theory and queer studies, either. Three major problems emerged. For one, possibly because many of the key thinkers of queer studies are trained in humanities fields, language is often treated not as a social entity but as a textual one. Further, when scholars thought about language as something that did not only live in texts, they turned to discourse and speech acts as performative aspects of language. While language as discourse has made important interventions, it ultimately overlooks the hermeneutic aspect of language, which is deeply intertwined with the social (Sakai 1997). And finally, again perhaps because most key thinkers of queer theory and studies have been trained in English departments, language easily becomes Language, which itself is equated with English. In other words, when queer studies theorizes how subjects are "gendered" by speech acts such as "It's a girl!" the speech act is always already imagined to take place in the English language. These issues with "language as textual," "language as discourse," and "language as Language/English" left me desiring a sociological and historical focus on language that understands it as a social practice (Bourdieu 1991; Williams 1977).

My understanding of language and my use of "translation" to understand the emergence of new sexual and gender idioms in contemporary Turkey owe a great debt to translation studies. Naoki Sakai (1997) has argued for the past two decades that we need to think about translation as a social practice, thereby undoing the false binary between language and practice. Departing from Sakai's question "What kind of a social relation is translation?" a number of critical translation studies scholars urge us to question the modern regime of translation and its role in contemporary global capitalist modernity (Mezzadra & Sakai 2014; Solomon 2014). They suggest that understanding translation as "a transfer of message from one clearly circumscribed language community into another" (Sakai 1997: 6) presumes languages to be homogenous and distinguishable entities, between which translation is supposed to act as a filter. Comparing this presumed linguistic equivalence to capitalist equivalence between commodities, Jon Solomon (2014) developed the term *translational accumulation* to define this modern system that assumes equivalence and commensurability between languages and systems of signs, where linguistic difference, assumed to be a gap, is traversed by translation. The contemporary "international" system comprising nation-states is shored up by "national languages" as markers of national, and presumedly cultural, difference. In other words, the modern regime of translation shores up anthropological difference by equating nation, culture, and language—the very structure that makes the universalism/cultural imperialism–versus–particularism/cultural authenticity double-bind possible.

Translation studies does not suggest, however, that we abandon translation as a concept and episteme altogether. Instead, scholars argue, what we need is to think of translation outside the homolingual address, which renders languages ahistorical and natural.[1] What does it mean, then, to employ translation critically as a lens or methodology without repeating the regime of anthropological difference? Following translation theorists, I suggest that we do not use the term to indicate a seamless move from one language to another in order to "bridge" a linguistic gap and find common ground, but instead to indicate social disjunctures (Mezzadra & Sakai 2014). "[T]ranslation can inscribe, erase, and distort borders," Sandro Mezzadra and Naoki Sakai suggest; "translation deterritorializes languages and . . . shows most persuasively the unstable, transformative, and political nature of border, of the differentiation of the inside from the outside, and of the multiplicity of belonging and nonbelonging" (2014: 11). Refusing the modern regime of translation and the homolingual address necessitates first and foremost that we refuse an ahistorical understanding of language, the model of languages as separable and countable entities, and a simple equation of language with (national) culture.

This definition of translation led me to look for social disjunctures in the understandings and uses of the concepts I was following: if not all subjects who employed the term *LGBT rights* meant the same thing when they expressed support for or objection to LGBT rights, what kinds of social and political outcomes would such disjunctures have? Using "translation as social disjuncture" as a methodology led me to pay ethnographic attention to the various and at times conflicting meanings and political positions the same terms could evoke. This methodology also inevitably complicated "the local," which is often homogenized in its opposition to "the global." Not only is this a problematic binary that has mapped onto others, such as "colonial" versus "authentic," but it also perpetuates the false assumption that careful attention to "the particular" is an intellectual and political solution to the homogenizing forces of globalization as universalism. I join Sakai (1997) in his caution that we do not forget that particularism is complicit with universalism. In other words, our critiques of universalism will not go very far if they are invested in producing and sustaining cultural and linguistic particularity. Understanding not only culture but also language as nonstatic, grounded, and historically changing, and as practical human activity deeply entwined with the material production of the world, allows us to see that it is precisely in those moments that trouble both the meanings of vocabularies of gender and sexuality, and the political regimes that employ them, that we can discover productive spaces for thinking and being otherwise. Understanding precisely how new forms of oppressive systems coalesce and erode our capacities to *think* of a different world is crucial not only to grasp the power of language and knowledge but also to start imagining life differently.

For instance, between 2008 and 2010, Turkey experienced what I claim were unprecedented levels of public discussion about the place of what was referred to as *eşcinsel hakları* (homosexual rights) in the nation. These debates happened in the context of the democratization efforts of the Justice and Development Party government (hereafter referred to by its Turkish abbreviation, AKP), which included plans to redraft the Turkish constitution, grant social rights to ethnic minorities, and extend the right to wear the headscarf to students of public universities and public office employees. Strangely, it was the headscarf debate that instigated the "homosexual rights" debate.[2] While many liberals in the country were excited to see these changes on the horizon, other leftists were suspicious of AKP's motives. They understood AKP as an anti-secular, Islamist party whose ultimate agenda was to weaken Turkish secularism by diminishing the constitutional power of the military—an institution that had historically intervened in governments feared to be undermining the country's constitutional commitment to secularism.

The right to wear the headscarf, on the other hand, was understood to be a more complicated affair; even secularists who suspected that AKP was Islamizing the country acknowledged that banning headscarf wearing at public universities was ultimately an infringement of women's right to education. In other words, even if all women who wore headscarves in the country represented Islamic insurgency and conspired against secularism, it was not fair to use criteria to weed out such people from higher education that applied only to women, and not men (since there is no Islamic requirement for men to wear headscarves). Headscarf activists increasingly framed the right to wear the headscarf as a woman's right, an educational right, and ultimately a human right. For instance, a petition by self-proclaimed "women with headscarves" demanded the right to wear the headscarf to public universities, but also added that this was simply one of many democratic rights the citizens of the country needed, along with ethnic rights, rights of religious minorities, and a judiciary that actually delivered justice. This framing of veiling as a human, and women's, right positioned it as a democratic right, as opposed to a practice that threatened (secular) democracy.

The opponents of the headscarf, on the other hand, argued that allowing headscarves at university campuses would create a slippery slope that would lead to demands to wear headscarves at high schools and eventually at elementary schools. Easily impressionable at a young age, many of the girl children of the nation would find themselves under peer pressure (presumably exercised by their friends wearing headscarves). These concerns became so prevalent that Minister of State Burhan Kuzu finally decided to issue a statement in the summer of 2008 to alleviate such fears. "We do not have to respond to every request," he stated, referring to possible future requests for headscarves at elementary schools. "There is also a high level of requests from homosexuals for equality and the right to marriage.[3] Are we going to give it to them simply because they are asking for it? We are obliged to act within the responsibilities of (the party in) power" (Çolak & Karakuş 2008). With power came the responsibility to distinguish between reasonable and unreasonable demands of the people, and with the obligation *not* to respond to unreasonable demands. The right to wear headscarves at elementary schools was, the minister claimed, as unreasonable as equality and marriage rights for "homosexuals."

LGBT activists (generically referred to as "homosexuals" by the minister) had indeed demanded inclusion in the new constitution—more specifically, they had requested that *cinsel yönelim* (sexual orientation) and *cinsiyet kimliği* (gender identity) be included in the new constitution's anti-discrimination clause. What Kuzu's statement did was to simultaneously set up headscarf rights and LGBT rights as *comparable,* and to indicate that there was a "limit" to what was demandable as a democratic right. While the minister seemingly used the analogy only to suggest that democratic rights did not constitute a slippery slope and that headscarf wearing at elementary schools was as unthinkable as a "right" as were demands of "homosexuals," this historical moment marked the beginning of the treatment of one's position on "homosexual rights" as a litmus test for one's commitment to democracy. Over the next couple of years, head-scarf activists were questioned in a number of public forums about their stance on "homosexual rights"—usually by secularists who did not trust that headscarf activists were genuinely invested in human rights at large. Now understood as a "package deal," democratic rights were presented as available only to those willing to stand up for any and all of them.

What this particular translation of "homosexual rights" revealed were the very limits of rights-based framings of social justice. The liberal logic that imagined and produced equivalence between "homosexual rights" and "headscarf rights," and that thereby turned the commitment to one to the prerequisite for (deserving) the other, did not necessarily make sense to people who did not experience the two as the same kind of thing. This was evident in one headscarf activist's reaction on a live TV show about the headscarf ban at universities. When asked whether she supported homo-sexual rights, since she was demanding the right to wear the headscarf at universities as a human right, she responded: "Excuse me, are there people who are not admitted to schools, or are beaten up by cops like us, because they are homosexuals?" Liberal logic countered, and liberal logic exposed: indeed there were no laws banning LGBT people from higher education in Turkey. Of course, legal or codified discrimination is not necessarily the key mechanism for the workings of actual inequalities in the world. Yet this abstract use of support for "homosexual rights" as a prerequisite for gain-ing the right to wear the headscarf did not make room for other (for instance, normative) violence and inequalities that LGBT and other people face in higher education. As to the second part of her question, had any LGBT activists been invited to the show, they could have shared their own experiences with police brutality, thus opening up the possibility for a col-lective conversation about state violence. Yet this sudden "concern" about LGBT rights was symbolic, and used only in abstraction to "expose" the assumed political insincerity of headscarf activists.

Further, this translation of "homosexual rights" to Turkey took place in the context of particular national anxieties and their specific articulations.

The logic that treated "fundamental rights and liberties" as a totality, and yet did not see everyone's relationship to the discourse (and exercise) of fundamental rights and liberties as *equally genuine*, was informed by secularist suspicions that Muslim subjects were using the rubric of democratic rights to further their Islamist agenda. Therefore, secularists demanded that Muslim headscarf activists produce proof of their sincerity, evidence that they *deserved* the fundamental rights and liberties they were requesting. This suspicion of Muslim headscarf activists was most clearly articulated in the phrase "Muslims to themselves" (*kendine Müslüman*). This expression not only indicates self-seeking motives on the part of those claiming to be Muslims to themselves—suggesting they are only after their own rights, liberties, and welfare—but also points out a deep-seated *insincerity* by underlining Islam's emphasis on justice and welfare for all. To be a true Muslim, therefore, is to be a Muslim to everyone. Accordingly, in this contemporary use of *kendine Müslüman* (Muslim to her/himself) *against* pious Muslim groups in Turkey, the expression married religious insincerity with political insincerity, simultaneously dismissing the religiosity and the political motives of Muslim groups, and particularly of women with headscarves. It also informed how "democratic rights" were understood, and how their discourses were mobilized. This logic of binary divisions between Islamists versus secularists ultimately strengthened the AKP government's hand, and served its discourse of secularist victimization of Muslims in the country and its increasingly conservative agenda.

Besides exemplifying the particular translation of "homosexual rights" discourses to contemporary Turkey, this story also illustrates the travel of gender identity and sexual orientation as markers of a kind of person, a type comparable to the "headscarf wearer." These markers are understood as grounds for political subjectivity that are imagined to be protectable by the law. While the liberal logic of human rights is often presented as historically unfolding in the direction of increasing inclusion of more and more marginalized people, this instance shows that the "translation" of the logic of human rights to various contexts can unveil its shortcomings empirically. This revelation happens, for instance, when not all subjects are understood to be (politically) genuine in their claims to human rights, or when the logic of one group's rights is abstracted and employed for particular political purposes by others. In fact, a common left logic in Turkey has historically articulated the rise of the religious (read: anti-democratic) political parties as proof that democracy can be undermined using its own structures. Therefore, while the logic of distrusting the democratic capabilities of pious Muslims in the country is not new, one's position on homosexual rights emerged as a new articulation of testing democracy's limits.

Understanding and analyzing LGBT rights, sexual orientation, and gender identity in contemporary Turkish politics as an instance of translation is helpful and productive in several ways. For one, translation emphasizes the interplay between language and experience by focusing on the ways in which the concepts we use affect how people come to understand their lived experiences, including their own and others' gender and sexuality. Yet treating translation as a method goes beyond asserting the concept dependency of meaning (Steinmetz 2005) and demands that we understand questions of method also as questions of methodology and epistemology. This is where translation becomes a *queer* methodology by refusing to reduce methodology to techniques of collecting "data" on already-existing social facts, and instead emphasizes the power of language to incite and shape what we perceive to be "reality."

One can argue that the above story is a "case" of many different things, yet one of the most valuable lessons to be learned from it has to do with the traveling and shifting meanings of a concept such as LGBT or, to use what stood in its place in the Turkish debates, "homosexual rights." At first, such widespread use of the term, and the sudden public concern for LGBT rights, might seem an exciting turn of events in Turkey. Yet the fact that LGBT activists were almost never invited to any of these debates, whether on TV shows or in newspaper columns, directs the question of "sincerity" from headscarf activists to those seemingly advocating for sexual rights. The work accomplished by this particular mobilization of "homosexual rights" in a national moment of some citizens hoping for democratization and others fearing Islamization reflects how transnational frames of thought (LGBT and human rights) meet with national ones (Muslim to oneself). Nonetheless, this story makes an easy global-versus-local binary impossible by showing the different ways in which human rights and LGBT rights were understood and evoked in the context of Turkey, and demands that instead of locking the discussion on

LGBT rights into a debate over "authentic" versus "colonized" culture, we transnationalize and complicate our understanding of "the local."

This mobilization of "homosexual rights" as a litmus test for democratic sincerity inevitably becomes a frame to contend with, both for LGBT activists and everyone else invested in social justice in Turkey. I am not making this point to evoke the tired debate of whether human or LGBT rights work as an imperial expansion of a Western liberal episteme or get reworked and resignified in creative ways in "local" contexts, but rather to issue an invitation to seek more *grounded* knowledges of which particular outcomes are produced in which *historical* contexts, which we always already should understand as transnational(ized). The travel of "homosexual rights" and "human rights" to this particular historical moment in Turkey happened in the context of a self-declared "mildly Islamist" government taking arguably the largest steps thus far toward European Union accession, while cultivating conservative gender and sexual politics in the nation at large, through which its members then positioned themselves as the true representatives of the public. Translation as a queer methodology, therefore, refuses both a desire for a radical alterity and for perfect translatability when it analyzes sexual and social formations.

Further, queer studies' emphasis on power and epistemology demands that we pay attention not only to whether everyone embraces particular frames of thought but also to who exactly has proper and *legitimate* access to them. The women headscarf activists' particular position in the secularist national imaginary resulted in the questioning of the sincerity of their claims to human rights, and the demand for their clear articulation of support for "homosexual rights" to prove their sincerity. Therefore, this story is distinctly not about whether certain subjects embrace human rights as a linguistic, narrative, and political device or reject it as "inauthentic," but about who gets to make claims to human rights without being interrogated and rendered *conditionally* legitimate.

Finally, the positioning of "homosexual rights" as an obstacle to women's right to wear the headscarf at public universities, and the "failure" of headscarf activists to utter an explicit statement of "I support LGBT rights," led to foreclosures of any possible dialogue that headscarf and LGBT activists could have had. This was unfortunate, especially because systematic state violence against "improper" citizen-subjects constituted a clear and important shared experience for both groups. It was unfortunate, also, in that while claiming that their faith as Muslims made it difficult for them to state that they supported "homosexual rights," a number of headscarf activists avowed that they were against all cruelty against "homosexuals." This position against cruelty could have resulted in productive conversations about what kind of coalitional politics might result from a "politics against cruelty" instead of a liberal, abstract "politics of rights." Yet this translation of "homosexual rights" that created liberal equivalence between "headscarf rights" and "homosexual rights" made it impossible to entertain a call for a politics *against* cruelty in return for the right *for* the headscarf.

Understanding language as practical human activity means that we pay close attention to the *lived* relationships between politics and language, focusing on the very material effects of what is enabled and rendered illegible by transnational travel of sexual epistemologies. Such travel cannot be captured with easy frameworks of local cultures either resisting or succumbing to forces of globalization. Yet we also cannot further "particularize" the local by suggesting that different locations creatively adopt these globally disseminating frameworks. Translation as disjuncture demands that we question the very premise of "the local," as well as the language-culture that is supposed to distinguish it. The historical understanding of language advocated by translation studies admonishes us not to confuse linguistic markers with authenticity (or lack thereof) and engages with queer studies' important demand that we as researchers constantly question the concepts, categories, and frameworks we operate with. This is not simply because we should worry that these categories might not properly "match" people's lived experiences, which is an empirical and positivist concern, but because the legitimate (and the illegitimate) ways of thinking about sexuality in particular, and the social in general, perpetuated by the legal, medical, and social scientific establishments shape how people come to understand their existence and experiences, which is an epistemological and political concern. I hope that "queering" sociological methods will result, among other things, in a deeper questioning of the concepts sociologists operate with, given that the social science researcher's political and ethical responsibilities cannot be addressed simply by listing the technicalities of data collection, or our own positionalities vis-à-vis our research.

NOTES

1. Some of these points will be familiar to those who work with transnational feminist scholarship. Transnational feminists have long critiqued tendencies that produce Third World difference (Mohanty 1988), that assume and reproduce clear distinctions between the global and the "local" (Swarr & Nagar 2010), and that locate hegemony squarely in "the West" (Grewal & Kaplan 1994; Hoang 2015), as well as those that yearn nostalgically for a precolonial, authentic past of the "Global South" (Abu-Lughod 2002). What translation studies contributes to these debates is the complication of *the linguistic,* which seems to remain the marker of culture par excellence.

2. Readers who were not following Turkish politics back in 2008 but are aware of the current authoritarianism of the Turkish government (extrajudicially) led by President Recep Tayyip Erdoğan might find such hopes surprising. Yet in 2008 AKP seemed to pursue fairly democratic political goals, focusing in particular on the civil rights of disenfranchised ethnic groups (but not the rights of disenfranchised religious groups or workers' rights).

3. In fact, during my fieldwork I traveled with Lambdaistanbul activists to Ankara to hand in the signatures collected over the previous few months on a petition demanding that "sexual orientation" and "gender identity" be included in the anti-discrimination law of the Constitution. The petition made no mention of gay marriage as an issue on the LGBT group's agenda, nor did the topic arise during any of the meetings or protests.

WORKS CITED

Abu-Lughod, Lila. 2002. "Do Muslim women really need saving? Anthropological reflections on cultural relativism and its others." *American Anthropologist* 104: 783–90.

Boellstorff, Tom. 2003. "Dubbing culture: Indonesian *gay* and *lesbi* subjectivities and ethnography in an already globalized world." *American Ethnologist* 30(2): 225–42.

Bourdieu, Pierre. 1991. *Language and symbolic power.* Cambridge, UK: Polity Press.

Çolak, Saliha, and Abdullah Karakuş. (2008). "Eşcinseller de eşitlik istiyor, verecek miyiz?" [The homosexuals are also demanding equality; are we going to bestow it?] *Milliyet,* January 28. http://www.milliyet.com.tr/2008/01/28/siyaset/asiy.html.

Ferguson, Roderick. 2003. *Aberrations in black: Toward a queer of color critique.* Minneapolis: University of Minnesota Press.

Grewal, Inderpal, and Caren Kaplan. 1994. *Scattered hegemonies: Postmodernity and transnational feminist practices*. Minneapolis: University of Minnesota Press.

Hoang, Kimberly. 2015. *Dealing in desire: Asian ascendency, Western decline, and the hidden currencies of global sex work*. Berkeley: University of California Press.

Mezzadra, Sandro, and Naoki Sakai. 2014. "Introduction." *Translation: A Transdisciplinary Journal* 2: 9–29.

Mohanty, Chandra. 1988. "Under Western eyes: Feminist scholarship and colonial discourses." *Feminist Review* 30: 60–88.

Said, Edward W. 1979. *Orientalism*. New York: Vintage Books.

Sakai, Naoki. 1997. *Translation and subjectivity: On "Japan" and cultural nationalism*. Minneapolis: University of Minnesota Press.

Solomon, Jon. 2014. "The post-imperial etiquette and the affective structure of areas." *Translation: A Transdisciplinary Journal* 2: 171–201.

Steinmetz, George. 2005. "The epistemological unconscious of U.S. sociology and the transition to post-Fordism: The case of historical sociology." In *Remaking Modernity: Politics, History, and Sociology*. Ed. Julia Adams, Elisabeth Clemens, and Ann Shola Orloff. Durham, NC: Duke University Press.

Swarr, Amanda Lock, and Richa Nagar. 2010. *Critical transnational feminist praxis*. Albany: State University of New York Press.

Williams, Raymond. 1977. *Marxism and literature*. Oxford: Oxford University Press.

16 Queer and Punishment

SEXUAL SOCIAL CONTROL AND THE LEGACY
OF "NUTS, SLUTS AND PREVERTS"

Trevor Hoppe

I have a confession to make: I have never particularly liked the word *queer*. Its definition is elusive. It sometimes serves as a catchall for all those who do not identify as heterosexual ("queer people"). Other times, it is used to signify a psychoanalytic approach to "reading" literature ("queer theory") that I find at times bewildering and woefully detached from the empirical social world. Even early in my career when I studied gay men, I did not study people who identified as queer. Now, as a scholar of the ways sex is regulated under punitive regimes, the concept of sexual orientation is even further removed from my research, as is any reference in my work to psychoanalytic theory. In short, it would seem at first glance that my work no longer qualifies as "queer" scholarship.

Despite my ambivalence toward the field, I did not refuse the invitation to contribute to this collection. As I wrote this piece, I often found myself wondering if I should have said no. Is my work truly representative of "queer methods"? What in Saint Foucault's name did that even mean? I wish to make some small effort to recuperate my relationship with the field by aligning my research with two now-distant traditions.

First, as Joshua Gamson and Dawne Moon (2004) note, the sociology of sexuality itself was born out of the sociology of deviance—a tradition

closely aligned with criminology. Deviance studies has had many iterations throughout sociology's history, but it includes a tradition of examining how society labels, controls, and regulates groups of people with a specific focus on stigmatized minorities (i.e., conflict and labeling theories).
Despite the utility offered by such an analytic lens for understanding inequalities, prejudices, and social stigmas based on sexuality, sexuality
scholars have long since put distance between themselves and the field's
deviant origins. This was largely due to the tendency of mainstream scholars to deploy those origins in ways that reinforced—rather than decon-
structed—pathology and social stigma associated with sexual minorities.
Deviance studies itself fell out of favor in the 1970s after sociologists
across the discipline lamented that it amounted to nothing more than a
fascination with, in the words of Alexander Liazos (1972), "nuts, sluts and
preverts." Instead, as Gamson and Moon argue, sexuality scholars
have focused on "sexuality as a basis of community and political life"
(2004: 47).

I argue that abandoning the literature on deviance studies—as well as
its twin concept, social control—is the academic equivalent of throwing
the baby out with the bathwater. Studying how the state labels, controls,
and punishes sex and sex crimes does not require scholars to reify sexual
identity categories—we can bring the deconstructionist insights of queer
theory to bear on the state, rather than on the pathologized subject. This
research is not driven by a prurient interest in explaining human perver-
sity (though I would *certainly* not object to such a research agenda, and
have myself participated in such an exercise); instead, my research aims to
understand how the state labels, controls, and punishes maligned
groups—*especially* those labeled as nuts, sluts, or perverts. Although I did
not fully realize it until I sat down to write this essay, situating my work in
this grand and thoroughly *debased* tradition turns out to have been a
decidedly queer thing to do.

Second, although much of what passes as "queer theory" today is deeply
rooted in psychoanalysis, the work of the field's unwitting founding father,
Michel Foucault, resonates deeply with the sociology of deviance and social
control. Although he died long before the birth of his posthumously attributed child, his social theory bears almost no resemblance to the endless
"queer" readings of texts in the humanities (for more on this topic, see

Halperin 2003). Foucault's *History of Sexuality* (1978) reveals how social institutions and scientific disciplines served to control how people experienced and understood sex; *Discipline and Punish* (1979) revealed much about how shifting approaches to punishment reflect deeper truths about the way power structures modern society; and although he did not predict the punitive turn toward mass incarceration in the United States, *Madness and Civilization* (1965) and other work on medical institutions were foundational for many of the insights now attributed to critical medical sociologists today. Although sociologists take pleasure in rebuking his methodological and empirical faults, Foucault's ideas inspired many of the social theorists whose work is foundational to the fields with which I most closely identity: the sociologies of sexuality, punishment, and medicine.

While the current state of queer studies might at times repel me, I also recognize that I am working within its oldest and perhaps even foundational traditions. "Queer" need not be synonymous with "sexual orientation" or "the sexual experience"; by challenging how sexuality is labeled, regulated, and controlled as "badness," "goodness," "crime," or "sin," and revealing the historical contingencies that enable these power relations, "queer" as an analytic might also be a way to understand the regulation and social control of sexual life.

This chapter traces how my own work has been shaped by two divergent literatures. First, Foucault's insights into the social control of sex led me to abandon the study of sexual experience. Second, the emerging literature on mass incarceration prompted me to view punishment as *the* definitive social problem of early-twenty-first-century American life. Bringing these literatures together, I began to investigate how the state regulates, controls, and punishes sex. Such a dramatic shift in my research agenda required me to develop an entirely new methodological toolkit that was not primarily rooted in phenomenology. Several epistemological problems emerged quickly—questions that I grapple with in this exploratory essay (and that I continue to grapple with in my research). I conclude by considering how this reorientation has reshaped my relationship to the field of queer studies and sexuality studies more broadly.

THE NIGHT FOUCAULT HISSED AT ME

As a young, aspiring gay male sociologist, I came to my graduate training with the intention of studying how individuals and communities experienced sex, pleasure, and desire and what social identities get attached to those lived practices. But my first publication left me with a sense of unease. In that article, I analyze gay men's sexual practices and identities as bottoms, taking a critical stance toward the cottage industry of public health scholarship that pathologizes gay men's desire to have receptive anal intercourse without condoms. Rather than tracing their desires to the subaltern or even to low self-esteem (as psychoanalysts and psychologists have done), I instead aimed to depsychologize their desires by demonstrating how particular configurations of sexual scripts about power and pleasure might prove to be social obstacles for practicing safer sex. Despite these efforts, I nonetheless came away from that project feeling as though I was guilty of the very charges I had levied against public health: by cataloguing and describing gay men's sexual lives and experiences, was I not simply facilitating their governance by a homophobic state—a state that viewed gay sex as risky, dangerous, and, in some cases, a punishable offense? What exactly was queer about this research? And, perhaps more important, what exactly *is* queer research and theory?

While some scholars use the term *queer* as a catchall for lesbian, gay, bisexual, or transgender (LGBT), others have argued that the theoretical purchase of queer scholarship is its power of deconstruction—typically referring to the analytic move to position sexual identity as constantly shifting and in a state of reformulation (Green 2007). However, while deconstructing the sexual subject has proven fruitful terrain for the sociology of sexuality, this chapter describes how my own research has been shaped by another tradition in queer studies—the work of French scholar Michel Foucault. Foucault's most important work revealed how expert discourses (psychology, penology, medicine) construct and shape human subjectivity. His work thereby reveals the critical link between knowledge and power. For sexuality scholars, this insight draws our focus away from sexual practice toward the power wielded by scientific and governmental institutions in their efforts to control human sexuality.

Foucault's "violent rejection" (Legrand 2008: 281) of phenomenology, or the study of consciousness and the human experience, challenged me to reimagine my own sexuality research agenda. To better set my current methodological choices in relief, in what follows, I first briefly describe the methodological toolkit I originally developed to study sexual behavior and experience. I then turn to the methodological and epistemological challenges that came with attempting to deploy this toolkit in the study of sex through the lens of punishment—as well as the strategies I developed to move past them.

STUDYING SEXUAL EXPERIENCE

When I began my doctoral studies, I was intent on studying how people interpret, understand, and experience sex. I employed the tools developed by the late, great John Gagnon and William Simon, who together developed the concept of "sexual script" to help theorize questions of desire and its social reproduction. In short, a sexual script is a set of expectations around sex that guide our behavior and experience. Scripts do not just guide spoken language, of course, but also our actions and reactions. This analytic tool is now widely used in the field and, for that reason, Simon and Gagnon's work on the subject is canonical to the sociology of sexuality.

In my study of gay men's bottom narratives, I used this conceptual apparatus to understand how gay men understood the "bottom" category, how it was socially enacted, and what its implications might be for HIV prevention. Conventional scripting studies relied largely on in-depth interviews, but I wanted to examine also the collective aspects of gay sex. To do that, I developed what I believe to be a mixed-methods approach that employed a combination of focus groups and in-depth interviews. In each focus group, four to six men collectively discussed a series of questions about gay sex, the "bottom" label, and HIV; a week later, I followed up with face-to-face individual interviews with each participant. In combining focus groups with follow-up interviews, I could observe not just how the men individually made sense of their desires but also how they understood these questions collectively. In the follow-up interviews, for example, many participants directly cited their peers' comments from the prior focus groups—allowing for a broader discussion that went beyond just their individual experience; for example, "That guy said that X makes for great sex, but I guess that made me realize that I think Y is really important." I found this methodological strategy to be highly productive for studying sex among gay men, since (at least in my own personal experience) gay men are quite willing to engage in free and open discussions about sex with their peers.

As I was analyzing the data, I was struck by the way that scripted expectations associated with being a bottom both constrained and gave possibility to these men's sexual lives. These scripts were neither solely the product of individual "agency" (e.g., the men's life choices) nor the result of social "structure" (e.g., the institutional and social contexts in which these men lived). To help theoretically make sense of this, I turned to Anthony Giddens (1986) and William Sewell's (1992) work on "structuration," or how social structures are reconstituted by individuals through language and practice. In doing so, I hoped to make this analysis relevant to a wider sociological audience.

I also sought to address what I saw as a gap in the literature. Many studies employing the concept of sexual script are often quite descriptive in that their primary aim is to simply identify which scripts exist in a particular population. However, we might expand our scope of inquiry from simply documenting their existence to considering what these scripts "do" in the world. In my 2011 article, I argued that bottoms who reported a particular nexus of scripts organized around principles of pleasure ("being a bottom means pleasing my partner") and power ("being a bottom means submitting to my partner's will") faced what I called pleasure/risk dilemmas when it came to navigating HIV risk. In short, if a bottom's partner doesn't wish to use a condom, these scripts can make it challenging for the bottom to object. In this way, scripts can coagulate into a structurated phenomenon that constrains individual agency.

The methods and analytic tools employed for this project—interviews and focus groups, on the one hand, and sexual scripts, on the other—were tailor-made for phenomenological questions of how people interpret and experience sexual practice. As I explain in the following section, however, adapting them to the study of how the state controls sex proved more challenging than anticipated.

STUDYING SEX THROUGH THE LENS OF PUNISHMENT

I came to the literature on punishment rather unexpectedly. As part of a committee tasked with putting together an undergraduate course, "The Global HIV/AIDS Epidemic," at the University of Michigan, I noticed occasional references to HIV-specific laws that made it a crime for HIV-positive people to have sex without first disclosing their HIV status. Thirty years into the epidemic, I assumed I could organize enough material to warrant a lecture. I was surprised to find that almost nothing academic had been written about these laws. Given the wealth of scholarship on HIV and the high stakes involved in incarcerating people, this omission presented a puzzle.

The criminalization of HIV also came to my attention at exactly the same time that the nation and sociologists were engaging in a critical conversation around mass incarceration (the term *mass imprisonment* was, in fact, was coined by sociologist David Garland). The sociology of punishment emerged directly out of this literature. Sociologists of punishment—including Garland, Bruce Western, and Becky Pettit—analyze how punishment operates as a social institution that shapes and reshapes our social landscape. Much of this literature examines how mass incarceration has buttressed and even deepened racial inequality in the United States, devastating black communities and particularly black men. Yet, while important studies have demonstrated how punishment is stratified by race and gender, sexuality has largely been absent from most analyses.

My dissertation was born out of these twin opportunities: the lack of empirical sociological research analyzing HIV-specific criminal laws, and the lack of sexuality-driven research in the sociology of punishment. As luck would have it, Michigan's law was typical of felony HIV disclosure laws nationwide, and it was one of the most aggressively enforced in the nation. These characteristics made Michigan an excellent case study for my project.

In my woefully naive mind, changing dissertation topics was as easy as that; HIV-specific criminal laws were a new topic, but I was still studying sexuality, right? I quickly realized that shifting from studying bottoms to studying the state would require me to become an altogether different kind of sociologist. The research questions that flow from analyzing how sexuality is punished and controlled required a very different methodo-logical toolkit. Indeed, even methods that seemed superficially the same in practice required vastly different executions on the ground—an episte-mological challenge I fully understood only once I was in the field.

My previous work examined how gay men understand, practice, and ultimately reproduce their sexual lives vis-à-vis sexual scripts. That project conceived of sexuality as a site of shared experience, pleasure, and social production and relied heavily on the qualitative toolkit familiar to sociolo-gists who study social identity. Before I conducted in-depth interviews with bottom-identified gay men about their sexual lives, I developed a range of probing questions that would walk participants through their sexual histo-ries, experiences, and interpretations of those experiences. But any sexual-ity scholar knows that opening an interview with probing questions about a participant's sex life is a very unwise strategy, indeed. Thus, I would begin these interviews with nonthreatening questions about a participant's biog-raphy, without even mentioning the word *sex*. Without much prompting, this preliminary questioning nearly always generated stories about the par-ticipant's adolescence, their coming-out process, and sometimes their deci-sion to move to San Francisco; this would eventually transition smoothly into a conversation about their early sexual experiences. This strategy helped gay men ease into a conversation about topics that are highly stig-matized in society (namely, a passion for receptive anal intercourse).

For my dissertation project, I was interested in a bird of a different feather: how prosecutors, judges, and health officials regulated the sex lives of HIV-positive defendants and clients. There is certainly an inter-pretative element to the ways authorities understand and apply the law, but their actions as agents of social control (pressing charges, sentencing, etc.) and the consequences of those actions (incarceration, probation, etc.) are equally important. When I sat down to conduct my first in-depth interview with a local health official for my dissertation, I began the inter-view as I had all the previous interviews with bottom-identified gay men: with nonthreatening questions about their biography. In this case, I expected the conversation to open with a brief discussion about their deci-sion to work in the public health sector, their understanding of HIV, and finally their current job and the strategies they employ in it to control and punish HIV-positive clients.

From the moment I hit "record" on my digital voice recorder, "Rosie" (a pseudonym chosen by the first participant I interviewed for the project) seemed flustered with my questions. I imagine my experience of this first interview as not entirely dissimilar from that of a dentist pulling teeth from an irritated patient. After the interview, I sat down to write a reaction memo to help me process this challenging experience—and to think about what went wrong. I wrote the following:

> [Rosie] was young and friendly but often seemed to be hostile to my questions. She seemed like she had something to prove to me, and thus resented questions that implied I needed her to explain things she seemed to think were obvious (e.g., "what does it mean for someone to slip through the social cracks?" which she replied "is that a serious question?"). That made this interview difficult, not the least of which because it was the first interview in this project.

From that reaction, I concluded that the interview "was largely a bust," as I wrote in my memo. "She evaded questions, gave overly broad answers (and then criticized me for asking overly broad questions), seemed unwilling to talk about her personal background. At the end, she basically told me how I should go about asking questions in the future."

Although I was largely flummoxed at the time (I wrote that "I appreciate the tips, but I also believe I asked her many of the questions she told me to ask others"), now, in hindsight, the cause of this frustrating dynamic is entirely clear. I had failed to adapt the interview method to this project. Health officials are busy professionals who do not wish to spend their valuable time at work discussing their early-career choices; rather than easing them into the interview, these kinds of questions tended to irritate participants—especially frontline workers like Rosie who are typically overworked and underpaid (it is perhaps worth noting that managerial staff more often enjoyed these kinds of questions). Moreover, many of the health officials whom I interviewed did not see their biography, their personal life, or even their subjective interpretation as relevant to their work.

By framing questions in personal and subjective terms, I was likely violating personal, private norms in the modern professional workplace. With each successive interview in the project, I was better able to assess whether these opening questions were necessary or productive. If I could do it all over again now, I would begin instead with a question originally much further down the protocol: "Could you describe for me a bit about your current role at the Health Department?" But more important, I would have reframed many of the questions; instead of asking for interviewees' interpretation ("What does it mean for someone to fall through the cracks?"), I would have been better served by framing questions in more practical terms (e.g., "Can you tell me about a time that a client fell through the cracks?"). Although such interpretive questions had been central to the interview protocol for my project on bottom identity ("Can you tell me what it means to you to identify as a bottom?"), putting them to health officials was often met with confusion or, in Rosie's case, outright criticism.

In addition to relearning how to apply the same methods to a new research project, studying the social control of sex also required that I learn entirely new methods. It is nearly impossible to contribute meaningfully to the sociology of punishment without grappling with questions of discrimination under the law. Studies demonstrating the uneven application of the law and, in particular, the overcriminalization of black men serve as the conceptual backbone of punishment studies. While one might use qualitative interviews to evaluate whether health officials or prosecutors hold discriminatory attitudes that might lead to discriminatory outcomes, the gold-standard approach is to use demographic data to compare the population of people impacted by the criminal justice system to the population at large. Evaluating whether HIV-specific criminal laws were unevenly applied across different communities required comparing the demographic composition of the population of individuals convicted under Michigan's HIV disclosure law to that of the HIV-positive population at large.

As anyone who has studied the criminal justice system will attest, accessing the data necessary to make such comparisons can be challenging. Each state compiles crime data differently; the agencies responsible for doing so vary from state to state; and the willingness of officials in those agencies to share that data also varies considerably. In the case of Michigan's HIV-specific felony disclosure law, I was lucky: the state police agreed to share a de-identified dataset of every conviction under the law from 1992 to 2010. But my excitement at this stroke of luck quickly gave way to terror when I opened the data delivered to discover that only two pieces of information were included for each case: the county in which the defendant was convicted and the date the defendant was sentenced. To ask the kinds of questions I had about the law's application, I would need to build out this dataset considerably.

To study these cases in greater detail, I first needed to identify the defendant in each case using public records. I devised a system for doing so that involved traveling across the state to local libraries to find local newspaper reports (typically preserved on microfilm) published in the week before and after the conviction date provided by the state police; I searched the newspaper for any reference to an HIV-related criminal case and archived any relevant news reports for later analysis (admittedly, I felt a bit like a detective in a film noir picture). I was able to identify roughly 50 percent of the cases listed in the state dataset in this manner. For those cases that were not reported in local media, I relied instead on the kindness of county clerks (in one case, a clerk searched for months on her own time for the case in question, emailing me the defendant's name and case number many weeks later) and on online search queries targeting websites that display criminal defendant mugshots. Using these strategies, I was able to identify more than 95 percent of all defendants ever convicted under Michigan's HIV disclosure law through 2010.

I then compiled a robust dataset of convicted cases that included the defendant's race and gender, as well as the gender of the complainant in the case (along with a litany of other variables). It was critical that I identify as close to 100 percent of defendants as could be reached for evaluating claims of discrimination under the law. Had I relied only on newspaper reports I would, as noted, have identified only 50 percent of the defendants; how could I be sure that the defendants reported in the media were not different from those whose cases went unreported? By compiling data on 95 percent of the cases, I was able to make strong claims about the population of defendants convicted under Michigan's HIV-specific criminal law.

But my interest in these cases was not just in the defendants' demographics. I was also interested in the language used in the courtroom by officials tasked with interpreting and enforcing the criminal law. To understand the discursive elements of the law, I also requested transcripts of the court proceedings for each of the identified cases for content analysis. This archival data revealed troubling stories, including that of an erotic dancer convicted in 2009 after the strip club she worked in was raided by police. Although she was originally charged for minor drug possession, court records strongly suggest that the police manufactured a case against the dancer under the HIV disclosure law once they learned that she was HIV-positive. The law requires that authorities demonstrate that a defendant had engaged in "sexual penetration" without disclosing their status. To make this case, the detective working the case testified at the defendant's plea hearing that a confidential informant reported that *his nose had penetrated her vagina during a lap dance*—clearly, neither a plausible pathway for HIV transmission nor a conventional example of "sexual penetration." Cases such as this one reveal the lengths to which authorities will go to punish HIV-positive people.

The resulting archive of news reports, court transcripts, and court documents ran to tens of thousands of pages and forms the basis of several papers as well as a book project. If anyone had told me when I enrolled in graduate school that I would one day be building archives and analyzing self-compiled datasets in order to study sexuality, I would have laughed at them. As someone who envisioned himself as a sociologist of sexual experience, these methods would likely have seemed foreign to me. Yet it is now clear that these are the methods that will drive my research for years to come. In my view, these are the methods best suited for critically analyzing the power of the carceral state.

I have now begun employing the methodological skills I honed in my HIV legal research in the study of sex offender registries. Although more than 800,000 Americans are registered as sex offenders, the sociological literature on these policies is almost nonexistent. As I show elsewhere (Hoppe 2016), these registries have ballooned in size over the past decade even as incarceration rates have leveled off, and declined nationally. More damning still, my research reveals the devastating impact these policies have on black communities; approximately 1 percent of all black men in the United States are currently registered sex offenders—twice the rate among white men in the United States.

The growth in sex offender registries reveals something about the social life of sex in the United States. Just as the war on drugs is losing its cultural legitimacy, legislators have declared a war on sex offenders that provides a new rationale for expanding the carceral state. I draw on Jonathan Simon's work (2009) to argue that legislators are now using Americans' fear of sex to "govern through sex crime." This trend reflects an understanding of sexual deviance rooted in biological determinism: if sex and desire are immutable characteristics, then the state must devise new forms of social control to regulate sex.

This research program was spawned by rethinking what a sociology of sexuality might look like—to consider how it might include a conception of sex as the object of social control, regulation, and punishment. The questions that emerged from this framework required me to develop new methodological strategies for studying sex. For example, although I might one day interview individuals registered as sex offenders about their experiences, my focus has turned to the decisions and practices of agents of social control. In my view, the most pressing research questions are not about the experience of being a registered sex offender (the literature on such questions is robust and, unsurprisingly, depressing); instead, it is urgent that social scientists shed light on the various authority figures who devise and execute these policies.

SEXUAL SOCIAL CONTROL: TOWARD A QUEER SOCIOLOGY OF PUNISHMENT

When I received the email inviting me to contribute to this collection, my initial reaction included a series of facial expressions best expressed via emoji. I no longer think of myself as studying gay people, queer people, or straight people; for that I matter, I do not think of myself as studying people of *any* sexual orientation. Instead, I think of myself as a scholar of the ways the state regulates, controls, and punishes sex. Do I (or does my research) really belong in a book about "queer" methods?

In truth, I do not believe there is such a thing as a "queer method." The methods I used in my study (and those used by many "queer" scholars) are the same ones used by many other scholars studying many other kinds of social problems. What's queer about my research is not truly the methods I use to answer questions, but rather their analytic purchase. While the meaning of "queer" may be deeply contested, most scholars would likely agree that its key feature is its deconstructive impulse. By analyzing discourses of sexuality, queer scholars can reveal, for example, the problematics that circulate beneath taken-for-granted systems of sexual control or medicalized notions of sexual orientation.

While I still consider myself a sociologist of sexuality, centering my work on the state shifted my focus from phenomenological experience toward the practical techniques of social control deployed by state authorities. Although the latter approach has deep roots in the sociology canon, it comes out of a tradition of deviance studies that was largely abandoned by sexuality scholars. As I argue, sexuality scholars might reclaim this tradition as a homegrown approach to studying sex—but doing so will require rethinking our methodological strategies.

Beyond my own specific trajectory, I hope that this reflection and my research more generally begin to open up new doors for thinking about the links between sexuality and punishment. As I have argued elsewhere (Hoppe 2016), punishing sex is not merely a mimeograph of other forms of punishment; sex brings its own unique social baggage. This is plainly observed in the heightened supervision required of individuals convicted of sex offenses, but not of other, nonsexual offenses, such as assault with a deadly weapon. Sex offender registries are premised on essentialized notions of sexual deviance—that sexuality is a fixed characteristic that cannot be changed and that sexual offenders therefore require special control. Clearly, queer scholars could contribute much toward the development of alternative counternarratives that would destabilize these naturalized underpinnings to sexual social control.

By returning to focus on the most marginalized, to those labeled and punished as nuts, sluts, and perverts, sociologists might find a refreshing path forward for future scholarship in a post–gay marriage world. Sociologists might also begin to destabilize and ultimately dismantle the now-conventional account of sexual progress left on the tongues of many observers in the wake of this profound legal achievement. With over 800,000 Americans (and counting) currently registered as sex offenders, the stakes for such a move have never been higher. Sexual social control is an urgent political problem. It is a criminological problem. But at its heart, it is a social problem—ripe for sociological analysis and theory.

WORKS CITED

Foucault, M. 1965. *Madness and civilization: A history of insanity in the age of reason*. New York: Pantheon Books.

———. 1978. *History of sexuality,* Volume1: *An introduction*. Trans. Robert Hurley. New York: Random House.

———. 1979. *Discipline and punish: The birth of the prison*. New York: Vintage Books

Gamson, Joshua, and Dawne Moon. 2004. "The sociology of sexualities: Queer and beyond." *Annual Review of Sociology* 30: 47–64.

Giddens, Anthony. 1986. *The constitution of society: Outline of the theory of structuration*. Berkeley: University of California Press.

Green, Adam Isaiah. 2007. "Queer theory and sociology: Locating the subject and the self in sexuality studies." *Sociological Theory* 25: 26–45.

Halperin, David. 2003. "The normalization of queer theory." In *Queer theory and communication: From disciplining queers to queering the discipline(s)*. Ed. Gust Yep, Karen E. Lovaas, and John P. Elia, 339–43. Binghamton, NY: Haworth Press.

Hoppe, Trevor. 2016. "Punishing sex: Sex offenders and the missing punitive turn in sexuality studies." *Law & Social Inquiry* 41(3): 573–94.

Legrand, Stéphane. 2008. "'As close as possible to the unlivable': (Michel Foucault and Phenomenology)." *Sophia* 47(3): 281–91.

Liazos, Alexander. 1972. "The poverty of the sociology of deviance: Nuts, sluts, and preverts." *Social Problems* 20(1): 103–20.

Sewell, William H., Jr. 1992. "A theory of structure: Duality, agency, and transformation." *American Journal of Sociology* 98(1): 1–29.

Simon, Jonathan. 2009. *Governing through crime: How the war on crime transformed American democracy and created a culture of fear*. Oxford: Oxford University Press.

17 The Demography of Sexuality

QUEERING DEMOGRAPHIC METHODS

Amanda K. Baumle

In 1976, in a move provocatively described by Harriet Presser (1998) as a "decapitation," feminist social scientists challenged the US Census Bureau's collection of data centered on the "head of household." Since 1880, the bureau's enumeration of households had focused on identifying the "head of family" or "head of household" and describing other household members in relation to the head. The presumption was not only that identifying the head of household was a simple task but that the category conveyed something meaningful about the household structure.

Although the Census Bureau ostensibly left the designation of "head" to the household members, if a wife was identified as head of household, the bureau edited the data to assign the position to the husband (Presser 1998). Feminist social scientists argued that the use of "headship," and the editing procedure to designate male heads in married households, indicated that the bureau was improperly imputing information about power and authority within the household from this indirect measure (Presser 1998). Ultimately, they led a successful challenge that resulted in the new designation of "householder," a category meant to capture an individual who owned or rented the home.

The "decapitation" of the census reflects how the incorporation of feminist perspectives and theory into population research has resulted in important shifts in how we approach methodological questions and, accordingly, what we know about demographic processes (see, e.g., Riley 1999; Presser 1998). Such changes have implications for what we know not just about the demography of women but also about that of men. The ways that feminist theory has shaped demographic research have caused me to reflect on whether and how we might experience similar changes within the discipline as a result of employing a queer theoretical perspective. Demographic research is infused with heteronormativity, ranging from the way data are collected and how sexual orientation is conceptualized and measured to how we model demographic outcomes.

The inclusion of nonheterosexual experiences in demographic research has revealed that many demographic outcomes are shaped by sexual identity. For example, research has established that sexual orientation affects both migration and the geographic distribution of individuals (see, e.g., Baumle, Compton, & Poston 2009). My own research and that of others has highlighted the role that sexual behavior and identity play in labor outcomes, such as earnings from employment (see, e.g., Badgett 1995; Baumle, Compton, & Poston 2009). And research emphasizes that sexual orientation shapes family structure, including partnership rates (Carpenter & Gates 2008), marital unions (Andersson et al. 2006), and the presence of children in the household (Baumle, Compton, & Poston 2009).

As a scholar focused on the demography of sexuality, I have witnessed the relatively rapid emergence over the past fifteen years of this new subfield of demographic research. When I first began using US Census data in 2003 to examine labor market outcomes of same-sex partners, relatively few demographers were engaged in work on population sexuality. This was reflected in the virtual absence of demography sessions on sexuality at conferences; sessions were frequently present only if organized by a small core group of researchers using the census data. And publication of our research in demographic journals was often met with obstacles due to critiques related to surveys designed with exclusively heterosexual experiences in mind.

Those of us engaged in research on population sexuality, then, frequently were in search of an academic home—in demography, sexualities studies, or other fields. Although our work seemed a natural fit for sexualities sessions or journals, we often encountered resistance from queer theorists and qualitative sexualities scholars regarding our measurement of sexual identities and, accordingly, the relevance of our findings for nonheterosexual individuals as a whole. I recall the excitement among a group of scholars in 2012 when they held a workshop devoted to quantitative sexualities research at the American Sociological Association's Sexualities pre-conference, a more formal mechanism for tying our work to the broader sexualities scholarship.

Navigating this tension between demographic and sexualities research was a fundamental aspect of the emergence of a demography of sexuality. Ultimately, I believe, the critical voices of demographers and queer scholars generated a stronger, more reflective scholarship on population sexuality. In this chapter, I draw upon my own experiences conducting research in this area, as well as the work of others on population sexuality, to describe some of the obstacles to engaging in this research, identify key issues for new scholars in the field, and offer suggestions for how to pursue research in this field. I argue that, while research on the demography of sexuality poses unique methodological challenges for demographers, our work has the potential to shift the way that we think about population studies, including the way that gender and sexuality intersect to shape demographic outcomes. I begin by describing the way that data collection influenced the growth of the demography of sexuality, including the challenges presented to those of us who straddle the fields of population and sexuality research, and the influences of heteronormative survey construction. I then draw upon my studies of asexuality and the motherhood penalty to highlight how traditional demographic approaches to modeling outcomes are challenged by centering nonheterosexual experiences. I conclude by discussing how demographic research might benefit from the incorporation of a queer methodological approach.

THE CENSUS BUREAU'S "ACCIDENT": MEASURING SEXUAL ORIENTATION

What we know about the demographics of the LGB population can largely be credited to a by-product of collecting data about straight couples. In

1990 the US Census Bureau added a new relationship identification category to the decennial census: "unmarried partner." A surge in the number of cohabiting couples prompted the bureau to more directly measure this population in order to examine the prevalence of cohabitation and the characteristics of those living together in committed relationships (Baumle, Compton, & Poston 2009). Although bureau officials were aware that same-sex couples might opt to use this category to identify their own relationships, the idea of deliberately measuring the LGB population through the census did not factor into the construction of the survey. Indeed, later, as a result of the Defense of Marriage Act, the bureau faced direct limitations on its ability to gather data about married same-sex couples.

Studies of the LGB population were certainly being conducted that did not rely on the US Census. In particular, a series of articles had appeared using datasets such as the General Social Survey and National Health and Social Life Survey to examine income inequality and sexual practices as related to sexually transmitted infections. But it was through the use of the unmarried-partner category on the census that researchers were able to examine a variety of demographic outcomes for the LGB population. The large sample size and geographic detail about same-sex unmarried partners allowed researchers to ask the types of questions that fall within the demographer's area of expertise, including those relating to spatial distribution, residential segregation, migration, family structure, and labor market outcomes (see, e.g., Baumle, Compton, & Poston 2009). Access to data such as these ignited interest in exploring demographic differences between same-sex and different-sex couples and opened the door for new lines of inquiry.

At the same time, problems with capturing sexual orientation through a partnership measure rather than identification, coupled with fears regarding measurement error, generated debates among scholars within and outside the area of demography. Scholars, including myself, who were submitting articles based on the same-sex partner data faced questions from both demographers and sexuality scholars regarding what segment of the LGB population was really being measured through such data and how findings might differ if we took an alternative approach to measuring orientation. In many respects, these questions raised the classic essentialist-versus–social constructionist debate regarding sexual orientation.

Demographers leaned toward an essentialist approach, urging a clear-cut definition of sexual orientation that would permit the classification of individuals into categories that would enable distinctions among hetero-sexual, gay, lesbian, and bisexual experiences. As Laura Durso and Gary Gates argued (2013), when individuals are presented with fewer options, they are more likely to select a category that produces adequate sample sizes for straightforward comparisons among groups.

In contrast, sexuality scholars tended to present a more constructionist viewpoint that supports viewing sexuality across a spectrum and encourag-ing individuals to self-identify with their preferred identity label. Some of these scholars are skeptical of analyses that purport to provide information about the "LGB population" based on limited conceptualizations of sexual identity measured by the sex of one's partner or by identity captured by three categories (straight, gay, or bisexual). The queer critique of these cat-egories as absent of real meaning (can we clearly delineate what character-istics, behaviors, or life choices render one "gay"?) translates into a distrust of measurement approaches that are categorical rather than continuous. Further, the reliance on proxies for sexual identity, such as sexual behavior or the sex of one's partner, raises questions regarding the degree to which any findings can be generalized to the LGB population as a whole.

For demographers engaged in sexuality research, then, traversing this divide requires careful statements regarding the limitations of the data and clear argumentation regarding why the findings are of import irre-spective of their inclusion or exclusion of different groups. I have been, and remain, sympathetic to both of these perspectives; I accept the prac-ticality of the demographer's essentialist viewpoint for much of quantita-tive research, yet believe that we must be cautious in generalizing from findings based on this approach given that it masks the greater complexity of sexual identity and behavior. With that in mind, I have adopted two approaches for addressing these challenges in my own work. The first involves the basic practice of disclosing the weaknesses and limitations of one's data, yet emphasizing the importance of generating new knowl-edge—both to better understand a segment of the nonheterosexual popu-lation and to garner support for collecting better data in future surveys. To this end, my coauthors and I have bluntly acknowledged the problems with the US Census data, offered some discussion of the ways they compare to findings from datasets with other measures of sexual orientation, and concluded that the data are not so problematic as to render them unworthy of examination (see, e.g., Baumle 2009; Baumle, Compton, & Poston 2009). In this way we convey that no dataset is problem-free for studying sexuality, but that consistent findings will emerge across individual research endeavors and ultimately contribute to the construction of knowledge in this field. Overall, this approach has served to quell some of the debate over measurement that demographic studies of sexual orientation are certain to generate. Further, more than one reviewer has observed that a key takeaway from articles using census data has been the urgent need for new and better surveys that incorporate thoughtful consideration of how to measure sexual identity.

A second approach I have used to address concerns about measurement of sexual orientation involves the utilization of multiple measures within a single study. On some surveys, such as the National Survey of Family Growth (NSFG) and the General Social Survey (GSS), information about sexual orientation can be gleaned from more than one variable. The NSFG, for example, includes questions on sexual identity, sexual behavior, and sexual desire. Authors who have used multiple measures of sexual orientation are able to present a more nuanced picture of how sexuality shapes key demographic outcomes, including whether and when outcomes vary across different components of sexuality. In one article, my coauthor and I examined predictors of asexual responses across all three dimensions of sexuality (Poston & Baumle 2010). All three of these measures on the NSFG are imperfect for assessing asexuality, yet using a measure for identity, behavior, and desire served to distinguish commonalities and differences in characteristics of individuals expressing one or more of these components of asexuality. In addition, our three-dimension approach allowed a more thoughtful consideration of what it means to be asexual: is asexuality the absence of sexual desire, the absence of sexual behavior, a sexual identity, or some combination of these? Qualitative research on individuals who identify as asexual has indicated that the absence of sexual behavior or, indeed, desire is not a necessary prerequisite for an asexual identity (Poston & Baumle 2010). The inclusion, then, of measures of all three of these dimensions of sexuality within demographic analysis is important for both methodological and substantive understandings of sexuality.

FAMILY DEMOGRAPHY AND HETERONORMATIVE SURVEY CONSTRUCTION

In addition to difficulties involved with capturing sexual orientation itself, my work in this field led me to more fully recognize how heteronormative survey construction often collides with the study of LGBTQ individuals and their families. The manner in which questions are asked presumes heteronormative relationships and family formation practices, rendering the examination of nonheterosexual families particularly problematic. The US Census, for example, delineates all household relationships relative to the "householder." This results in children within households being identified only with respect to their relationship to the householder and not to other individuals residing in the household. This approach can reflect parent-child relationships fairly accurately within married heterosexual households where children hold the same relationship to both parents. Outside the nuclear family context, however, the collection of data on parent-child relationships between a child and only a single parent can generate a biased portrait of the household structure.

These data problems arise for any complex family structures, including cohabiting families and stepfamilies, in which boundary ambiguities can generate discrepancies among family members regarding who is, and who is not, part of a family (Brown & Manning 2009). For same-sex couples with children, however, this approach to capturing family relationships is especially problematic. After interviewing a number of LGBT parents about their relationships with their children, my coauthor and I discovered that the collection of parent-child relationships on surveys and forms was a regular source of tension for our participants. We examined this issue more closely through interviews with one hundred individuals about the ways that they identify relationships to children on census surveys (Baumle & Compton 2014). Our results reflected the tension that LGBTQ individuals experience between their identities and the identification process on surveys. Participants described how, given that both biological and legal limitations prohibited most of them from holding the same relationship to their child as that of their partner, they reasoned through their options in order to select a relationship on the form. For example, a couple who together had a child who was biologically related to only one parent might (1) choose to list the biological parent as the householder in order to simplify the relationship designation, (2) list the child as adopted if the nonbiological parent had secured a second-parent adoption, or (3) list the child as biological for the nonbiological parent because it reflected their lived experience. Overall, our results suggested that LGBTQ individuals considered the intention of the survey, the legal relationship (or lack thereof) to their partner and child or children, or their lived experiences in determining the identification option.

The stories of our participants about census identification struggles emphasized to me, as a demographer, the importance of exercising caution when using family data on census or other surveys to describe the relationships of LGBTQ persons. An indication that a child is "adopted" might not mean the same thing for same-sex couples as for different-sex couples, given the greater likelihood in the former case that the child is the biological offspring of the other household member. Further, because same-sex couples have only recently been permitted to adopt jointly in many jurisdictions, adopted children are more likely to hold that legal relationship with only one household member. When reporting on "adopted" children, therefore, the meaning of this category may be quite different for children in same-sex households than for those in different-sex households.

Many complex families, both heterosexual and nonheterosexual, encounter these survey identification challenges, and they highlight how heteronormative assumptions about procreation and family structure pervade survey instruments. The experience of LGBTQ individuals with identifying parent-child relationships underscores how we must be careful about data interpretation for complex families as a whole, as well as suggesting the need for "queer theory–informed instrumentation" (Grzanka 2016).

DEMOGRAPHIC MODELS: INTERSECTIONS OF SEX, GENDER, AND SEXUALITY

For demographers studying sexual orientation, methodological challenges are not restricted to the measurement of sexual identity or survey construction. In many instances, I have found that traditional approaches to studying demographic outcomes do not translate to nonheterosexual individuals. These difficulties are tied to the interplay between demographic theory and modeling that often rests upon heteronormative assumptions regarding sex and gender. Frequently, sex is used as a proxy measure for other gendered concepts such as parenthood responsibilities, household division of other labor, workplace behavior, and decision-making power. These assumptions do not necessarily translate to nonheterosexuals, in part because of greater variation in gender identity and performance and in part because of differences in terms of how gender operates within different-sex versus same-sex relationships. As many gender scholars have observed, gender is relational; that is, how gender operates depends partly on whether an individual is interacting with someone of the same sex or different sex. These differences render many of the traditional demographic models problematic for nonheterosexual individuals and, in turn, problematize more generally the use of sex as a proxy for gendered behaviors. As reflected by my own research and that of others, this issue arises in the areas of migration, family formation, and the motherhood wage penalty.

One example involves the way that sex is frequently incorporated into models to capture demographic outcomes as a consequence of power differentials. In migration studies, the female in a relationship is often deemed less influential for migration decisions due to unequal power relations associated with factors such as earnings and education; this is particularly the case in studies of international migration. When one considers same-sex couples, however, using sex as a proxy for power differentials becomes problematic and forces a reevaluation of current understandings of these models. As Martin Manalansan notes, incorporating sexuality into migration studies "not only expands the meaning of migration but also alters our understanding of gender and challenges migration studies' reliance on heteronormative meanings, institutions, and practices" (2006: 224).

Similar questions are raised when examining the formation of family relationships and the benefits that might be expected to accrue from them. In particular, demographers have asked whether marriage or cohabitation has the same effects on demographic outcomes for same-sex as it does for different-sex couples. A notable body of research has found a relationship between marital status and health and economic outcomes within hetero-sexual relationships, with marriage improving health and longevity for men and being positively related to earnings in the workforce (see, e.g., Waite 1995). Some have attributed married men's improved outcomes relative to unmarried men to a gendered division of labor, with married men experiencing an advantage from the presence of a female partner who might take on more of the household obligations (Waite 1995). In contrast, studies examining the division of labor in same-sex households have generally found more egalitarian arrangements (e.g., Kurdek 2004).

Such findings raise questions as to whether marriage would result in economic or health benefits for same-sex couples similar to those seen with different-sex couples. Inquiries into these areas will require a reevaluation of the types of questions asked and the models employed when assessing health and economic outcomes for same-sex couples. In particular, demographers must rely less on employing sex as having substantive importance in distinguishing differences in outcomes for married couples and, instead, consider whether a more direct assessment of labor division or gender performance must be developed. Such an approach could ultimately prove beneficial in further unraveling the manner in which marriage operates on health and economic outcomes within different-sex relationships.

Similarly, demographic models of economic outcomes have included variables grounded in gendered assumptions about work and child care. The presence of children in the household is a traditional variable employed in demographic analyses of labor outcomes, and a large body of research has found a motherhood penalty experienced by heterosexual women that is not experienced by fathers. In contrast, my own research shows that women in same-sex relationships do not experience the same penalty; rather, mothers in same-sex relationships earn more on average than do nonmothers (Baumle 2009). Although these findings do not suggest that we abandon the child variable when modeling economic outcomes, they nonetheless emphasize that the variable is measuring something other than parenthood itself and, arguably, something different from the gendered dynamics of caretaking. Is this a story about female same-sex couples dividing child care in a different way than do different-sex couples? Is it about employers' differential assessments of women whom they perceive as likely to have children versus those whom they presume not to be potential mothers? Or is it attributable to differences in entry into and exit from the labor force? By focusing on same-sex couples, demographers are becoming more thoughtful regarding what exactly is being measured and, in turn, what these results might suggest about how gender and parenthood operate within the workplace.

CONCLUSION: QUEERING DEMOGRAPHY

The field of demography has shifted in response to the incorporation of both feminist and critical race theories. These changes have resulted in a move from focusing on demographic experiences as homogenous toward recognizing the ways that characteristics such as sex and race shape demographic outcomes, including migration, mortality, fertility, economic effects, and family structure. Increasingly, scholars of race and gender demography have encouraged going beyond simply including sex or race as a variable in demographic models, toward a consideration of how demographic models and theories might need to be modified to capture differing experiences. Similarly, queering demography holds promise, I believe, for not only better capturing the characteristics of the LGBTQ population but also for provoking reflection upon our approaches to studying the heterosexual population.

Incorporating a queer theoretical perspective into demographic research emphasizes the ways that survey construction, and the resulting data, is imbued with heteronormative assumptions about sexuality and relationship formation. Push-back from queer theorists and qualitative sociologists challenged, and created an environment in which to debate, how to best measure sexual orientation. This dialogue with sexuality scholars has encouraged demographers to consider the best questions to include on surveys, as well as who is really captured by any of these measurements. This involves demographers being more thoughtful about whether "different-sex couples" or individuals who identify primarily as different-sex sex partners can be presumed heterosexual. Questions about how to measure the transgender population have also sparked conversation about the lack of exhaustive categories within traditional methods of collecting data about sex. And the study of family relationships within same-sex households has emphasized how many household-level questions about relationships are ill-suited for those that do not embody the heteronormative nuclear family. Bringing a queer perspective to demography, therefore, has the capacity to lead to improved measurement of sex, gender, sexuality, and relationships for both heterosexual and nonheterosexual populations. In this respect, the way that the demography of sexuality has straddled multiple disciplines has encouraged demographers to reflect on our choices in ways that might otherwise have been absent.

As my own experience with article reviewers suggests, part of the response to the dissemination of demographic information about LGBTQ populations has involved a growing recognition of the need for better data. Since the US Supreme Court struck down key portions of the Defense of Marriage Act in *United States v. Windsor* (2013), the US Census Bureau has taken measures to both count and release data on same-sex marriages. This includes testing relationship options for "same-sex husband/wife/spouse," "same-sex unmarried partner," and "opposite sex" counterparts. The availability of these response options should dramatically improve data quality, given that they will provide a second validity check that will reduce the likelihood of contaminating the same-sex couple pool with different-sex couples whose sex has been misreported. In addition, Representative Raul Grijalva introduced the LGBT Data Inclusion Act in the US House of Representatives in May 2016. This act called for the inclusion of LGBT identity questions on government surveys, including the National Health Interview Survey, the American Community Survey, and the Behavioral Risk Factor Surveillance System. The push for more and better data about the LGBTQ population on large, nationally representative surveys has the potential to spur additional inquiry into questions surrounding population sexuality.

In addition to discussions regarding survey construction, focusing on LGBTQ experiences has thus far problematized the practice of using variables such as sex or presence of children in demographic models. Both variables have been used as proxy measures for gendered behaviors, but assumptions regarding gender do not necessarily translate to the LGBTQ population. In particular, the ways in which gender is relational can result in different relationship dynamics for same-sex versus different-sex couples that alter demographic outcomes (Umberson et al. 2015). Queering demography requires, in part, a closer examination of how we measure concepts in our models and, in turn, what varying outcomes for same-sex couples might mean for our models and theories as a whole.

Bringing a queer theoretical perspective to demographic research holds promise for the development of knowledge on how sex, gender, and sexuality shape populations. Queer theory's focus on the deconstruction of identity categories and on centering minority experiences serves to expose gender-normative and heteronormative assumptions underlying demographic research. In this respect, I believe that incorporating a queer perspective into demography could prompt demographers to engage in a self-conscious reassessment of the manner in which hegemonic power differentials within sexuality and gender have shaped our analyses. To continue to advance research about population sexuality, we must acknowledge that methodological rigor requires our approaches to be both reflexive and evolving, responsive to influences from scholarship outside more traditional demographic approaches. In these respects, collaboration between demographers and sexuality scholars builds upon and strengthens what we know about how to study sexuality.

WORKS CITED

Andersson, Gunnar, Turid Noack, Ane Seierstad, and Harald Weedon-Fekjaer. 2006. "The demographics of same-sex marriages in Norway and Sweden." *Demography* 43: 79–98.

Badgett, M. V. Lee. 1995. "The wage effects of sexual orientation discrimination." *Industrial and Labor Relations Review* 48: 726–739.

Baumle, Amanda K. 2009. "The cost of parenthood: Unraveling the effects of sexual orientation and gender on income." *Social Science Quarterly* 90: 983–1002.

Baumle, Amanda K., D'Lane Compton, and Dudley L. Poston Jr. 2009. *Same-sex partners: The social demography of sexual orientation.* Albany: State University of New York Press.

Baumle, Amanda K., and D'Lane R. Compton. 2014. "Identity versus identification: How LGBTQ parents identify their children on census surveys." *Journal of Marriage and Family* 76: 94–104.

Brown, Susan L., & Wendy D. Manning 2009. "Family boundary ambiguity and the measurement of family structure: The significance of cohabitation." *Demography* 46: 85–101.

Carpenter, Christopher, and Gary J. Gates. 2008. "Gay and lesbian partnership: Evidence from California." *Demography* 45: 573–90.

Durso, Laura, and Gary Gates. 2013. "Best practices: Collecting and analyzing data on sexual minorities." In *International Handbook on the Demography of Sexuality*. Ed. Amanda K. Baumle, 21–42. Dordrecht, The Netherlands: Springer.

Grzanka, Patrick R. 2016. "Queer survey research and the ontological dimensions of heterosexism." *WSQ: Women's Studies Quarterly* 44: 131–49.

Kurdek, Lawrence A. 2004. "Are gay and lesbian cohabitating couples really different from heterosexual married couples?" *Journal of Marriage and Family* 66(4): 880–900.

Manalansan, Martin F., IV. 2006. "Queer intersections: Sexuality and gender in migration studies." *International Migration Review* 40: 224–49.

Poston, Dudley L., and Amanda K. Baumle. 2010. "Patterns of asexuality in the United States." *Demographic Research* 23: 509–30.

Presser, Harriet B. 1998. "Decapitating the U.S. Census Bureau's 'head of household': Feminist mobilization in the 1970s." *Feminist Economics* 4(3): 145–58.

Riley, Nancy E. 1999. "Challenging demography: Contributions from feminist theory." *Sociological Forum* 14: 369–97.

Umberson, Debra, Mieke Beth Thomeer, Rhiannon A. Kroeger, Amy C. Lodge, and Minle Xu. 2015. "Challenges and opportunities for research on same-sex relationships." *Journal of Marriage and Family* 77: 96–111.

Waite, Linda. 1995. "Does marriage matter?" *Demography* 32: 483–507.

18 What to Do with Actual People?

THINKING THROUGH A QUEER SOCIAL
SCIENCE METHOD

C. J. Pascoe

About a decade ago, as a newly minted PhD, I attended a public discussion between psychoanalyst Ken Corbett and queer theorist Judith Butler. I forget the actual topic of the discussion, these years later. But I remember vividly Dr. Corbett sharing a vignette about the complicated emotional terrain of masculinity that would later appear in his book *Boyhoods*.

"It is summer, and I am driving to the beach. The top is down. My seven-year-old nephew Alex is in the back seat, his blond hair wild and in the wind. Eminem raps from the stereo speakers. . . . I turn around and Alex is standing on the seat, raising one fist in the air, grabbing his crotch with his other hand, and doing his best Eminem. He shouts, 'This is the life!'" (Corbett 2009: 208). Corbett proceeded to unpack this tender and complicated moment in terms of masculine play, pleasure, and performance. Professor Butler responded with an equally compelling analysis about the nature of gender, sexuality, inequality, and power. I, who only moments before was imagining myself in the car rapping along with Alex and Eminem about not missing our one shot, was seduced, totally thrilled by her heady deconstructive discourse about performativity and abject identities. With a soft smile Corbett slowly shook his head and said, "Well, of course *you* can say that, Jude, *because you don't have to deal with actual people.*"[1]

"You don't have to deal with actual people." Indeed, like many social science graduate students who were introduced to and enthralled by queer theory in the late 1990s,[2] I wanted to use all queer theory All The Time to analyze All Things. However, as a social scientist in training, I found my concern summed up in Corbett's comment—What *do* you do with actual people? While I tend to the humanistic side of sociology as a discipline, I'm still, by comparison, an empiricist. I found myself knee-deep in writings by Sedgwick, Butler, Halberstam, and Bersani, among others, wondering how to take theory designed for literary criticism and close readings, theory focused on exploring heteronormative assumptions underpinning great literary works, art, and philosophic claims, and use it to deal with and understand *actual flesh-and-blood people in their everyday worlds,* not just literary, filmic, or artistic representations of them. When one has been trained as a sociologist, even a feminist sociologist, to look for patterns, develop categories out of those patterns, and provide a perhaps replicable analysis about those categories, according to the critical research stance that sociology entails, how does one invoke a theoretical sensibility designed to interrogate the very basis of those categories and is suspicious of the categories themselves as examples of the workings of power? As Steven Seidman (1994) and others point out, the sensibilities and many of the insights embraced by queer theory were originally given voice by radical social constructionist sociological theories as well as interdisciplinary feminist theories, neither of which are optimally acknowledged by queer theorists.

The question is, How does this translate methodologically—when one is dealing with actual people—from the very conception of a project to its execution, its analysis, its writing and publication? After all, I had been trained in a disciplinary tradition that, as Regina Kunzel (2008) points out, had been a central part of the normative project of constructing sexuality itself. As a graduate student stumbling through ethnographic research and analysis, somewhere along the way and in large part due to the feminist mentorship I received, I developed what I am calling a queer social science method. A queer social science method at its core is one that brings the patterned, lived experiences of actual people into conversation with queer theoretical insights. In this essay I suggest that scholars who want to further develop a queer social science method might start with the

following propositions: embracing failure, deploying categorical ambivalence, and emphasizing a critical focus on the center, not the periphery.

EMBRACE OF FAILURE

"Failing is something queers do and have always done exceptionally well,"
writes Jack Halberstam in the introduction to *The Queer Art of Failure*
(2011: 3). For me, stumbling into a queer social science method was,
indeed, a process of failure. Even writing this particular essay is an experience fraught with the pain, embarrassment, and stigma that characterized
the dissertation research, analysis, writing, publishing, and job search
process. Then, and to some extent now, a sense of failure characterized
those endeavors. When I read Halberstam's book,[3] some of the shame,
embarrassment, and stigma began to ebb as I realized that perhaps this
wasn't my experience alone, but a shared one. A queer one. My dissertation, which was subsequently published as the book *Dude, You're a Fag:
Masculinity and Sexuality in High School* (2007), is the result of multiple
failures, the sort of failures Halberstam in *The Queer Art of Failure* rechar-
acterizes as inherently queer. These are the sort of failures I am going to
suggest might be central to a queer social science method.

Here is an incomplete and brief list of the failures behind *Dude:*

- *Failure* to find a research site. I contacted school after school after
  school after school, more than fifty, if I recall correctly. No public school
  wanted to admit a graduate student researcher to study adolescent
  masculinity, it seemed to me. One school even went so far as to say it
  had someone conducting the exact project I described at the school
  already. I haven't seen the results of that study.

- *Failure* to move the project through the institutional review board.
  Multiple iterations of my human subjects proposals were rejected. I
  tried to ask for help, in person and by phone. Repeatedly I was told by
  the IRB representative in charge of my proposal some version of, "Tell us
  what you want to do, and we'll tell you whether or not you can do it."
  Without their guidance I changed the wording of my proposal over and
  over again, guessing as to what phrasing might please them until finally
  they passed it through, even though the proposed research itself
  remained relatively unchanged.

- *Failure* to get a job. Perhaps like many of us, my first year on the job market was an abysmal one. Was this due to my research topic? It turns out, sociology departments weren't exactly outdoing each other to recruit sexuality scholars. Was it due to my recommendations? Rumors emerged about a less-than-optimal letter of recommendation in my file suggesting that *Dude* lacked an argument. Still other rumors suggested less-than-optimal relations between that letter writer and graduate students. I still wonder to this day what was in that letter and if it or my research was the problem.

- *Failure* to be a sociologist. I have often described myself as a very bad sociologist. In fact I published an article in a *sociology* journal for the first time in 2015. Until then, I had published in interdisciplinary journals. When I was invited for talks, it was rarely to sociology departments.[4] I instead spoke to sexuality programs, psychology programs, gender and women's studies programs, and gave university keynote lectures, often never hearing from any representative in a sociology department during my visit.

To be honest, it never occurred to me that these experiences, among myriad others, were anything more than my own. Certainly, we all have our job, research, and publishing struggles. Graduate student life is emotionally, financially, and intellectually challenging for many of us. However, my understanding of these struggles began to shift when I found myself sitting in the audience of the ASA Sexuality pre-conference in 2012.[5] I listened as Janice Irvine documented unique struggles of sexuality researchers by sharing the initial results of her study of sociologists of sexuality. Her study indicated that as sexuality scholars, we are faced with unique challenges throughout our professional lives—harassment in the field site, harassment and intellectual dismissal by our colleagues, difficulty getting published in journals, to name a few (Irvine 2014). I wasn't alone as tears streamed down my face listening to Irvine tell our stories in our words. I remember hearing her quote other scholars, and thinking, "Wait, did I write that?" Our stories were shared stories. The stories of sexuality research were ones of failure in so many ways: failure to avoid sexual harassment, failure to be gendered correctly, failure to be understood as legitimate sociologists, failure to reproduce normative messages about sexuality, failure to publish in the right venues for tenure, failure to get jobs, failure to hold on to those jobs—stories of violent tenure denials some of us witnessed firsthand. We were, collectively in that room, the queer art of failure.

It turns out I was not alone in my failures. Rather as I detail below, my inability to do a more traditional sociological analysis of sexuality was a failure to be part of the normative project of social science. As Halberstam writes, "Disciplines qualify and disqualify, legitimate and delegitimate, reward and punish: most important, they statically reproduce themselves and inhibit dissent" (2011: 10). The discipline of sociology itself, into which so many of us entered, perhaps because of fantasies about how research and knowledge production can inform social action and social change, was the same discipline that, because of its epistemological engagement with the production of "the norm," relegated us and our research to the sidelines at best, and to failure at worst.

QUEER POSITIONALITY

Queer positionality itself might be part of that failure. Feminist method-ologies tell us that the researcher herself is a central part of the research process (see, for instance, England 1994). A queer social science method builds on this insight, suggesting that the researcher's sexuality is also a central part of the research process. In fact, the failure to inhabit a binary social organization of researcher-researched, adult-child (1988), boy-girl (Pascoe 2007) may be an important part of the findings. In researching *Dude*, I found that my particular queer positionality as a twenty-some-thing researcher embodied a wide variety of failures to conform to bina-ries like these, failures that were central to the research process: failure to be a role model for sexual-minority students (as recommended by liberal out-and-proud narratives; Connell 2014); failure to be a normatively gen-dered woman; failure to be readable as an adult; failure to be readable as a student; failure to maintain expected age, geographic, temporal, and social boundaries; and, finally, failure to leave the field.

Upon first arriving at the field site for *Dude*, "River High," I pulled the rainbow sticker off my car in violation of that "out-and-proud" expectation. But lack of a rainbow symbol did not stop the LGBTQ young people at the school from recognizing me as one of their own. As I tried to conform to social science research methods about the divide between researcher and researched, I attempted to evade answers about my sexual life. Shawna, a tangential member of one of the groups I studied, the Basketball Girls, once followed me out of the school cafeteria, saying, "I have to ask you my question but I'm not sure how." I joked with her, hoping to skirt questions about my sexuality by asking, "Do you want to know how much I weigh?" Shawna responded, "No," and the other Basketball Girls laughed. I threw out a few more joking questions: "How old I am? What my favorite color is? How many kids I have?" As Shawna and I continued to walk, the other girls fell away, and she asked me, "So are you into girls?" I replied, "What makes you ask that?" She murmured, "I dunno," as she shuffled uncomfortably. "'Cause you wear that big jacket and 'cause the way you like move and talk and stuff, and 'cause you used to have your hair all short." I nodded to indicate that I understood why she was asking that question and responded by saying that I could answer her when I was done with my research in December. I found myself wanting to be out to these girls as a role model because there were no other out gay adults at River High. Even years later I get asked by audiences why I didn't stand up for Ricky to the administration or why I wasn't out to the sexual-minority students at River. A sense that I somehow failed these young people in need of an adult role model still haunts me these years later.

Similarly, I struggled and perhaps failed, to encourage the boys I was studying to maintain socially sanctioned, age-based sexual boundaries. In part, perhaps, to render my queer positionality as legible in their world, some boys I studied did their best to frame me as a potential (hetero)sexual conquest. For instance, one day as I was sitting around with some of the boys in the weight room, one of them, J.W., was looking pensive, sheepish, or mopey, I couldn't tell which. He finally sidled up to me and asked, in a saccharine bashful voice, "Can I ask you a personal question?" This question always gave me pause. I had been asking these young people all sorts of personal questions for over a year. I felt that I should reciprocate, as per the guidelines of feminist research methodology, to a certain extent, with information about myself. I answered "Sure," thinking I could talk myself out of inappropriate questions about whether or not I was married, gay, or straight, usually the vein of these personal questions. Instead, J.W. surprised me with a question I didn't fully understand but inferred the meaning of quite quickly: "Have you ever had your walls ripped?" Given the context of the boys' previous discussions about making girlfriends bleed by "ripping their walls," I assumed this particular sexual experience had something to do with their penises being so large that they produced bloody tears in their girlfriends' vaginal walls. Responding neutrally and hoping to see if my interpretation was correct, I asked, "What do you mean, 'walls ripped'?" J.W. stammered trying to answer the question. After an awkward moment and feeling uncomfortable myself, I said, "I know what it means. Why do you want to know?" He responded, "Cuz, I like to know if girls are freaky or not. I like freaky girls." That is, he wanted to know if I was a "girl" he could like because of my unconventional sexual practices.

Both Shawna and J.W. were trying to render my sexuality legible and, in doing so, produce meanings about sexuality in general. Shawna wanted to know if she was reading my sexual "sign equipment" (Goffman 1978 [1956]) of black shirts, cargo pants, and bodily comportment correctly. J.W. was trying to make those signs legible as well—through discursive sexual violence. J.W. wasn't alone. In the course of my research boys grabbed me, physically confined me, and joked about "banging" me. The way in which the young people I was researching dealt with my queer positionality—looking to me as a role model or as an object of sexual harassment—became an important part of the research process and indeed a finding itself.

In a way I never anticipated, this queer positionality also blurred the lines around the boundary site itself in terms of leaving the field. Years after *Dude* was published, I found myself a devoted member of an online community of queer parents. Over the years, we shared our challenges and successes with fertility struggles, parenting adventures, and partnership formations and dissolutions. The group's members still remain in almost daily contact with one another. A year or so into my participation in this group, a member private-messaged me to ask if I was C.J. Pascoe, the one who interviewed her at River High in the early 2000s? In that instant, I discovered that I had been sharing some of my most intimate struggles around queer family making with a member of this group who had indeed been a student at River High. Years after I had left the field, this member of one of the student groups I had studied, the GSA Girls, and I found ourselves bonding over being queer parents.

Queer positionalities blur the boundaries of the field, the boundaries of
age, and perhaps, with the help of the internet, the boundaries of space.
Forging a friendship with my former respondent felt in some ways like
violating expectations that had been premised on discrete communities,
on ways of knowing that assumed a researcher who was not part of the
community of the researched. This queer positionality itself, as negotiated
by me and by my respondents, is a central component of a queer social
science method.

CATEGORICAL AMBIVALENCE

A queer social science method embraces an ambivalent stance toward categories. This is no easy task given sociologists' love of categories. We are a
social science after all, one that emerged from Auguste Comte's project to
extend the method of scientific classification from the natural to the social.
However, feminist sociologists, such as those who populated my PhD program and made up the internal members of my dissertation committee,
had developed a robust critique of ways of knowing that constituted social
scientific findings. That critique and the training I received from them in
feminist methodologies laid the groundwork for uncovering findings that
perhaps might not square with existing scholarship. Even so, as a nascent
social scientist, I entered the field ready to fit my findings firmly into the
literature about youth culture, literature that detailed the wide array of
groups that defined adolescent life. I entered River High primed to look
for the organization of students into the distinct categories I had read so
much about in the literature on young people.

Armed with my notebook, I looked around, eager to record the River
High versions of the Hallway Hangers, Brothers, Lads, Ear'ols, Rednecks,
Rutters, Cool Kids, Jocks, Dropouts, Freaks. Soon I had my answer: students were talking about "fags." Whoever these guys were, they were refer-
enced constantly. Male students used this phrase incessantly and seemingly apropos of nothing. Walking down a hallway, for instance, a boy
would yell, "Fucking faggot!" at no one in particular. Curious, I began to
ask students who the "fags" were. Where would I find them? Who was in
this group? Student responses soon told me that that was the wrong set of

questions to be asking. There was only one student who others held up as an example of a fag, not a group of them.

In other words, the social category or group to which students belonged was not the finding; the production of the very category itself was. I shifted my focus from a traditionally sociological approach emphasizing categories of young people, to a focus on the discursive production of masculinity. I came to call this process, by which boys disciplined one another into normatively masculine identities, enactments, and values through joking and serious forms of gendered homophobia, a "fag discourse." As such, instead of following classifications, I followed the discursive nature of the classification *process*, focusing on how gendered and sexualized meanings were mobilized and deployed across a range of students, contexts, and situations. In the failure to find groups, I found discourses. This failure, in this case, was the finding. Thanks to the feminist scholars on my dissertation committee, this failure was allowed to be the finding.

FOCUS ON THE CENTER

Perhaps because of the word *fag* in the title, after the publication of *Dude*, I came to be seen as an expert on LGBTQ youth. I was asked to serve on advisory boards for organizations working on behalf of LGBTQ youth, to comment on research on sexual-minority young people, to advise on LGBTQ issues in education, and frequently received press calls requesting comment and expertise on LGBTQ youth suicide or victimization. The problem was, I did not actually research queer youth. In fact, I found myself frequently reading up on all the research *others* had conducted on LGBTQ young people in order to answer these questions. Among the fifty young people I interviewed for *Dude*, one boy identified as gay and five girls identified as some variation of queer or lesbian. Whom did I know a lot about? Heterosexual teenage boys. *Dude*, at its core, is a book about heterosexual masculinity.

Why did people repeatedly fail to ask me about heterosexuality? It may indeed be because I use the word *fag* in the book's title. But I would suggest that this failure is due to a reaction to the book's request that readers turn their focus from the margin, the other, the victimized LGBTQ youth, to the center, to heterosexuality. To, perhaps, themselves. Repeatedly, academic and nonacademic audiences alike would, in a variety of ways, ask me to tell the story about how bad it was for gay kids in school. Repeatedly, I would answer by refocusing the conversation on institutional, discursive, and interactional productions of gender, especially heterosexual masculinity. Audience reactions to this refocus ranged from cool dismissal to downright anger. At one talk to a psychological staff at a large state prison, a listener stood up, interrupted me, and insisted that I used the phrase "homophobic discourse" rather than "fag discourse" as *fag* was offensive. When I unpacked for him the gendered nature of the use of this word and why the boys' practices did not, in fact, constitute the sort of homophobia he wanted me to talk about, he angrily walked out of the room. But not before first lecturing me about why I was wrong.

Indeed, even journal reviewers weren't keen on the story I was telling about heterosexual masculinity. As one reviewer wrote of the article "'Dude You're a Fag': Adolescent Masculinity and the Fag Discourse" (2005), which eventually appeared in the journal *Sexualities,* "At times, it almost seems as if he is taking revenge on male heterosexuality by both emptying 'it' (p. 10) and parodying 'it.'" Note that I am a "he" and that there are confusing scare quotes around "it." At that time and to this day I could not find evidence of this "revenge" and so changed nothing in the article. This comment, however, is instructive in that it encapsulates a larger discomfort with the way in which this research focuses on the center. To analyze heterosexual masculinity and its production is to take revenge on it. Analysis, in this line of thinking, is reserved for the *other,* the categories about which we can know, catalogue, and pathologize.

As queer theorists point out, turning an analytic lens on the center destabilizes the very category of the norm itself. That, apparently, is profoundly unsettling to reviewers, popular audiences, and other academics as they continually attempt to pull the discussion toward a narrative focusing on the suffering LGBTQ youth. This is indeed an important story, but it's not the story of *Dude.* The story of *Dude* is one of normative heterosexual masculinity and the institutional, interactional, and discursive violence that produces it. When I'm talking to audiences, I often remember how when one of my children was a toddler and wanted me to focus on something he didn't yet have words for, he would take my head, place a hand on either cheek, and gently turn it again and again toward the thing he wanted to talk about until I acknowledged The Thing. To maintain a useful analytic focus, a queer social science method might require acting like that toddler, continually reminding the audience of the center, no matter how many times they look away.

STUMBLING THROUGH A QUEER SOCIAL SCIENCE METHOD

As Halberstam reminds us, "Under certain circumstances failing, losing, forgetting, unmaking, undoing, unbecoming, not knowing may in fact offer more creative, more cooperative, more surprising ways of being in the world" (Halberstam 2011: 2). This sort of failure, of not knowing, captures what it felt like to me to research *Dude*, a process that I now think of as stumbling into a queer social science method. The failures in this particular research project, as Halberstam might say, were deeply queer, and reflection on them helps to elaborate a queer social science method that embraces failure as a way of knowing, as a finding in itself. It is a method that suggests ways to bring the experiences of "actual people" into dialogue with queer theory through an embrace of queer positionality, expressions of categorical ambivalence, and a focus on the center.

All that said, even as I share some of these embarrassing and perhaps shameful moments in the research process, I'm not sure at this point that *Dude* can be read as a failure. After its publication the book sold exceedingly well. Chapters have been reprinted, some multiple times. It's been favorably cited frequently. To continue with the failure metaphor, did I fail to fail? What had felt like "outsider research" for so long has made its way, perhaps, to the "inside." But with that move comes a certain loss. That queerness—the repeated failures that informed who I was, how I worked, and what I did—was central to the research findings featured in *Dude*. I question what will be lost as I enter the ethnographic field once again in the next few months. As an insider with a job, a reputation, and an influential book, the stakes of failure are different. As such, the ways of knowing in this next project will be different. I do not enter into this particular ethnography accompanied by "ways of being and knowing that stand outside of conventional understandings of success" (Halberstam 2011: 2). This time I'm situated well within the bounds of the discipline. While this means that my graduate students' intellectual trajectory will not be shaped by watching mentors experience tenure denial based on their research topics, it also raises questions about what will be elided by insider ways of knowing. Can a queer social science method exist as an "insider method"?

A queer social science method is informed at once by queer theory and by sociology, a discipline whose claim to science and systematic data collection pushes back against the destabilizing impulse of queer theory. This method embraces the margins and boundary transgression. It casts a critical eye at the "normal." It interrogates the very categories upon which social scientists rely to make claims, while perhaps gathering information about the operation of those categories. It is a method in tension with itself. It is precisely by embracing this tension that a queer social science can deploy the best of both disciplines—the deconstructionist theoretical sensibilities of queer theory and attention to systemic research on the experiences of "actual people" embodied by sociology. This is the project of a queer social science.

NOTES

1. This may not be the direct quote, as I've been telling this story for years. But, I promise, he did say "Jude."

2. Thanks to the inspiration and forethought of my youngest and queerest, Doc Marten–wearing dissertation committee member, who after reading my research memos, quickly handed me work by Leo Bersani and Judith Butler.

3. Which indeed I *failed* to do for many years because I was too busy building a family and having babies . . .

4. Save for Brandeis University, my alma mater and a school still blessedly informed by the Frankfurt School—one of my earliest intellectual influences.

5. The first ASA Sexuality pre-conference. Ever. In 2012. Let that sink in.

WORKS CITED

Connell, Catherine. 2014. *School's out: Gay and lesbian teachers in the classroom*. Berkeley: University of California Press.

Corbett, Ken. 2009. *Boyhoods: Rethinking masculinities*. New Haven: Yale University Press.

England, Kim V. L. 1994. "Getting personal: Reflexivity, positionality, and feminist research." *Professional Geographer* 46(1): 80–89.

Goffman, Erving. 1978 [1956]. *The presentation of self in everyday life*. Harmondsworth, UK: Penguin.

Halberstam, Jack. 2011. *The queer art of failure*. Durham, NC: Duke University Press.

Irvine, Janice M. 2014. "Is sexuality research 'dirty work'? Institutionalized stigma in the production of sexual knowledge." *Sexualities* 17(5–6): 632–56.

Kunzel, Regina G. 2008. *Criminal intimacy: Prison and the uneven history of modern American sexuality*. Chicago: University of Chicago Press.

Pascoe, C. J. 2005. "Dude, you're a fag: Adolescent masculinity and the fag discourse." *Sexualities* 8(3): 329–46.

———. 2007. *Dude, you're a fag: Masculinity and sexuality in high school*. Berkeley: University of California Press.

———. 2007. "What if a guy hits on you?" In *Representing Youth: Methodological Issues in Critical Youth Studies*. Ed. Amy L. Best. New York: New York University Press.

Seidman, Steven. 1994. "Queer-ing sociology, sociologizing queer theory: An introduction." *Sociological Theory* 12(2): 166–77.

19 Queer Accounting

METHODOLOGICAL INVESTMENTS
AND DISINVESTMENTS

Carla A. Pfeffer

In 1998, I was working on an undergraduate honors thesis focusing on lesbians' experiences in psychotherapy. As I conducted interviews, several of my participants began discussing either their partner's or their own intention to "transition," or move from self- and social identification as a woman to that as a man (or transgender man). I was not very familiar with what it meant to transition, so I asked my research participants to tell me more. I quickly learned that this phenomenon I had stumbled upon was potentially more interesting, and less defined in existing research literatures, than the one I had initially set out to study. Seven years later, just two years after beginning my doctoral studies, my own lesbian-identified partner at the time began to identify as transmasculine. Over the next several years, my then-partner began using "he" and "his" pronouns, legally changed his name, and had "top surgery" to bring his chest into closer alignment with his transmasculine identity.

My academic interests and personal life converged. I became more invested in finding information about the sort of relationship that I was developing with my trans partner. There were very few guideposts then for women in partnerships with trans men, and the writings about relationships most closely resembling them seemed to be those focusing on lesbian butch-femme identity and relationship dynamics. I was also deeply entrenched in the early stages of professional socialization. I attended conferences and engaged in pre-conference conversations and workshop sessions wherein graduate students learned, ultimately, normative expectations for how we should style and present both our selves and our work. This professional socialization process also involved careful observation of how these processes unfold among others in departmental colloquia and conference sessions. I watched as both budding and senior scholars dismissed and derided some scholarship as "me-search," that dreaded brand that marks researchers who have either an explicitly stated or assumed personal connection to the subject or population on which their research focuses. Through these early professional socialization experiences, I learned that this sort of research was selfish navel gazing, zealotry, nonrigorous, nonobjective, and nonneutral—always at risk of becoming advocacy or activism rather than "real" or legitimate scholarship (see also Schilt, this volume).

INVESTING IN "ME-SEARCH": ACCOUNTS AND ACCOUNTABILITY

The graduate courses I took that focused on research logic, sociological theory, and quantitative and qualitative methods offered ways for me to think through and develop critiques of flippant and routinized dismissals of so-called me-search. My coursework in feminist epistemologies and methodologies (for an excellent overview, see Hesse-Biber 2012) provided me with tools for disinvesting from normative values and assumptions about how best to study, understand, and write about lives lived on the margins. These normative values and assumptions include, but are not limited to, commitments to researcher total objectivity, detachment, and neutrality (which include practices such as double-blind peer review and avoidance of "me-search"); viewing researchers as entirely separate from (or irrelevant to) their data and analysis; the belief that social science research involves the collection of facts and absolute truths; viewing quantitative methods as more objective and value-neutral than qualitative methods; comparative case analysis as a gold standard for qualitative approaches; belief that research is published or not published on the basis of its rigor, import, and merit alone; and viewing studies of marginal individuals, groups, or topics as appropriately targeted to specialist rather than generalist journals.

Let us consider just one of these normative assumptions: that quantitative methods of data collection are less value-laden and more objective than qualitative methods. Researchers who use quantitative approaches must make decisions across a broad array of matters—from initial research conceptualization to dissemination—that are often imbued with their values and interpretations. Consider the ways in which questions about sex, gender, and sexuality are often posed to survey participants. The response options researchers offer may reveal critical disparities between the conceptual interpretations of researcher and participant. For example, researchers often operationalize the concept of sex by using only two binary options rather than the fuller spectrum of possible variants (including intersex), or by employing terms such as *woman* or *man,* rather than *female* or *male.* Researchers may fail to include categories that reflect the identities of their participants, who then either become "missing data" or shoehorn themselves into ill-fitting conceptual categories. Do researchers even become aware of such elisions and data distortions, let alone seek to redress them? How researchers "collapse" their variables for analysis may reflect their views about sex, gender, and sexuality self-identifications that may be directly at odds with their participants' self-identifications, thereby imposing researchers' values onto both their research participants and their analytic constructs.

Rather than shy away from these muddy and potentially contentious intersections between self-representation, interpretation, and understanding, I came to invest my energies, instead, in all that may be learned by leaning and peering into them. I came to consider researchers' talk about (or avoidance of talking about) their own personal connections to the topics and populations they study as an issue of personal accountability and other researchers' inquiries into those connections a matter of professional accountability. Does the white male researcher studying family formation practices discuss the contours of his own family growing up or his family today in his research, and do these contours seem to have any bearing on his research as revealed by questions he fields about his research from his peers—and why or why not?

As with the narrative data I collect from research participants, I came to view researchers' discussion of their connection to their topics or populations under study (and the presence or absence of such discussion) as situated "accounts" that are externally motivated and compelled in myriad ways. Marvin Scott and Stanford Lyman (1968) proposed the notion of "accounts" as part of their sociology of talk, which theorized that what we say to one another (and how we say it) reflects not only the reality or facts of a situation but also our attempts to bridge or smooth over actual or potential inconsistencies between our actions and others' stated or perceived expectations. I became less interested in searching for "the objective truth" or what is "real" than in listening to people's accounts of their own actions, research, and the patterns that emerge across these accounts. My aim is to learn more about how people make meaning, how they work to shape the way that others account and make meaning, and the systematicity across these accounts.

I disinvested from the notion that distance and detachment provide the optimal context for rigorous empirical investigation and, instead, invested in the idea that we must work toward personal accountability in our research, developing the willingness to identify our various connections and disconnections with the populations we study and to invest the effort to challenge normatively proscriptive research practices. Dorothy Smith wrote about the potential dangers of "conceptual imperialism" (1974: 8) within the discipline of sociology, as researchers develop a bifurcated consciousness and become alienated, as a methodological imperative, from that which they research. Investing in researcher accountability, I argue, allows researchers—including those engaged in research with communities in which they are a part—to offer more holistic (and potentially less alienating) insights about the dynamic social processes, strengths, and tensions that exist within the communities they study.

Investing in Researcher Accountability

I recall from an interdisciplinary seminar a heated discussion of Susan Krieger's *The Mirror Dance: Identity in a Women's Community* (1983). In this foundational work in lesbian history, Krieger offers narrative excerpts from ethnography and research interviews. There is virtually no interpretation or analysis, simply a series of interview snippets. My first assessment of this work was that it constituted the very best in feminist research possibilities on queer communities—an ability to quite literally "give voice" to an underrepresented community without researcher intervention. By the end of the class and my methods training, however, my perspective shifted entirely. I came to consider such an approach not simply inadequate but possibly an abrogation of responsibility to make sense of research participants' accounts and explicate their potential contributions, limitations, and implications.

Imagine a railroad conductor who observes an obstacle on the tracks ahead of the train but who merely notates it rather than pulling the brake cord; a physician who draws a blood sample revealing elevated glucose and who notes the figure in the patient's chart but offers no prescription and does not discuss diabetes management with the patient; a teacher who tests students but never lets them know what grade they received. In each of these scenarios, a critical feedback loop has been interrupted with professional responsibility breached along the way. Why should research be any different? It is not that the conductor's, physician's, teacher's, or researcher's feedback and analysis are necessarily infallible, but that the very purpose of their specialized training and knowledge development is to render them accountable for providing it as a matter of professional and ethical responsibility. I came to invest in standpoint feminist epistemology, which values the particular insights and analytic interpretations of researchers situated within their own communities and social networks, as one method for becoming accountable in the practice of conducting my work and developing and disseminating knowledge.

In a graduate course on qualitative methods, I learned to put knowledge into practice as I entered the field and gathered data. I was urged to consider how my presence, questions, and verbal and nonverbal responses constitute an intervention, as researchers are always part of the account and the accounting process. Accountability here meant acknowledging these realities and becoming systematic in the ways that we recognized and documented our own situated subjectivities. I wrote memos during my research to note that which would never be captured in verbatim transcripts of audio-recorded interviews with research participants: nonverbal cues of expressed discomfort, gazes averted or held, a crossing and uncrossing of legs, a fidgety foot—either my own or that of a participant. I was also taught to maintain awareness of the limitations of my own vantage point, reinforcing the need for multiple and diversely situated accounts and accounting processes.

Disinvesting from the Comparative Case Mandate as an Investment in Understudied Communities

As I drafted my dissertation proposal in 2005, I was urged to aim, if at all possible, for fifty interviews. If qualitative methods were generally considered suspect, one way to grant them more disciplinary legitimacy was to make the number of participants "respectably" large (for excellent overviews of qualitative methods, see Compton, this volume; Denzin & Lincoln 2005). I was also urged to develop a comparative sample and analytic framework. For my proposed project, this most often manifested as advice that I should interview the trans partners of the women I wished to interview. Yet following this advice posed a dilemma.

With finite amounts of time and money to invest, I wanted to ensure that I had an adequate sample of women alone, especially as I had been reading about and from the perspectives and experiences of trans men for years. I decided to dig my heels in and invest in a sample consisting exclusively of women partners of trans men. I argued that the existing literature focusing on trans men, fairly well developed by this time, could serve as a literature-based comparison group. So, too, could the existing literatures on the experiences of lesbians and heterosexual women in partnerships with cisgender men. The project's most imperative goal was to reach data saturation (the point at which additional interviews fail to yield new substantive themes or reveal variations between groups under study) on key issues of import for women partners of trans men.

QUEER VALUATION: FINANCIAL AND DISCIPLINARY INVESTMENTS AND DISINVESTMENTS

My dissertation committee members had expressed concerns that it would be difficult to recruit so many individuals from what they assumed was an

exceedingly small and hidden minority population. Incentivizing participation through a modest participant payment could, accordingly, increase
the likelihood of successful recruitment. I applied for funding from the
National Science Foundation (NSF) Dissertation Improvement Grant
program and the Andrew W. Mellon/American Council of Learned
Societies Dissertation Completion Fellowship program. I was invited to
revise my NSF proposal and was ultimately disappointed to receive a
rejection that caused me to question not only the quality of my proposal
but the relative value of my research and future career possibilities altogether. One sociologist reviewer of the proposal wrote in feedback to me:
"It is unclear to this reader how this research will provide a foundation
from which the Ph.D. candidate can build a career . . . [or will place] the
Ph.D. candidate on a trajectory that yields high possibility of publications,
at least in the most prestigious sociological outlets."

The fact is that the majority of proposals submitted to NSF are rejected.
While rejection always stings, that was not so much what stuck with me as
the feedback that accompanied the decision. Feedback may carry a particularly shaming valence for queer scholars if they are told, essentially,
that projects reflecting their lives carry little broader import or value. This
may be especially acute for queer scholars who have also experienced
rejection from their families or other crucial sources of support on the
basis of their gender or sexual identity. In the context of this pointed and
deeply personal rejection, it is perhaps unsurprising that when I received
an email months later congratulating me on winning the prestigious
Andrew W. Mellon/American Council of Learned Societies Dissertation
Completion Fellowship, my immediate emotional reaction was not one of
joy or vindication, but shock and disbelief. What I did next is now, with
nearly a decade's hindsight, cringe-worthy and breaks my heart a bit. Yet
I want to tell you more, because I find my own reaction emblematic of the
sorts of bracing and emotional labor that queer scholars often embody—
we become shaken by the discipline, left unsteady and unsure of the value
of ourselves and our work.

Rather than celebrating the competitive and substantial fellowship I
had just been awarded, I emailed the program officer with an earnest
inquiry about whether the email had actually been intended for me and
my project or if it was perhaps sent in error. I cried when I heard back

that the fellowship was genuinely intended to support me in doing this work, this project that I had been told was so queer that it would surely be irrelevant to my discipline. Learning that this project had been deemed worthy of significant financial investment was a game changer for me. Yet what if that game changer had never arrived? We do not share these experiences of failure, shame, and doubt with one another nearly enough as we busily craft shells of invulnerability, telling ourselves and one another that we must develop thicker skins and overcome "imposter syndrome." Jodi O'Brien cautions against such stripping of painful affect from sociologists' methodological approaches. Instead, she urges us to lean in to the "inescapable scratchiness" of emotionally difficult experiences and testimonies, and to discern the ways in which such experiences tend to congeal and aggregate among specific groups (2009: 12).

Despite the initial concerns of my supportive mentors, I had no difficulties recruiting fifty women to interview for the project. Some were so eager to tell their stories, with the hope that their experiences might illuminate the pathways of others like them, that they refused the twenty-five-dollar participant payment I offered. Like a wildfire, my sample size exploded, drawing participants across thirteen states in the United States, three Canadian provinces, and one territory in Australia. I was dismayed that my sample was largely white and consisted entirely of cis women, since my call for participants had been intentionally broad and I wished to interview a broadly diverse group of women partners of trans men. At the beginning of data collection for this project in 2005, internet social media and networks were just beginning to flourish and become more broadly accessible. Sources of support for women partners of trans men at that time were limited mainly to university-affiliated support groups for LGBTQ students, online message boards, and burgeoning social media sites such as MySpace. Participants thanked me for conducting the research, expressing their desire to learn if their own experiences were typical or atypical, whether there were others like them, and what the future for them and their relationships might hold.

Paying Our Dues: Intellectual and Community Investments

My interview protocol for the study was inspired and informed by the previous work of sociologists of gender, sexuality, and the family—Arlie

Hochschild, Marjorie DeVault, Philip Blumstein, Pepper Schwartz, and Christopher Carrington, to name just a handful. Despite the exploratory nature of my study, I wanted to develop a systematic method for collecting information across a broad range of areas likely critical to the lives and everyday experiences of cis women partners of trans men. My interview protocol was holistic, addressing topics connected to demographics and intersectional identities of research participants, their partner, and their relationship; focused inquiry into gender and sexual identities of oneself and one's partner; how the couple met; sources of social support and strain; household division of labor and child care; relationship structure and legal recognition; transition-related processes and care; sexuality and intimacy between partners; and issues connected to the body and embodiment.

Throughout recruitment and interviewing, participants sometimes asked me about how my interest in studying women partners of trans men had developed. Some asked me if I was a partner of a trans man. Others told me that I probably found their story strange, revealing through their comments that they assumed I was heterosexual and partnered with a cis man. In other words, participants were attempting to gauge my level of engagement and investment in their community. Whenever participants directly inquired, I disclosed my identity as a fellow partner of a trans-identified person. Methodologically speaking, this may have helped to generate rapport with some participants. On the other hand, I did find that some participants used phrases such as "you know what I mean" or "you know how it is" when talking about their lives once they had established our shared membership in the queer community of cis women partners of trans men. In these instances, it became methodologically imperative for me to probe further by asking participants if they could tell me more about their experiences or perspectives, rather than filling in the blanks with my own experiences or assumptions.

Risky Portfolios: Balancing Our Investments

My quest to situate work on nontraditional individuals, partnerships, and families within the most visible mainstream outlets in sociology was motivated by my deep-seated belief that the experiences and perspectives of the cis women I interviewed deserved broader dissemination and could illuminate existing gaps in sociological literature on sex and gender, sexualities, and families. This motivation was further galvanized by my disinvestment from the notion that research involving participants whose gender or sexual identities are queer is best reserved for sociology journals focusing primarily on gender and sexuality—namely, *Gender & Society* and *Sexualities*. In conversations with other gender and sexualities scholars between sessions at the annual meeting of the American Sociological Association, we bemoaned the fact that research focusing on queer populations was often summarily routed to a few specialty journals, where it joined a tremendous backlog of research focusing on gender and sexuality, and where it sometimes seemed to signal acceptance of trans-related work while inclusion of such scholarship remained relatively tokenistic in the discipline more broadly. While these journals remain some of our most favored and trusted sources for research that is both timely and critically important, we were concerned about the continuing ghettoization of our work and discussed strategies for garnering greater entrée into generalist journals with broader distribution and higher impact. If getting our queer research placed in specialty journals could make small but steady waves in the pool of disciplinary progress, placing such work in top-tier generalist journals might be more akin to a cannonball.

Yet as many gender and sexuality scholars have discovered, just making it through the locker room to get to the pool can be exceedingly difficult. When submitting work on queer populations to more mainstream journals, we noticed some demoralizing trends. First, our research was often summarily dismissed by editors through the practice of "deflection" or "desk rejection," meaning that editors determined that the article did not merit further peer review at the journal, along with the suggestion that it be sent to journals specifically focusing on gender and sexuality. When it was sent out for review, we noticed that it often landed in the laps of reviewers who seemingly understood nothing about our queer participant groups, the challenges of sampling with these populations, or the theoretical literatures we incorporated into our frameworks and analyses, which often drew on interdisciplinary insights and approaches. In these reviews, our samples were often described as too small or methodologically weak because they drew upon "convenience" samples. Our findings were then dismissed as nonrepresentative or nongeneralizable and, therefore, largely anecdotal rather than valid as contributions to social science.

It was through these conversations with other scholars, and the pooling of our collective frustrations, that I decided to disinvest from (and position myself against) some of the prevailing disciplinary norms within sociology. I want to claim here that queer methods do not begin and end with our individual research projects but, rather, must be conceptualized as a complex interplay between and among the structures and institutions that guide and shape our projects from start to finish, with possibilities for queer intervention, in the form of investments and disinvestments, all along the way. First, I pushed against the notion that qualitative research with queer populations was less systematic and rigorous than research with other populations for which demographic parameters had been established. I began to describe my sampling strategy in my written work and conference presentations as "purposive social network sampling," rather than "convenience sampling" or "snowball sampling" (see Patton 1990). When you are conducting research with a population that is hidden and for which population parameters have not yet been established, one way to gather data purposively is to locate key informants who then disseminate information about the research to other members of the social network, allowing for the largest possible recruitment of subjects. With a broader base of possible participants, researchers may choose to target particular aspects of the population or trend of interest. For me, because almost nothing had been written about women partners of trans men, my aim was maximum variation among participants.

Second, I began to reconsider the ethics and pragmatics of double-blind peer review in the context of how research is conducted in the twenty-first century, particularly research that is highly distinct because of its substantive content or its unique population of interest. For years, I declined to peer-review any paper whose title or topic rendered its author identifiable to me. In those ASA meetings with fellow scholars of queer populations, we would reveal that we received peer review requests for one another's papers but declined to review them because it was obvious to us who the author was. While not all in our discipline would decline to review under such circumstances, and others might check in with an editor first for advice, graduate students and early-career scholars may be more likely to doggedly follow double-blind review standards more conventionally or be reticent to "bother" editors for advice.

Clearly, we were acting in accordance with normative researcher ideals of distanced objectivity and neutrality at all stages of the research process—including peer review. Yet this strategy ultimately was self-defeating, as it limited the advancement of social scientific knowledge on queer populations. In declining to review one another's papers, we indirectly pushed articles into protracted limbo as editors struggled to find suitable reviewers. Far too often, the reviewers who were found submitted reviews that revealed their lack of expertise on the populations and topics under investigation. These dismissive and unhelpful reviews only made it more likely that research involving queer populations would remain ever outside the discipline's center.

The ability of reviewers to search for paper titles on the internet has already rendered much of the premise of double-blind review pragmatically false in the twenty-first century as more and more of us place titles of works-in-progress on our vitae or on conference presentations, often allowing our identities to be easily discerned should a reviewer wish to do so. In sociology, communities of researchers studying queer genders and sexualities have generally been small enough that many people can easily match a specific topic or community being studied with particular scholars even when asked to do a blind review. In turn, I disinvested from claims that double-blind peer review is the most objective method of assuring a fair process and that I should decline to review papers on queer genders and sexualities if I think I can identify their authors.

Such a position is inconsonant with feminist research ethics stressing the critical importance of attending and responding to inequities across all stages of the research process—from research conceptualization to review and dissemination. I have found my recommendation rates to accept, revise, or reject do not differ based on whether I feel I know or have a hunch about the author's identity. I do, however, feel much more personal angst about recommending rejection for papers whose authors I presume I know, and have found this both humbling and of value to me in working to create constructive reviews that help authors to craft stronger and more compelling papers. Ultimately, it is my determination that papers should be reviewed by those most qualified to assess their relative merits, and substantive content expertise is, in my estimation, no small part of such qualification—particularly when considering populations that have been historically stigmatized and rendered marginal.

I invested in a strategy in which I aspired to publish not only in journals that I have always loved and faithfully read, but also in journals that reach the broadest possible sociological audiences. On one hand, we might think of this as a methodological approach to queering the discipline. On the other hand, aiming to publish queer work, in all of its messy contradiction, in the most mainstream journals also reflects deep investment in the normative. Our work is often steeped in these sorts of tensions, a precarious balance between delicious and distasteful, assimilation and resistance. Research on queer identities, communities, and social practices holds the power to challenge and broaden regulated disciplinary spaces. Yet even as we celebrate what may seem disciplinary trailblazing and inroads, we must always contemplate which of us gets to be behind the wheel, who is most at risk of being run over, how long it will be until another traveler joins us, and whether the demands of the journey will transform us or our work so that we or it become unrecognizable to ourselves or to those we seek to represent.

Appreciation and Depreciation: Publication as Risky Investment

I first set my sights on publishing my work in the *Journal of Marriage and Family*, as I viewed this journal as the flagship family studies specialty journal in sociology. I had gathered extensive data on household division of labor and emotional labor from my research participants' accounts and felt that my data could illuminate existing conversations about the role of gender in structuring relationships and household labor. I believed that insights from my data were especially critical as a bifurcation had emerged in the family studies literature that characterized heterosexual unions as fairly inegalitarian with regard to the division of family labor, while gay and lesbian unions were depicted as much more egalitarian. In a way, this bifurcation seemed to suggest that, in the absence of sex differences between partners, gender differences were eradicated. In contrast, my data with women partners of trans men suggested that same-sex was not synonymous with same-gender. In other words, it mattered relatively little that the genitals and reproductive organs of both my research participants and their trans partners were most often the same. Instead, I found that masculine gender identification was reportedly associated with greater uptake of masculine-typed family labor (taking out the garbage, maintaining the cars, mowing the grass) and reduced uptake of feminine-typed family labor (cleaning, cooking, attending to emotional needs).

Several years after the article was accepted for publication, I met Ralph LaRossa, the deputy editor at the *Journal of Marriage and Family*, who had offered detailed feedback as I revised my submission multiple times. He congratulated me and told me how much he appreciated the work and how happy he was to publish it. It was not until years after its acceptance that I came to more fully understand and value LaRossa's contributions to the shape and contours of this work as an investment on his part—and a potentially risky one at that. Prior to the publication of this article, there had been no substantive inclusion or representation of transgender people, partnerships, or families in the pages of the *Journal of Marriage and Family* over its seventy-year history. LaRossa's careful and tireless engagement with this paper was a reflection of his commitment to the belief that an investment in scholarship that included these previously neglected queer populations was both timely and worth taking a chance on.

Because I was actively working on this paper when I was on the job market in 2008, the campus visit talks and conference presentations that I gave focused on this work specifically. It was during the question-and-answer period following these talks that I first began to realize that the ways in which our work is understood and interpreted always happens through existing cultural lenses and frameworks. While I underscored in the *Journal of Marriage and Family* article that structural forces and gendered socialization processes constrain and shape personal choices and family structures for *all* of us, many of those who engaged with this work focused on the specific details of household labor and emotion work that I describe in the paper.

In giving these talks, I got the same question again and again, even from some of the most celebrated feminist sociologists in the discipline: "Aren't these supposedly queer couples and families just a repackaged, contemporary version of Ozzie and Harriet?" This question was frustrating because, in some ways, it was a fair characterization. The stereotypically gendered family labor some cis women partners of trans men described performing did, indeed, seem regressive. On the other hand, why would sociologists of gender and the family be surprised by this? Previous work on cisgender partnerships had revealed patterns in division of household labor wherein the bulk of such labor was performed, disproportionately, by more-feminine partners—even within same-sex partnerships. I was unsettled by the embedded assumption in this line of questioning that partnerships between cis women and trans men would somehow magically transcend gender socialization practices and the social and structural dimensions of gendered interaction.

In addition to questions from sociologists that seemed to suggest that the partnerships and families of cis women partners of trans men held particular responsibility or power to embody the politics and vision of queer liberation, there emerged a strange bedfellow: trans-exclusionary radical feminists (often abbreviated as "TERFs"). Excerpts from my *Journal of Marriage and Family* article appeared online in *The Dirt from Dirt* blog, a relatively high-traffic site maintained by a self-identified lesbian who views transgender identity as both fraudulent and a site of intentional lesbian and cis women's erasure. In one blog post, "Dirt" provides an alternative interpretation of my findings, describing my research participants as "50's housewives."[1] In a more recent, book-length volume, noted TERF Sheila Jeffreys misgenders the trans partners of my research participants and characterizes cis women partners of trans men as tragic dupes in a system of patriarchy.[2]

Despite my disappointment and anger with these public mischaracterizations of my research participants and their partnerships and families, in taking responsibility for my own work and its reception, I committed my next publications to engaging with just these sort of questions of structure and agency in a much more direct way. I knew that I would need to work to better distinguish the nuance and complexity of the lives of the cis women who had invested me with their accounts and the responsibility to interpret, analyze, and publish them. Shortly after publishing the *Journal of Marriage and Family* article, I began to work on disentangling two distinct articles from one behemoth chapter of my dissertation. I knew that I wished to send one of these articles, on concepts I termed "normative resistance" and "inventive pragmatism," to *Gender & Society*, the leading journal in gender studies and a top-ten journal in sociology. The second article was shaping up to be the most radical piece that I had written and drew heavily on queer theory and a critique of normative assumptions surrounding queer identities and belonging.

QUEERING THE DISCIPLINE THROUGH NORMATIVE INVESTMENTS?

In 2010 I held my breath and submitted this article, "'I Don't Like Passing as a Straight Woman': Queer Negotiations of Identity and Social Group Membership," to *Social Problems*, a well-regarded generalist journal in sociology that focuses on publishing scholarship on social inequalities. Nearly one month later, I received a desk rejection from the editor. In his letter, the editor explained that he had decided not to send the manuscript out for peer review, because it lacked broader appeal to the discipline. Reading that review brought me back to the NSF reviews I had received years earlier. Yet, rather than feeling hopeless, sad, or ashamed, I felt angry.

By this time, I had heard this same story from other scholars of queer genders and sexualities far too often. I came to believe that the barrier I was facing was less a reflection of the inadequacy or irrelevance of my own work than of systematic trans scholarship marginalization within the discipline. When we talk to our senior mentors about publishing, they often offer us some version of the "aim high, work down" strategy, whereby you submit your work to the top journal at which you believe your work might reasonably be accepted and, upon receiving rejections, move down the hierarchy of journal status and impact. The editorial outcome I had just received should have meant that I moved down to the next journal tier in the hierarchy, perhaps targeting a more sexualities- or gender-focused subdisciplinary journal, as the editor suggested would be more appropriate.

Instead, I crafted a new cover letter, did not change a word in the manuscript, and sent it immediately to the *American Journal of Sociology*. In the cover letter, I explicitly detailed why it was time for the *American Journal of Sociology* to publish an article focusing substantively on transgender issues and why it was better suited for mainstream than for subdisciplinary journal placement. One of the issues with investing in reasonable-sounding and moderate advice is that it fails to account for the often unreasonable and immoderate degree of serendipity that imbues many social processes, including publishing. In addition to the potential quality and contributions of your work, publishing outcomes depend heavily on (1) the editorial staff and their constellation of personal, professional, and political proclivities as well as the backlog they face on the particular day they encounter your submission; (2) current events provoking broader social interest and salience for particular topics; (3) reviewers (see point one on editorial staff); (4) the perceived status of the author and their existing contributions; and (5) a metric fuckton of good or bad luck.

After seven months under review, during which time a message from the editorial office conveyed apologies because they were having difficulties finding reviewers for the piece, I received a "revise and resubmit" decision. The reviews were generally positive and supportive, though they required extensive revisions. Rather than balking at the inclusion of a queer theoretical framework, reviewers urged me to push this analysis and critique of normativity even further. Indeed, it was an *AJS* reviewer who initially suggested to me that my uncritical use of the term *women* to describe my participants, while denoting their partners as "trans men," revealed a normatizing imbalance, situating the cis women I interviewed as not requiring an adjective to delineate their claim to womanhood. In all subsequent publications, I shifted my language to refer to my participants as "cis women."

It took me just over a year to make the requested revisions for the *American Journal of Sociology* article while I also worked on other publications, fulfilled my duties as a new faculty member, applied for academic jobs that could provide greater resources for research, and was terrified about any missteps that might derail the possibility of the article ultimately being accepted. Five months later, I received a "contingent acceptance" (also known as conditional acceptance). The requested revisions were actually quite substantial and required significant reworking of the manuscript once again, yet this decision could not have come at a better time.

My partner and I had just lost our home and possessions in a massive fire, and my partner was four months pregnant. During what was one of the most challenging times of our lives, we found a reason to celebrate. We moved into a new home, began all over again, and had a baby. Given the messiness of my life at this time, this round of revisions took eight months, and I submitted the revised manuscript in April 2013. It took nearly one year (and many phone and email requests for status updates) for the paper to be accepted in late March 2014 and another four months for it to appear online. The paper appeared in print in December 2014, nearly four and a half years following its initial submission.

Acknowledging Our Investments and Disinvestments

Following the release of the *American Journal of Sociology* article (and throughout the period from its conditional acceptance to publication), scholars of sex and gender and sexualities expressed amazement that an article like this one—with "queer" in the title, focusing on transgender partnerships and families, using qualitative methods, and employing a queer theoretical framing—could or would be published by one of the flagship mainstream journals in the discipline. In general, I shared in their incredulity throughout the process, but remained ever invested in this possible outcome as something much larger than this paper or my personal career. Cannonball! I see the publication of work like this as the culmination of decades of struggle by scholars pushed to the margins and forced to create their own subdisciplinary journals and niches just to be able to talk to one another and exchange knowledge and empirical and theoretical insights.

Publication of this article felt like elbowing and squeezing one's way into a seat at the table. I am not so naïve to believe that a single paper will open floodgates for broader inclusion of work employing queer populations, queer methods, or queer theory in mainstream disciplinary journals. I understand the function of tokens even as I hope this article will not ultimately become one. I do believe, however, that articles like these—when they manage to breach the fortress—tend to keep us moving forward and invested with hope, with possibility (despite low probabilities) even as we are often left shaken by our encounters with disciplinary boundaries and borders. I will always owe many debts to those sociologists who carved out similar spaces at earlier points in time, giving me hope along my way.

To that end, I also wanted to engage directly with other scholars of queer genders and sexualities whose work has been dismissed or consigned to the

margins. I wanted to publicly disinvest from the idea that scholars studying queer topics or communities should feel shame or reshape their interests into something more palatable. In the acknowledgments section of my
American Journal of Sociology article, with more than a bit of trepidation,
I dedicated this publication to "my interview participants and to gender
and sexualities researchers who have pushed beyond feedback like that
which I received from sociologist reviewers at the National Science
Foundation. . . . Your lives and work are important and deserve to be valued, understood, and recognized—thank you for the inspiration to always
keep pushing forward." Once the article was published, the dedication garnered a bit of attention.

On Twitter, Beth Popp Berman wrote: "Carla Pfeffer challenges Smith
in category of bitter-yet-accurate acknowledgements in a major sociology
journal." Saida Grundy responded to this assessment by tweeting: "my
friend carla pfeffer's words here shouldn't be described as 'bitter,' for she is
brilliantly exercising the queer art of *shade*." I would be disingenuous if
I said that I did not enjoy this vision of myself as the sociological equivalent of Drew Barrymore in *Firestarter,* hair blowing back and eyes glinting
as barriers to full disciplinary inclusion for sociologists studying queer
genders and sexualities are incinerated. There is no shade to be found in
that hot queer utopia.

Investing in Queer Research, Researchers, and Methods

In this chapter, I wrest the concepts of investment and disinvestment
from the domain of economics for the purposes of considering the ways
that we might invest in particular disciplinary norms and of exploring just
what is at stake when we resist, reject, or disinvest from these norms. I do
so as an extension of Jodi O'Brien's description of sociology as "an epistemology of contradiction" that requires "going inward" to understand the
system of human interconnections through which we carve out our lives.
O'Brien argues that "our most engaging work—that which has the greatest
impact—reflects a bold confrontation with the messiness of human social
life, and this necessarily includes our personal experience of this messiness" (2009: 7–8). By sharing some of my own messy entanglements here,
I hope to offer the sorts of accounts that will allow other researchers to

make meaning of this work in which we are collectively and vulnerably investing our lives, our energies, our hopes, and our careers.

The investment-disinvestment framework that I sketch here is imbued with several assumptions. First, I assume that scholars have finite resources when it comes to the amount of time, energy, and resources they can invest in their various pursuits. Second, I assume that some scholars have access to greater time, energy, and resources than others. Third, I assume that scholars compel, and are compelled by, others to invest time, energy, and resources in particular ways and that the pressure to invest and ability to resist or reject investment depend on the relative power of those involved. I argue that it makes good sense for scholars to consider not just who they are and what it is that they do, but also how they arrived at that doing.

There was a time when I almost dropped out of graduate school. I even went so far as to notify one of my mentors and apply for admission to a local pastry arts program. Along the way, many of those with whom I used to chat between sessions at ASA or whom I saw give brilliant talks on queer genders and sexualities started to disappear, having no luck in publishing or no luck on the job market. But it is rarely simply bad luck, is it? As I move forward in my career, I have become more invested in mentorship, especially mentorship for those deemed risky investments. I recently served as an NSF proposal reviewer and worked to ensure that proposals on queer topics and communities received a fair review and substantive, nonshaming feedback. I see little value in complaining about or calling out systematic problems if one does not invest in finding or enacting viable solutions to address them.

As we work toward addressing systemic and structural barriers to our individual and collective success, we must also, more immediately, attend to ourselves and one another. For more than a decade, I have remained connected with a group of friends and fellow scholars focusing on (among other topics) sex, gender, and sexualities. We first crossed paths in graduate school and developed a working group to develop intellectual scaffolding where none yet existed. We still video-teleconference with one another monthly via Skype, Google Hangout, or Zoom. Our group's membership now spans every time zone in the United States, so this is sometimes challenging. We have workshopped and supported one another through papers and presentations, job and conference talks, grant applications, teaching materials, tenure cases, departmental political dramas, births, deaths, and all that life throws our way.

It truly takes a queer village, and often we invest in carving out pathways for these spaces and communities when their absence becomes too painful. Our methods, when guided by ethics and integrity, are necessarily imbued with care and caring. Indeed, *method* must be understood as extending far beyond simply how we conceptualize, propose, and conduct a study. Though the following is by no means a complete list, queer methods also encompass and reflect an understanding of the power and limitations of our own situated identities and partial perspectives as researchers; attention to the affective dimension of experience and knowledge; ethical conduct in the field and in interactions with participants, researchers, and the broader public; taking responsibility for our work when we talk and write about it and through responding to its uptake; acknowledgment that all research is interventional; and consideration of the potential immediate and broader impacts and implications of our investments and disinvestments all along the way.

This is challenging yet rewarding work that we do. Sociologists must resist the urge to pursue difficult and marginalized scholarship in isolation from one another or to hold both their successes and failures close to their, and only their, hearts. Ultimately, there is much to gain in understanding sociology as an epistemology of messy and valuable contradictions. Sociology needs "rogue scholars" and rogue scholarship (O'Brien 2009: 11). The advancement of queer scholarship, scholars, and methods in sociology is an ongoing and collective social accomplishment worthy of all our various risky investments and disinvestments.

NOTES

1. See "50's Housewives the Future of TMates?" *The Dirt from Dirt,* March 16, 2011, http://dirtywhiteboi67.blogspot.com/2011/03/50s-housewives-future-of-tmates.html.

2. For an overview, see Carla Pfeffer, "(Trans) gender culture clashes: Social recognition and determining the 'real.'" *Gender & Society,* posted August 20, 2014, https://gendersociety.wordpress.com/2014/08/20/transgender-culture-clashes/.

WORKS CITED

Denzin, Norman K., and Yvonna S. Lincoln (eds.). 2005. *The SAGE handbook of qualitative research,* 3rd ed. Thousand Oaks, CA: SAGE.

Hesse-Biber, Sharlene Nagy (ed.). 2012. *The handbook of feminist research: Theory and praxis.* Thousand Oaks, CA: SAGE.

Krieger, Susan, 1983. *The mirror dance: Identity in a women's community.* Philadelphia: Temple University Press.

O'Brien, Jodi. 2009. "Sociology as an epistemology of contradiction." *Sociological Perspectives* 52(1): 5–22.

Patton, Michael Q. 1990. *Qualitative evaluation and research methods.* Beverly Hills, CA: Sage.

Scott, Marvin B., and Stanford M. Lyman (eds.). 1968. "Accounts." *American Sociological Review* 33(1): 46–62.

Smith, Dorothy E. 1974. "Women's perspective as a radical critique of sociology." *Sociological Inquiry* 44(1): 7–13.

Contributors

AMANDA K. BAUMLE, JD, PhD, is Associate Professor of Sociology at the University of Houston and conducts research on the demography of sexuality and sociology of law. She is the coauthor of *Legalizing LGBT Families: How the Law Shapes Parenthood* (NYU Press, 2015) and *Same-Sex Partners: The Demography of Sexual Orientation* (SUNY Press, 2009) and the editor of *The International Handbook on the Demography of Sexuality* (Springer, 2013).

D'LANE R. COMPTON is Associate Professor of Sociology at the University of New Orleans. Her career and research interests include social psychology, the social demography of sexual orientation, and qualitative and quantitative methods including experimental. Compton is the coauthor of *Same-Sex Partners: The Social Demography of Sexual Orientation* (SUNY Press, 2009) and *Legalizing LGBT Families: How the Law Shapes Parenthood* (NYU Press 2015).

CATHERINE CONNELL is Associate Professor of Sociology and Women and Gender Studies at Boston University and Director of BU's Women, Gender, and Sexuality Studies Program. Her work focuses on the intersections of gender, sexuality, and work and organizations. Her book, *School's Out: Gay and Lesbian Teachers in the Classroom,* was published by University of California Press in 2015. Her current research focuses on recent gender and sexuality policy changes in the US military.

TINA FETNER is a sociologist at McMaster University. Her research interests are in the area of sexualities, social movements, and political sociology. Her focus on right-wing politics includes analyses of the Tea Party movement as well as her book, *How the Religious Right Shaped Lesbian and Gay Activism,* which examines the dynamic relationship between these two opposing movements. She also researches the social-contextual determinants of attitudes toward lesbian and gay people and the meanings of marriage and the wedding ritual in the context of legal recognition of same-sex marriage. Her work has appeared in *Social Problems, Sociological Perspectives,* and *Public Opinion Quarterly.*

GARY J. GATES studies the demographics of the LGBT population. US Supreme Court justice Anthony Kennedy cited Gates's research in his majority opinion holding that same-sex couples have a constitutional right to marry. Gates retired as a Distinguished Scholar at the Williams Institute, UCLA School of Law, and serves as Senior Researcher at Gallup Inc. He holds a PhD in public policy and management from the Heinz College, Carnegie Mellon University.

AMIN GHAZIANI is Associate Professor of Sociology and Canada Research Chair in Sexuality and Urban Studies at the University of British Columbia. He is the author or coeditor of four books: *The Dividends of Dissent, A Decade of HAART, There Goes the Gayborhood?* and *Sex Cultures.* His work has appeared in the *American Sociological Review, Annual Review of Sociology, Contexts, International Journal of Urban and Regional Research, Social Problems,* and *Theory and Society,* among other outlets.

MELANIE HEATH is Associate Professor of Sociology at McMaster University. Her research interests include sexualities, gender, family, and global politics. She has studied the conservative religious men's group the Promise Keepers and marriage promotion initiatives. She is author of *One Marriage Under God: The Campaign to Promote Marriage in America,* an in-depth examination of conservative politics that have promoted heterosexual marriage and banned same-sex marriage. Her work considers the legal consequences of outlawing family forms and sexual practices, such as polygamy and prostitution, and the meanings of marriage and the wedding ritual for same-sex couples. Her work has been published in *Gender & Society, Signs, Sociological Perspectives, Qualitative Sociology,* and *Sociological Quarterly.*

JODY L. HERMAN is Scholar of Public Policy at the Williams Institute, UCLA School of Law. She studies the demographics of the transgender population, as well as the prevalence and impact of discrimination against transgender people. She holds a PhD in public policy and public administration from George Washington University.

KIMBERLY KAY HOANG is Associate Professor of Sociology at the University of Chicago and author of *Dealing in Desire: Asian Ascendancy, Western Decline, and the Hidden Currencies of Global Sex Work* (University of California Press, 2015).

Dealing in Desire is the winner of seven national book awards from the American Sociological Association, National Women's Studies Association, Association for Asian Studies, and Society for the Study of Social Problems.

TREVOR HOPPE is Assistant Professor of Sociology at the University at Albany, State University of New York. His research examines the institutional social control of sex and disease. Hoppe has published two books, *The War on Sex* (Duke University Press, 2017) and *Punishing Disease: HIV and the Criminalization of Sickness* (University of California Press, 2017).

CAYCE C. HUGHES received his PhD in sociology from the University of Chicago in 2017 and is currently a postdoctoral fellow at Rice University in Houston, TX. His research interests include the sociology of privacy, urban poverty, social inequality, health and well-being, and culture. Hughes's dissertation, "Negotiating Privacy in the Context of Poverty: Poor Mothers and the Social Safety Net," examines how African American urban women navigate privacy in the face of the extensive surveillance they encounter as they seek assistance from the social safety net.

ANGELA JONES is Associate Professor of Sociology at Farmingdale State College, State University of New York. Jones obtained her PhD from the New School for Social Research. Jones is conducting a mixed method study of adult webcam performers, and her book based on this research, "Camming: The Intersectional Politics of Online Sex Work" is forthcoming with NYU Press. Jones is the author of another monograph, *African American Civil Rights: Early Activism and the Niagara Movement* (Praeger, 2011) and the editor of *The Modern African American Political Thought Reader: From David Walker to Barack Obama* (Routledge, 2012) and *A Critical Inquiry into Queer Utopias* (Palgrave, 2013) and the coeditor of the After Marriage Equality book series (Routledge). She has also authored numerous scholarly articles published in peer-reviewed journals. She is a mother, a paddle boarder, and a runner and loves to grow vegetables.

EMILIA LOMBARDI is Assistant Professor in Baldwin Wallace University's Department of Public Health. She holds a PhD in sociology from the University of Akron and has been examining health disparities among lesbian, gay, bisexual, and especially transgender populations since the mid-1990s. Lombardi is heavily involved in transgender-related research and social activism.

TEY MEADOW is Assistant Professor of Sociology at Columbia University. Her writing on gender and sexual classifications has appeared in academic journals including *Gender & Society, Politics & Society, Sexualities,* and the *Journal of Contemporary Ethnography.* Her first book manuscript, "Trans Kids: Being Gendered in the Twenty-First Century," will be published by the University of California Press in 2018.

MIGNON R. MOORE is Associate Professor of Sociology at Barnard College, Columbia University. She writes on the intersections of race and sexual minority status. Her first book, *Invisible Families: Gay Identities, Relationships, and Motherhood among Black Women* (University of California Press, 2011) focuses on African American lesbian identity and family formation. Her current research (funded by the National Institutes of Health) examines LGBT health and aging. She is researching a book on the coming-of-age experiences of sexual minority seniors in the 1950s, 1960s, and 1970s and is tentatively titled "In the Shadow of Sexuality: Social Histories and Social Support of Black LGBT Elders."

C. J. PASCOE is Associate Professor of Sociology and the David M. and Nancy L. Petrone Faculty Scholar at the University of Oregon. She is the author of *Dude, You're Fag: Masculinity and Sexuality in High School* and coeditor of *Exploring Masculinities: Identity, Inequality, Continuity, and Change*. Her work focuses on sexuality, gender, inequality, and young people.

CARLA A. PFEFFER holds a PhD in sociology and a graduate certificate in women's studies from the University of Michigan. She is currently Associate Professor of Sociology and Women's and Gender Studies at the University of South Carolina. Pfeffer's sociological research inquires into contemporary families, genders, sexualities, and bodies considered marginal, as well as social actors' management of stigma and discrimination. In a new project, funded by the Economic and Social Research Council, she will be working with international colleagues to explore the reproductive experiences and practices of transgender men.

EVREN SAVCI is Assistant Professor in the Women, Gender, & Sexuality Studies Program and the Lesbian, Gay, Bisexual, & Transgender Studies Program at Yale University. She received her PhD in sociology (with a graduate emphasis in gender studies) at the University of Southern California and held a postdoctoral fellowship at the Sexualities Project (SPAN) at Northwestern University, Evanston, Illinois. Her areas of interest include transnational sexualities, queer theory, language and epistemology, religion, and political economy. Her work has appeared in *Sexualities, Political Power and Social Theory, Ethnography,* and *Theory & Event,* among other venues. She is currently finishing a book manuscript, "Queer in Translation: Sexual Politics under Neoliberal Islam."

KRISTEN SCHILT is Associate Professor of Sociology at the University of Chicago, where she directs the Center for the Study of Gender and Sexuality. She is the author of *Just One of the Guys? Transgender Men and the Persistence of Workplace Inequality* (University of Chicago Press, 2010). With multimedia artist Chase Joynt, she is working on a book manuscript and experimental film that examine the history of transgender research in sociology.

AMY L. STONE is Associate Professor of Sociology and Anthropology at Trinity University in San Antonio. Her research includes the study of lesbian, gay, bisexual, and transgender (LGBT) politics, communities, and the law. She is the author of

Gay *Rights at the Ballot Box* (University of Minnesota Press, 2012), *Cornyation: San Antonio's Outrageous Fiesta Tradition* (Maverick Books, 2017), and editor, with Jaime Cantrell, of *Out of the Closet, into the Archives: Researching Sexual Histories* (SUNY Press, 2015). She has published in such journals as the *Annual Review of Sociology, Sexualities,* the *Journal of Homosexuality, GLQ,* and the *Journal of the History of Sexuality.*

JANE WARD is Professor of Gender and Sexuality Studies at the University of California, Riverside, where she teaches courses in feminist, queer, and hetero-sexuality studies. She is the author of *Not Gay: Sex between Straight White Men* (NYU Press, 2015) and *Respectably Queer: Diversity Culture in LGBT Activist Organizations* (Vanderbilt University Press, 2008).

Index

Religious Right. *See* conservative, anti-LGBT movements and respondents

representativeness, 191–92

research design: access and recruitment, 171–75, 189–90; conscientiousness in methodological decision making, 199–200; demographer resistance to LGBTQ studies, 187; empirical research as gold standard, 185; LGBTQ populations as too "messy," 186; reception and the believability problem, 192–93; sample representativeness, 191–92; sample size and saturation, 194–98; sampling, 188–89

research encounter, queerness of, 136

resistance gatekeeping strategy, 39, 41–44

respectability politics, heteronormative, 101–2

respondent-driven sampling (RDS), 204–6

ridicule as gatekeeping, 39, 45–47

rights-based framings of social justice, limits of, 255–56

Rodgers, Philip, 90–91

Rooke, Alison, 129–30, 131

Rosenfeld, Michael, 87–89

Rowse, Jayne, 87

Rubin, Gayle, 101–2

Sakai, Naoki, 251–53

Salcedo, Bamby, 71

Salganik, Matthew, 204–5

sample size, 87, 194–98

sampling: purposive social network sampling, 314; research design and population size knowledge gap, 188–89; respondent-driven sampling and chain referral techniques, 204–6; snowball, 127, 205, 314; as threat to privacy, 127, 129

saturation, 196–97, 309

Savci, Evren, 64

Schippers, Mimi, 13, 102, 104

Schneider, Beth, 13, 54

Scott, Marvin, 307

scripts, sexual, 266–67

Seidman, Steven, 4, 7–10

self-presentation and identity management in interviews, 129–33, 142–44. *See also* positionality; privacy and disclosure

Sewell, William, 267

sex: decoupling gender from, 76; demographic models and intersection with gender and sexuality, 285–87; as proxy for power differentials, 285

sex offender registries, 273–74, 275

"Sexualities in the Social World" (ASA 2015), 63–64, 95–96

sexualities research: absence of sex in, 95–96, 101–2; demography of sexuality, 277–89; dirty-work stigma, 98–102; failure and, 294–95; pornographics as queer method, 102–7; sociology, need for pornographic imagination in, 96–98

sexual orientation and identity: as composite concept, 204; demographic models and intersection with sex and gender, 285–87; demographic outcomes shaped by, 278; essentialist-vs.-constructionist debate, 280–81; measuring from survey data, 279–83; travel of, as marker of kind of person, 256–57

sex work research. *See* carnal ethnography in Ho Chi Minh City, Vietnam; pornographics

Simon, Jonathan, 274

Simon, William, 266

Small, Mario, 186, 196

Smart, Michael, 206

Smith, Dorothy, 307

snowball sampling, 127, 205, 314

social construction: of biological sex, 76; of body, 238; of heterosexuality, 13, 141–42; of homosexuality, 8; quare studies and, 15; queer theory and, 292; of sexuality vs. homosexuality, 9; of sexual orientation vs. demographic essentialism, 280–81

social control. *See* punitive state regimes and social control of sex

social events in the field, organizing, 173–76

social network sampling, purposive, 314

Social Problems, 319

sociology: carnal, 230; of deviance, 262–63, 275; as epistemology of contradiction, 322; institutionalization of once-marginalized subfields and power of exclusion, 48–49. *See also* feminist sociology

sociology, queering of: areas of queer inquiry, 12–16; barriers to, 4–6; feminist challenge to, 38; new developments, 11–12; from outside in, 63–64; progress and lack of legitimation, 10–11; Seidman's *Queer Theory/Sociology*, 4, 7–10, 12, 14; trans-inclusivity, 75–77; vision for queer sociology, 17–20

Solnit, Rebecca, 51

Solomon, Jon, 251

Sontag, Susan, 96–97

www.ingramcontent.com/pod-product-compliance
Lightning Source LLC
Chambersburg PA
CBHW020822270326
41928CB00006B/405